88044

Teaching in the Knowledge Society:
New Skills and Instruments for Teachers

Antonio Cartelli
University of Cassino, Italy

 Information Science Publishing

Hershey • London • Melbourne • Singapore

Acquisitions Editor:	Michelle Potter
Development Editor:	Kristin Roth
Senior Managing Editor:	Amanda Appicello
Managing Editor:	Jennifer Neidig
Copy Editor:	Larissa Vinci
Typesetter:	Cindy Consonery
Cover Design:	Lisa Tosheff
Printed at:	Yurchak Printing Inc.

Published in the United States of America by
   Information Science Publishing (an imprint of Idea Group Inc.)
   701 E. Chocolate Avenue
   Hershey PA 17033
   Tel: 717-533-8845
   Fax: 717-533-8661
   E-mail: cust@idea-group.com
   Web site: http://www.idea-group.com

and in the United Kingdom by
   Information Science Publishing (an imprint of Idea Group Inc.)
   3 Henrietta Street
   Covent Garden
   London WC2E 8LU
   Tel: 44 20 7240 0856
   Fax: 44 20 7379 0609
   Web site: http://www.eurospanonline.com

 Library of Congress Cataloging-in-Publication Data

Teaching in the knowledge society : new skills and instruments for
   teachers / Antonio Cartelli, editor.
    p. cm.
   Summary: "This book investigates changes induced by information
 and communications technology in today's education system"
 --Provided by publisher.
   Includes bibliographical references.
   ISBN 1-59140-953-5 (hardcover) -- ISBN 1-59140-954-3
 (softcover) -- ISBN 1-59140-955-1 (ebook)
   1. Educational technology. 2. Internet in education. 3. Distance
 education.   I. Cartelli, Antonio, 1954-   .
   LB1028.3.T385 2006
   371.3'5--dc22
                                                2006000269

British Cataloguing in Publication Data
A Cataloguing in Publication record for this book is available from the British Library.

Teaching in the Knowledge Society:
New Skills and Instruments for Teachers

Table of Contents

Preface

We all are persuaded that ICTs are strongly influencing our lives and are changing our way of thinking. Since their first appearance in everyday life, many scholars have tried to find possible explanations for the effects they could have on mankind. They have also drafted possible scenarios for the evolution of human activities and ways of living under the influence of these new instruments or prostheses, as someone likes to define them. The same happened in education.

In this book, together with well known hypotheses on the influence of ICT on education, and the attempt of finding and defining a pedagogy of ICT, special perspectives for the analysis of that phenomenon are adopted to better describe the context to teachers, tutors, and all actors involved in the teaching-learning process.

First of all three different levels of intervention for the ICTs on knowledge construction are recognized and proposed for the discussion. They are subject, community/organization and society. Secondly, the reference frame teachers/professors are immersed in is analyzed and the changes on their ways of working are discussed. Thirdly, the experiences some authors are carrying out with their students are reported and two main points of view are analyzed: the former one looks at the ICT as the instrument for overcoming students' difficulties or helping them in obtaining better performances; the latter one is mostly concerned with the review of already known teaching-learning theories strongly modified by the intervention of ICT, and on the suggestion of new teaching-learning environments and scenarios. They make sure they are not missing hypotheses for the complete reorganization of teaching work, and more generally for the analysis and restructuring of educational environments and settings, and some instruments and strategies for teaching are reported.

If the role of the ICT is very important in all chapters of the book, not less important is the way information is managed and especially: (a) the information/knowledge spread by means of new technologies, (b) the actors of teaching-learning and educational process and their interaction with technologies, (c) the places and times involved in the use of ICT in educational contexts.

The perspectives outlined above instantiate in six different sections.

The first section analyzes the changes induced by ICT on the ways of knowing and learning. Different points of view for the discussion are suggested from the following entities: the subject, the community/organization, and the society. Further elements proposed from the authors emerge from the need of answering to new individual or social needs in the changing environments, or from the hypothesis of new ways of organizing and planning teaching processes.

In the second section, the analysis of the environments where teachers and professors are involved in is discussed. Two main themes clearly emerge from the debate: (a) teaching style as the main way for teacher/student interaction, and (b) learning environment and the teacher's role and function within this environment.

The third section focuses on students' success in e-learning and distance education courses and on the use of ICT for improving teaching-learning success. First of all, students' dropping out of e-learning is discussed and some variables marking the phenomenon are analyzed. Secondly, the influence of individuals' learning styles on students' performances in e-learning courses is described as emerging from the literature and from the experience. At last, the systematic use of ICT for letting people access teaching-learning phenomenon/evolution in real time is analyzed and the paradigmatic change for didactics and education administration is proposed.

The fourth section is mostly concerned with students' environments, management, and with strategies to be adopted from teachers in well settled theoretic contexts, with the help of ICT. Two main fields of interest emerge from the discussion: (a) collaborative and cooperative learning and the strategies to obtain the best results from them, and (b) the use of simulation as systematic teaching strategy.

The fifth section proposes ICT solutions for the use of special virtual environments devoted to teaching-learning. First, an e-education scenario is proposed, next a virtual reality environment is depicted and, lastly, an instrument for the use of knowledge management in e-learning is discussed.

The sixth section discusses two different kinds of resources teachers must include in their pedagogy: Web and its transformation in Semantic Web and media selection for better results in teaching.

The first section is made up of five chapters.

Chapter I: "Space, Time, and Process." Fundamental for a better understanding of the whole book is the introduction made by Giuseppe Refrigeri. It describes the context within, which all other chapters are included, and depicts a reference frame useful for further readings. While describing the main features of distance education and e-learning, the author reports the changes induced from this way of teaching-learning practice on space and time, considered as two essential factors of education. The following elements are then analyzed: space ubiquity (with special attention paid to space physical extension, its functions and identity), simultaneity and logical-psychological concomitance.

Chapter II: "Contributions of Psychopedagogy to the Inclusion of ICT in the Pedagogical Environment." Maria Apparecida Mamede-Neves critically analyzes distance education and the interactions between ICT and teaching and knowledge structures (with special attention paid to psychopedagogical phenomena). First, she examines the innovation induced in psychopedagogy by the concept of virtual classroom with respect to traditional physical classroom. Next, she analyzes learning through ICT, the incorporation of the Web in pedagogical practices, and the use of the Web by youngsters. Last, the need for the acknowledgment of the value of the interrelationship between the culture of physical presence and cyber culture in teaching environments is shown, as well as the need for teachers to become effectively enabled in adding ICT to their pedagogical practice.

Chapter III: "ICT, Knowledge Construction, and Evolution: Subject, Community, and Society." Antonio Cartelli reports the hypotheses scholars developed for explaining knowledge construction and evolution in mankind, and the role that ICT is playing on this phenomenon. While analyzing the separation emerging today between human knowledge and corporate knowledge, he considers the results of studies on wrong ideas and proposes a tri-partition of knowledge contexts: the individual, the community, and the social (scientific) ones. In the author's opinion, ICTs not only play a relevant role in each one of the above contexts, but they influence all the others. These effects are deduced from the analysis of some studies the author made on groups of students attending courses where special information systems for teaching and researching were developed.

Chapter IV: "Education and Organization: ICT, Assets, and Values." Pier Cesare Rivoltella describes the implementation of technology in education according to the theory of organization, and especially Norman's perspective. He shows how the implementation of ICT in the schools can be seen in the perspective of society transitions from fordist and tayloristic structures, to the service management paradigm, to the building values together with consumers. In doing this he criticizes the deterministic solution (which states that implementing technology changes everything and produces innovation) and adopts a systemic vision with the characteristics of presumption, community, and value constellation.

Chapter V: "Some Insights into the Impact of ICTs on Learning Agency and Seamless Learning." Hitendra Pillay, John A. Clarke, and Peter G. Taylor start from the assumption that the learning capacity of individuals is recognized as the most valued commodity in a knowledge and information society. As a consequence, they hypothesize the need of moving beyond what has traditionally been conceived of as a learning environment and develop alternative models, which acknowledge and accommodate the learning competencies required to successfully engage with a contingent and dynamic learning environment, like the one today's learners have to face. The concept of a learning agency incorporating the intelligence inherent in learning environments is proposed as a mechanism to explain seamless learning within and across environments, particularly those that are rich in technology.

The second section is made of three chapters.

Chapter VI: "Cultural Agents: Who They Are and What Role They Play." Salvatore Colazzo states that, in online education, teaching involves cultural, pedagogical, and didactical mediation more than in presence education. In this environment, teaching aims at improving the aptitudes and the intelligence and personal qualities of the students by starting from the competences already in their possession, by raising to consciousness their implicit knowledge and by favoring group interaction. Teaching function conceived as a mediating function leads the author to state that the socio-constructivist paradigm is the key factor for post-modern pedagogy development.

Chapter VII: "A Model to Measure the Impact of Web-Based Technologies in Different Teaching Styles." Carmen de Pablos Heredero observes that in higher education we can differentiate three different teaching styles: (a) the traditional one, with the presence of students and teacher in a classical classroom, (b) the distance teaching style, substituting the personal interaction between student and professor with a distance relation based on different materials, and (c) the virtual style, in which a permanent relation between students and lectures is established via a network. While starting from previous studies analyzing the variables better describing the impact of ICTs on the final results achieved from the different teaching styles, the author depicts a model based on those variables.

Chapter VIII: "Teachers, Tutors, and Mentors: New Roles or Professionals?" Paolo Ardizzone and Pier Cesare Rivoltella show the main transformations of our Information Society and their influence on teaching role in schools and universities are described. Particularly, the focus is on teachers and tutors in online education. The first is gradually passing from the "sage on the stage" to the "guide on the side" (of the learner), the second is really important because the learner, in an online environment, needs more than a presence to be helped from the cognitive and emotive point of view. The chapter also provides a description of main activities of these professionals: organization, knowledge and experience sharing, and evaluation.

The third section is made of three chapters.

Chapter IX: "Assessing Satisfaction and Academic Locus of Control of Dropout Students in Online Learning Courses." Yair Levy analyzes dropouts from on-campus and distance education courses. As literature suggests, students attending e-learning courses dropout at substantially higher rates than their counterparts in on-campus courses and the author explores two main constructs (students' satisfaction and academic locus of control) with online learning. Results show that students' satisfaction with e-learning is a key indicator in students' decision to dropout from online courses; furthermore, completer students report to have significantly higher satisfaction with online learning than students who dropped out from the same courses. At last the author reports that the academic locus of control appears to have no significant impact on students' decision to drop from online learning courses.

Chapter X: "Learning Styles and Adaptive ICT-Based Learning Environment." Zlatko J. Kovačić has two aims. Firstly, he provides an overview of learning styles research and secondly, he provides an overview of research in adaptive hypermedia learning environment systems (i.e., those where different learning styles are considered and used to create a personalized learning environment). It clearly emerges that distance education institutions must seriously consider the individualization of learning environment not only as an option because of economies of scale, but as a key factor for the success of teaching-learning actions and educational programs.

Chapter XI: "From the Monitoring of the Teaching-Learning Process to Didactics' Transparency." Antonio Cartelli proposes further elements of innovation induced by ICT in school management. First, students' assessment, school evaluation, and the great changes which invested them in the last decades are described. Next, the same topics are deeply analyzed with respect to results coming from educational research and to the use of ICT; as a consequence the limits of the use and application of ICT and information systems to separated educational fields clearly emerges. Last, the author's hypothesis of a paradigmatic change in education management, strongly based on the use of information systems and ICT, is reported; contextually it is described how the above change leads to didactics transparency in teaching-learning processes.

The fourth section is made of three chapters.

Chapter XII: "Teaching Team Competencies." Tony Jewels and Rozz Albon observe the incorporation of various types of group work into pedagogies in higher education institutions, yet many examples fail to embrace a rationale for, or the potential benefits of, multiple contributor environments essential in a knowledge intensive society. The authors propose that for optimum IT workplace effectiveness, in which principles of knowledge management need to be applied, it is necessary to take into account the competencies of the teams in which individuals work and to explicitly teach team competency skills.

Chapter XIII: "Cooperative Learning and ICT." Nicoletta Sala emphasizes the role computers and ICT can play in a teaching environment based on cooperative learning. The author discusses an educational experience she made on 45 high school students involved in the development of a database letting their school evaluations be available online. This educational approach used cooperative learning and learning by doing strategies and proved very useful both for students and teachers.

Chapter XIV: "Simulation, Training, and Education Between Theory and Practice." Angela Piu reports the results of theoretical and practical research work on simulation both as a teaching strategy creating a dynamic and experiential situation which enables participants to take on roles in relation to the variables to be tested or modified, and the learning content the students need to acquire. On the basis of recent research the author carried out, the suggestion of a reflection on the synergy triggered through simulation is made and the role of simulation in integrating different skills and types of knowledge is emphasized.

The fifth section is made of three chapters.

Chapter XV: "E-Teaching Scenarios." Manfred Schertler suggests a modern approach to e-teaching scenarios at the university level. This approach covers content-related and communicational components of an e-education scenario. Content creation and delivery via the Internet, as well as teacher/learner communication is shown from the point of view of the teacher. The content related part of an e-teaching scenario uses the well-known variety of computer-assisted training applications. The communication part refers to all aspects of teacher/learner and learner/learner communication within e-teaching scenarios. Based on elementary communication patterns and an easy-to-use technical infrastructure, a set of reference communication processes for e-education is created and carried out depending on the chosen teaching method. To prove the technical feasibility of the concept, the whole e-teaching process is supported by prototypic software solutions.

Chapter XVI: "Distributed Virtual Reality Learning Environments." Sam Redfern, Micheál Colhoun, Jordi Hernandez, Niall Naughton and Damien Noonan discuss emerging technologies for Collaborative Virtual Environments (CVEs), and outline their suitability for improving the pedagogical support provided by online learning environments. Starting points for their analyses are modern approaches to collaborative learning and their force in terms of supporting sociability and community, which are powerful mechanisms for combating isolation. Last, they present and discuss their own prototype CVE learning environments, their virtual campus architecture, and their model for complex task-based synchronous and asynchronous interaction.

Chapter XVII: "The Meaning and Development of KM in E-Learning According to the CARID Experience." Marco Pedroni firstly talks about common elements featuring knowledge management and e-learning, with special attention paid to knowledge structure and representation. Soon after he describes the software developed at CARID (Academic Centre for Didactic Research and Innovation at the University of Ferrara), for the representation of knowledge contexts and the support to information streaming, based on indexes and expansible concept maps.

The sixth and last section is made of two chapters.

Chapter XVIII: "Semantic Web and Digital Libraries." Giorgio Poletti starts his chapter by observing that the main objective of the Web was to define and build a universal archive, a virtual site in which the access to documents could be possible with no time or space limits. In this digital library, documents are equipped with logical connections that make it possible to each user, a definition of a reading "map" that expands according to the demands for knowledge that are gradually built up. This perspective is pointed in the direction of the "Semantic Web," a network capable of satisfying and understanding our requests, not by some "magical" telepathic communication between browser and navigator, but rather a data warehouse in which documents are matched to meta-data that permit specialized software to distinguish fields, importance, and correlation between documents.

Chapter XIX: "Media Selection from the Teacher's Point of View." Donatella Persico analyzes the problem choosing the most suitable media for achieving educational purposes as seen from the teacher's point of view. While observing the importance of the variables at play in the educational setting and the characteristics and potentialities of the various media, the author suggests some criteria for media choice, with particular attention towards the teacher's needs. She also discusses how a teacher's decision making must happen on the basis of the educational strategies the same teacher deems most appropriate and how techniques for material retrieval and reuse rather than new development must be favored.

Section I

Chapter I

Space, Time, and Process

Giuseppe Refrigeri
University of Cassino, Italy

Abstract

This chapter starts by describing the main features of distance education and by analyzing the changes induced from this way of the teaching-learning practice on space and time, which are considered as two constitutive factors of traditional education. The chapter then focuses on the following aspects: space ubiquity, simultaneity, and logical-psychological concomitance and depicts new scenarios for education while describing the changes induced on those aspects by distance.

Introduction

In the past years,[1] we have had a more marked diffusion of distance education and the rising of online education, which is replacing the former one in many cases. As a consequence, not only are the methods and techniques of the teaching-learning processes experiencing deep changes, but so is the whole didactical process. We can say that a real Khun revolution is happening, a paradigmatic fracture compared to the ultra millenary past experience of traditional education, which was based on the presence of the educational actors.

Obviously, the revolution described above has many different origins, but we can refer to it as the introduction of "distance" into teaching and, more in general, into the educational process. Such a distance because of different and rather known economic, social, and technical reasons seems to satisfy the ever increasing and different requests from education and mass-formation.

Distance is considered the feature of the formative and teaching process giving the student the chance of attending his or her studies in a time, place, and logical order far from the teacher's. Distance has caused a general change in today's teaching because it modifies identity, role, and the functions of space and time, two essential factors in the educational process.[2]

The change in the above two factors is considered the main cause of the deep innovations of today's education. Before the distance advent, teaching space and time were marked by the constitutive aspects of presence, that is, (a) space *ubiquity*, considered to be the coexistence of the process subjects, pupil and teacher, and of all other educational factors in a given, well delimited place; (b) *simultaneity*, as the coexistence of the above constitutive subjects during the whole process and sometimes over (as it happened in total institutions); and (c) context *concomitance*, intended as the assimilation of the educational offer, derived from the logical order of teaching programs and chronological times and rhythms of curricula units, with its psychological identification in the atmosphere of the educational environment.

Space and time, for their characteristics, have for a long time been considered natural granted factors, having little or no influence on educational and teaching dynamic processes traditionally dominated by human factors, that is, teacher, pupil, and their relationship. Just the same happened after the discoveries of evolutionary psychology. Many scholars were induced to think of space and time as natural elements in the didactical process. The introduction of "distance" has interrupted such an ultra-millenary tradition and has increased the dimension of space and time in education. Space has reached global dimensions and time has become longer and wider to embrace the whole day and life; as a consequence the subject has gained new opportunities for the fruition of education and the formative offer has become individualized. The above changes deeply influenced teaching process both on its theoretical and practical sides.

Many different reasons can be found to explain the advent of distance in educational processes and its influence on space ubiquity, time simultaneity, and logical-psychological contextuality. First of all, they can be referred to much more availability of free time by people in today's society depending on a clean decrease of manual work, everyday more and more is given to machines, robots, and automatons, or on social reasons, among which a more careful work organization. In a more decisive way, the introduction of the ICT in education intervened in changing teaching-learning contexts. Networks and especially the

Internet let the subjects of the educational process interact at planetary and interplanetary distances, synchronously and asynchronously and modifies the way people communicate.

In the following paragraphs, the three dimensions of distance will be analyzed and the modifications induced on all process factors and on the teaching process in its systemic entirety will be discussed.

The Expansion of Space Ubiquity in Education

First of all we have to remember that the spatial factor in education is usually intended as whatever physical environment where the actions have taken and currently take place directly or indirectly referred to the teaching-learning process. The Apollo Licius' Temple in Athens, where Aristotle taught his followers, can be considered an instructive space like the peripato (the shadowy avenues) where the Stagirite taught his disciples while walking. In the same way, but some centuries after in the Middle Ages it can still be considered educational spaces with the sacristies and the conventual rooms, or the Episcopal and parish schools where the Holy Writs, and in most favorable cases reading and writing, were learned.

Today educational spaces include classrooms, laboratories, (where special teaching activities are carried out, i.e., science, foreign language, computer, gym, and playground) libraries, and video libraries, etc.[3] It clearly emerges from what has been reported until now that "space" as an educational factor has always been considered essential for the teaching process because it was the physical environment where activities could be developed, but it was, and is still today, of secondary importance if compared to the process itself and to all other factors. The space subsidiary with respect to other educational factors is demonstrated, in the author's opinion, from the lack of exclusivity, role and function of the spaces devoted to education. They are in fact very often considered multiuse places to be used for administrative and political elections, or to be adapted to repositories and retirements during wars and natural disasters, etc.

Today the changes we are discussing are about the introduction of distance due to ICT, are making the educational space a primary element or, at least, a second lead actor in the teaching process and are assigning to it the power of intervention on identity and results of the process itself.

Physical Modifications of Space

It has to be noted that space as an educational factor is having modifications both inside and outside the formal school environment.

Inside, the typical presence elements are: classrooms, libraries, reading halls, labs, gyms, executive and administrative management offices, re-structuring to satisfy the distance needs while maintaining their traditional functions in the oral and written communication. In other words, their structure and organization are changing and enriching of more equipments; that is, traditional furnishings are replaced by multimedia and computer instruments and like desks, they are built with special attention to technical peculiarities for multimedia and networking communication. Furthermore, new places and structures are made, particularly labs for preparation of teaching material, group work, etc.

Outside, we have architectonic innovations, new places for distance needs and ICT services. In new and renovated buildings the traditional structure of schools (classroom and offices) is changing its architectonic configuration, more and better equipped spaces are assigned to individual and group work. In many schools and universities there are rooms with computer services and procedures to be used from single students and/or groups of them.

More radical changes in the features of the educational space factor are induced from the introduction of virtuality; it has to be intended as an extension of space dimension in flexible and global terms, enlarging the educational space to dimensions we couldn't image a few years ago.

A virtual classroom is now a teaching-learning place which dimensions can vary from a single room to the earth globe, where students can work alone or in groups and different communities can coexist.[4] This new meaning of educational space is a very important innovation, because it overcomes the physical nature of the classroom and reaches the mental and psychological extension of every possible dimension. In Western philosophical tradition this meaning is new and introduces further changes in educational contexts.

As regards specifically teaching process a remark is needed: together with the constitutive feature of space described above we have many other innovations, which can be referred to the separation today existing among the different educational context factors. First, we must remember what happens to the two subjects of the process: teacher and student, who can be physically separated. It is a paradigmatic innovation, which many pedagogists often consider skeptically and sometimes refuse, being faithfully bound to physical presence. This new paradigm must be still metabolized in its importance and appropriate use; experiences, on another side, show that we are in front of a change producing great teaching and social advantages since many people can attend lessons at any age and any condition of life, jobs, and geographical distribution. Secondly, we can see the enlargement of the teaching-learning context. It extends from a very narrow school building to very far physical environments and to virtual environments. In other words research institutions, libraries, and databases all over the world overbearingly enter in the new classroom and determine the need of new literacy skills. Furthermore a successful implementation of the didactic process needs new learning and social skills both in students and teachers. In regards to the last ones, a more specialized and complex professionalism is needed based upon IT and ICT literacy, networking, netsurfing, etc., which are all useful in crossing and going along these new global spaces.

Thirdly, the teaching-learning communication enriches new languages of a greater iconic function and of a higher heuristic depth, due to greater data amount availability and to more rational enquiry processes. Last, even if it may be obvious, the changes in the physical space of education induce the pluralization of teaching methods.

Modifications in the Functions of Space

The introduction of distance in education modifies all didactical functions of space. The schools and all other educational places, besides keeping their main functions, are enriching of planning, organizing, and evaluating functions better pertaining to the management of educational processes and systems. In Italy, for example, traditional education has been usually conceived in places different from the classroom, under the influence of subjects different from students and teachers (mainly by central and local government or by publishing houses and firms producing different teaching materials). Today the school is acquiring a new plurality of functions thanks to the introduction of school autonomy. POFs (*Piani dell'offerta formativa*—Formative Offer Plans), which all Italian schools must prepare at the beginning of the school year, are an emblematic expression of this recent function.

With respect to teaching programming, which was introduced in Italian schools about 40 years ago to overcome the Ministry centrality and rigidity[6], the POF now has relevant elements of innovation; it originates in fact from a more place-joined conception of education, partially more respectful of the real learning need and competence of the student.

As a consequence of school autonomy, the places of education, at least in Italy, have gained more and more importance in regards to planning and programming functions and strategies for the control of the teaching process and the use of evaluation instruments. Furthermore, experimentation and research in teaching methodology, which are more and more important today in school and educational places, due to the need of making teaching and learning effective, can be included among the new functions of educational space.

Teachers' initial and in-service training have changed their features for the space expansion. Only a few teachers each time could attend courses, which were usually made in their school and needed the presence of special professionals in that school. Now all teachers, or special categories among them, can be involved in training courses and can use ICT for distance and online training. Good examples of the changes described above can be found in Italy in the training courses for novice teachers, mostly based on the use of e-learning platforms, and in-service teachers' computing literacy, where thousands of teachers are attending online computing courses.

In regards to the teaching process, the changes in space function are chiefly concerning teacher and teaching methods and instruments. Today's teacher is involved in functions very different from teaching ones, but not less important with respect to them. The guidance control and management and the tutoring are good examples for these new functions. We must remember that the expansion of educational space caused important changes in teaching methods and instruments, so that the whole process itself deeply changed[7].

In regards to the teaching methods, the specialization of educational space for different subjects involved in the educational-training processes must be noted (i.e., extra-schooling for adults, recovering from drop-outs, high professional education for firms and corporations, special education for disabled persons, etc.) In all of the above cases, educational space increases the number of its functions and the well known and traditional individualization method, dating back to R. Dottrens, assumes global and virtual features. The changes concerning teaching instruments are as much important as the methods. With computing and networking new languages and possible environments are allowed, the whole teaching plan has to be reconsidered and continuous professional re-conversion has to become a common feature of teachers.

Modifications in Space's Identity

The introduction of distance is also changing the identity of educational space as a process factor. It is, in fact, strengthening the plural meaning of classrooms and any other place in educational agencies. Some decades ago, the places of education were quite exclusively identified with school spaces. Recently, educational spaces have expanded to embrace a great plurality of environments. Today home is an educational space more than in the past, (for the presence of ICT instruments together with books, magazines, multimedia, and mass media) organizations and corporations are other educational places, as are local Authorities and Administrations. Municipalities, for example, provide not only occasional educational spaces, they have special equipped rooms for training and education of their workers and other people. If this metamorphosis is evident in non-formal educational agencies, things are not very different in the informal ones. Informal agencies, mostly made by different environment expressions like town and natural habitat, are considered for their aspects, a more powerful educational place when compared to non-formal agencies, both for their positive potentials, and for the risks and dangers one can meet within them. Environment, agreeing with F. Frabboni and F. Pinto Minerva (2001), can be considered as a "Knowledge data bank" because "town and landscape are like reading copybooks, information encyclopedias…," a natural warehouse of "both signs-traces of the past ages and witnesses of present culture: sounds, images, words, objects and so on." There is no doubt that pluralization of educational space identity is due to more reasons, among which the expansion of educational into social, life-level raising, and social space fruition all play a relevant role.

The Expansion of Time Simultaneity

Time, as an educational and teaching process factor, has to be intended as every moment, every period, and all these together when the teaching-learning actions take place. Every hour and every day of lesson, the duration of every exercise, every lab activity, etc., can be seen as elements of the educational time. In the same way every period in the school year and/or academic year and every cycle in education (trimester, semester, school year, and the same educational cycle) can be considered educational times too.[8] We can consider time to be devoted to education, also the hour amounts periodically and annually dedicated to each topic, subject, and/or discipline. Finally, we can consider every human life as an educational time devoted to this function: babyhood, childhood, adolescence, youth, and maturity, and the school levels and periods referred to them. Infant school, concerning the first introduction of a child into the school system; primary school, where the first knowledge elements are acquired; high school, where pupils go after the primary school, are all examples of educational times, even if the whole compulsory period (as the set of part or all the above periods) is an educational time itself.[9] The university and any advanced educational period, which follow all other school times, are further educational times.

After the distance introduction, the school time and any other educational time, had and are having deep changes, to be intended chiefly as chronological expansions of different kind and duration. The changes have such an importance and significance that they are revolutionizing the factors of the teaching process with respect to "presence" characteristics. There are two changes concerning time factor. They are: a vertical one and a horizontal one.

Time Vertical Expansion

The vertical expansion of time has to be intended as a linear extension, or more properly, the age raising of schooling and education in each individual. Some decades ago, it was limited at the first age period and, only in some more fortunate cases, it was extended to youth; today, vice versa. It has dilated until the life's end for a higher number of people and potentially for everyone. This phenomenon cannot be mistaken with compulsory schooling period evolution, marking school social function in many industrialized world countries.[10] In this case the different extension of schooling compulsory periods never went over the youth years and was mostly concerned with the presence feature of education.

The vertical extension of chronological distance cannot be confused with continuous professional and management training, during work life and until retiring age. In this case, the extension is only occasional or recurring, developed in special courses for qualification, or re-qualification, organization, or re-organization, and technical make up.

Time extension caused by distance is a new situation, marked by a permanent availability of time to devote to education; a new life condition giving each person the chance to learn and train all along his life. Vertical time extension has induced at least two more relevant changes on the teaching process. First of all it produced the student diversification; it contributed to changing students' typology from the traditional and general pupil, exclusively devoted to studies for the preparation to future life and to young people, who came to the end of their school period and were ready to enter in working world, and finally, to operators of every adult age (unskilled workers, highly skilled workers, technicians, employees, managers, etc.) or to people retired from work who came back to the university for the pleasure of doing something they couldn't when they were young.

Depending on the above diversification, time vertical extension introduced new methods and instruments in teaching. It led to the personalization of didactical communication by means of ICT with a great variety of students having different features. Due to students' differences it is necessary to use specific teaching communication methods and instruments (mostly starting from personal working experience and life sense); mass media and computers became permanent factors in the teaching process while helping teachers and students in finding personal ways of communication. It changed the meaning and use of science and technology in education.

At last the student-teacher relationship expanded, it turned from simultaneous interaction into diachronic educational time; otherwise stated, distance introduced in a systematic way asynchronous communication in the teaching process.

Time Horizontal Extension

Time extension as a school and educational factor also happened horizontally. By this expression we mean the modular availability people have of different time periods during the day, the week, and the year to freely devote to study and education. Besides the morning or afternoon hours traditionally devoted to school, other hours and new day hours have become educational time, including the evening and night (i.e., for each week day, including the holidays, happened just the same). Also if a great role in the horizontal extension of educational time has to be assigned to the organization of industrial work and to the advent of service society, we must remember the distance contribution in the same phenomenon and especially the value introduced by the features of mass media, computer, and ICT. The main consequence of this time extension has been the change induced in the meaning of school and educational time; it mostly belonged to youth in the common sense, but it is now expanding more and more to all life periods. Further consequences of this time extension can be found in the social and existential meanings of life periods; life time is no more structured in three separate and sequential segments: study time, work time, and retiring age time. Every life period, except the first one is now multifunctional because it can be devoted to work, study, and amusement. The lifetime itself finally gets a multifunctional meaning, in the sense that living time can be used with more intents and aims.

The most important modification in time concept is less perceived by contemporary culture and can be found in the passage from needing time to possibility time, it is evidenced in some contemporary philosophical currents (among which phenomenology and existentialism).

The Diversification of
Logical-Psychological Concomitance

The third and last modification induced by distance can be found in the diversification of the subject's logical concomitance and in the dissipation of the psychological atmosphere, mostly due to presence teaching. Logical-psychological concomitance is present in traditional lessons including everywhere they take place: in conferences, in group works, in training, and on the job siding experiences, etc. On these occasions all subjects are involved in the same place and all together, all along the event time, and in the same situations.

The diversification of logical concomitance induced by distance has to be intended as the individualization of the logical order of the topics to be learned and of the study and lessons' sequence, which are more rigid in the presence teaching. The psychological dissipation must be intended as the dissipation of the existential atmosphere in the teaching-learning relation; it is traditionally marked by reciprocal influences, by transfer of emotional experiences, and by various support forms and mutual growth.

With distance students immersed in a "cold" psychological atmosphere (i.e., teacher doesn't influence him or her psychologically both in negative and positive terms). Due to this modification, students feel free to choose their personal route among planned teaching units and individualize their learning. For what has been reported until now, logical-psychological concomitance is a new feature of distance education often seen in its negative aspects, more than in its positive features. By many educators, and even by some pedagogists, the logical-psychological context diversification is accused of coldness of teacher-pupil relation detachment, all leaving the student in an uncertain state negatively acting on his or her development. On the contrary, recent psychopedagogy research assigns to the above diversification and to the consequent learning individualization meta-cognitive functions positively acting on students' development.

References

Frabboni, F., & Pinto Minerva, F. (2001). *Manuale di pedagogia generale*. Roma-Bari: Laterza.

Further Reading

1.   Space and time in education

Barman, Z. (1999). *Dentro la globalizzazione. Le conseguenze sulle persone.* Bari: Laterza.

de Kerckhove, D. (1993). *Brainframes, mente, tecnologia,mercato.* Bologna: Baskerville.

de Kerckhove, D. (2000). *La pelle della cultura.* Ancona-Milano: Costa & Nolan.

de Kerckhove D. (2003). *La conquista del tempo*. Roma: Editori Riuniti.

Delors, J. (1997). *Nell' educazione un tesoro. Rapporto dell' UNESCO della Comissione Internazionale sull' Educazione per il XXI secolo*. Roma: Armando.

Elias, N. (1993) *Time: An Essay*. Oxford: Blackwell.

Elias, N. (1994). *The civilizing process: The history of manners and state formation and civilization*. Oxford: Blackwell Publishers.

Farn, M. (1970). *La percezione dello spazio*. Bologna: Cappelli.

Featerstone, M. (Ed.). (1990). *Global culture. Nationalism, globalism and modernity*. London: Sage.

Fraisse, P. (1971). *La percezione del tempo*. Torino: SEI.

Hawking, S., & Penrose, R. (2002). *La natura dello spazio e del tempo* (trad.it.). Milano: Rizzoli.

Huntington, S. P. (2000). *Lo scontro delle civiltà e il nuovo ordine mondiale*. Milano: Garzanti.

Lachiéze-Rey, M. (1999). *L' infini. De la philosophie à l' astrophisique*, Paris: Hatier.

Lacroix, P. (2001). *E-formation*. Paris: Dunod.

Levy, P. (1997). *Il virtuale*. Milano: Cortina.

Mansell, R., Samarajiva, R., & Mahan, E. (Eds.). (2002). *Networking knowledge for information societies: Institution & intervention*. Delft University Press.

Mazure, A., Mathez, G., & Mellier, Y. (1994). *Chronique de l' espace-temps*. Paris: Masson.

McLuhan, M. (1962). *La galassia Gutenberg*. Roma: Armando.

McLuhan, M. (1964). *Gli strumenti del comunicare*. Milano: Il Saggiatore.

Merleau Ponty, J. (1974). *Cosmologia del XX secolo. Studio epistemologico e storico sulle teorie cosmologiche contemporanee*. Milano: Il Saggiatore.

Morin, E. (1999). *I sette saperi necessari all'educazione del futuro*. Milano: Raffaello Cortina.

Morin, E. (2001). *La testa ben fatta*. Milano: Raffaello Cortina.

Morin, E. (2002). *L' identità umana*. Milano: Cortina.

Refrigeri, G. (2002). Le modificazioni didattiche nella scuola multiculturale, in *Quaderni di antropologia e scienze del linguaggi*, n. 8/2002 (pp. 205-216).

Vicario, G. B. (1973). *Tempo psicologico ed eventi*. Firenze: Giunti-Barbera.

2.   Teaching and didactics

Cambi, F. (2000). *L' arcipelago dei saperi. Progettazione curricolare e percorsi didattici nella scuola dell' autonomia.* IRRSAE-Toscana, vol.1. Firenze: Le Monnier.

Cambi, F. (Ed.). (2002). *La progettazione curricolare nella scuola contemporanea.* Roma: Carocci.

Damiano, E. (1993). *L' azione didattica, Per una teoria dell' insegnamento.* Roma: Armando.

Erdas, E. (1991). *Didattica e formazione. La professionalità docente come processo.* Roma: Armando.

Galliani, L. (1998). Didattica e comunicazione. In *Studium educationis* (Vol. 4, pp. 626-662).

Iori, M. L., & Migliore, A. (2001). *Imparare a insegnare. I ferri del mestiere.* Milano: Franco Angeli.

Margiotta, U. (Ed.). (1999). *L' insegnante di qualità. Valutazione e performance.* Roma: Armando.

OCDE (1994). *La qualité de l' enseignement.* Paris: OCDE.

Semeraro, R. (1999). *La progettazione didattica. Teoria, metodi, contesti.* Firenze: Giunti.

Vertecchi, B. (1993). *Decisione didattica e valutazione.* Firenze: La Nuova Italia.

Endnotes

[1]   Distance education (in Italian *"Formazione a Distanza"*—*FAD*) has been operating since the 19th century, mostly by mail when the distance wideness, the roads' lack, and the severity of weather and all obstacles of personal order didn't permit the school attendance, to promote literacy and technical-professional skill learning. In the second half of the 20th century, electric and electronic media gave new strength to distance education and online education was born due to computing and networking diffusion.

[2]   Together, space and time must be considered essential factors of the educational process: pupil, teacher, discipline topics, (values, knowledge, skills, behaviors, etc.) teaching methods and instruments, educational and social aims of each educational action. The identity of each of them, the role and the functions they played in the educational process, and their weights

within the same process have always been defined by educational theories and educational models.

3   With context services must be intended all teaching actions developed in concomitance with the proper and complete teaching process: guidance actions, tutorship, training, internationalization, placement, etc. They are not only simple support services to teaching process, but real and complete interventions, all containing educational contents together with the assistance ones.

4   "Virtual" substantially means not real, but possible. When applying this term to teaching-learning physical environments, we must refer not only to really existing contexts, but to wider ones, maybe not available today, but possible, if we are able to know them or discover their existence.

5   School autonomy has been introduced into Italian school by Law n. 59/1997 (March 17th 1997, better known as Bassanini Law) and subsequent regulations on the autonomy of school institutions (March 8th 1999, M.D. n.275).

6   Teaching planning has been introduced into Italian schools by Delegate Decrees in 1974. The first time they gave to the teacher council the function of "planning care of educational action." Later, this function has strengthened by the EIP (Educational Institute Plan) and by FOP (Formative Offer Plan).

7   Teaching methodology has expressed a great variety of models until now. Firstly we have Socrates' maieutic, surviving for many centuries, subsequently we have Comenius and Herbart methods in XVII and XVIII centuries; very recently, in XX century, we have Bruner spiral structure, Gagné-Briggs rationalization lesson, Bloom mastery learning. All these methods, though very different, are marked by presence, or face-to-face interaction. The first breaking element with respect to tradition is based on teaching individualization according to Robert Dottrens ideas. With respect to this first individualization, always based on the "presence," we have a new kind of individualization (second generation) based on the "distance."

8   The cycle concept (circle) is old. It describes a close phase which is proposed more times in curricula progression. Nowadays, it is present again with Moratti reform just to indicate a definite time, and an approximately long period before being a course.

9   The compulsory schooling, besides being a duty to get a formation in order to enter actively and consciously the society, takes the significance in the literature of approximately long attending period.

10   The compulsory schooling has been introduced into many European countries including Italy in the second half of 19th century. The Italian children

of the post-unity period had to go to school for 2/3 years compulsorily, later the compulsory schooling time has taken wider dimensions to reach the actual 12 years of the formative compulsory schooling introduced by the Moratti reform. But this dilation is referring to young schooling and the situation of the considering process.

Chapter II

Contributions of Psychopedagogy to the Inclusion of ICT in the Pedagogical Environment

Maria Apparecida Mamede-Neves
Catholic University of Rio de Janeiro, Brazil

Abstract

This chapter aims at critically analyzing distance education and the interactions between ICT, teaching, and knowledge structures based on the contributions of psychopedagogy. The first section examines the innovations currently taking place in the field of psychopedagogy, in which the concept of the physical classroom is being replaced by that of the virtual classroom. The second and third sections analyze, respectively, the learning through ICT and the incorporation of the Web in the pedagogical practices, their possibilities, and limitations. A fourth segment regards the use of the Web by the youngsters and analyses the possible reasons for its great significance and use among youngsters. The conclusion of this chapter stresses the need to acknowledge the value of the interrelationship between the culture of physical presence and cyberculture in the teaching environment, as well as the need for teachers to change their mentality and to become effectively enabled to add ICT to their pedagogical practice.

Introduction

Why speak of psychopedagogy, instead of pedagogy, when the heart of the current debate is teaching in the knowledge society? Maybe because in the field of pedagogy, we have witnessed, with a certain degree of apprehension, several attempts to find the decisive factor in guaranteeing effective learning. Searching for answers to this question, pedagogy has dichotomized the individual and the group, the natural and the social, ignoring the fact that the answers do not solely depend on those who teach or those who learn, or on society only. This has been so for several decades, resulting, for example, in the decline of biological factors as determining in the success or failure of learning after years of excessive biologist; in the prevalence of psychology; in the prevalence of educational technology; in the prevalence of the social factor, considered for a long time, the only architect of knowledge, and so forth. There were several theories and several innovative proposals which became disused because they did not achieve the goal they longed for.

Looking into this trail, it is clearly not enough that factors considered essential to learning are individually announced and enunciated. Certainly, the human being cannot be studied in parts, made of hermetic departments, as if he were a collage of different clippings, a fragmented being. Current studies are increasingly showing that people are both singular and collective, always inserted in a certain social context, expressing their way of thinking in their daily lives and informal communication. Therefore, human beings are part of a natural and of a social order (Elias, 1994). From this perspective, the heart of the matter is trying to find out how this takes place. In other words, one should work with a complex approach to the act of learning, not only because cognition and emotion are structural elements in learning, simultaneously dependent on the body, the context, and the relationship, but also because there is always a connection between the individual and the environment which necessarily places them in a position of interdependence.

Psychopedagogy, such as it is known today, goes beyond the isolated fields of pedagogy and psychology. Formerly used as an adjective as a way of rendering the pedagogical function more psychological, it now exists as a noun, as organized knowledge which, adopting complex thinking, on the terms proposed by theorists that, based on ideas proposed by Prigogine and Morin among others, dare to go beyond their strict fields of study to reflect upon the global culture that today, more than ever, is at this level mostly stimulated by the technological advances that, chiefly, allow us to shorten distances (Carvalho & Mendonça, 2003). Along that line of thinking, the theoretical advances in the field of psychopedagogy seek to know the dimensions that, in an insoluble way, constitute the individual that learns, this active relation being, seeker of the knowledge of himself and the universe. On the psychological point of view, knowledge always floats in a zone of uncertainties of large proportions and, exactly because of that, the gathering of knowledge takes an important ethical-political function.

The building of knowledge takes place where reason and affection intersect: in the tension between cultural diversity and the universality of knowledge; between personal fate and social/historical fate—such tensions being regarded as dimensions, at the same time distinct and inseparable. On the other hand, the construction of knowledge, from this perspective, presupposes that the individual takes a step beyond the acquisition of information to incorporate and manipulate the instruments of questioning, logically assuming that learning is being able to question. For that reason, the individual's presuppositions are fundamental when we study the new skills and tools necessary for teachers to act in the current pedagogical environments, in which the use of ICTs (information and communication technologies) and distance education are increasingly more widespread (Santos, 2003).

On that sense, one of the most significant experiences in e-learning, among the ones I have participated in, was carried out between the end of the 90s until 2002 and will be reinstated in 2005, after a period which was destined to the critical analysis of the project. I am referring to the "Curriculum and Educational Practice Specialization Course", most of which is carried out long distance and has been developed by the Education Department at the Catholic University of Rio de Janeiro (PUC-Rio), with the duration of up to two years for conclusion. My participation in this work occurs in different levels: as a member of the team that organized and implemented the project and now executes a critical evaluation of the collected data; as a general coordinator of the project in several stages of the process; and as a teacher in more than one subject in all the classes formed. This initiative allowed 1,000 teachers, who are located in 14 states in Brazil, to attend and be certified up to 2002, separated by great distances, considering the extension of the country. In order to have an idea of that magnitude, it is important to know that the average distances between the cities attended was 1,690 Km, except that the largest distance was 3,409 Km and the smallest was 380 Km!

Considering the magnitude of the process, only with the use of e-learning would it be possible to reach those professionals and obtain the proposed objectives, because it was essential that this formation occurred without having to take the teacher away from the classroom and for having, as consequence, to face the great distances that separated the groups.

Aiming at the continuous formation of managers and Elementary, Junior High, and High school teachers, the central proposal of the course divides into two segments:

- Provide these professionals with an update and a deepening into central educational issues in Brazil, with emphasis on those that have a direct implication with the problems related to the content and the psychopedagogical practices of their subjects, through the theoretical discussion and practical actions the make the establishment of cooperative learning and the development of inter-subject actions and practices.

- Offer the teacher who takes the course the possibility to reflect upon the practice of citizenship in a world that is filled with science and technology, stimulating the critical appropriation of knowledge of those areas and developing competence that allows them to use them critically.

Exactly because of this second segment, one of the specific objectives of the course is to introduce the teacher, in a critical way, in the use of technology and digital information, since the group being attended is very far from the appropriation of these possibilities. In reality, this project has been very well succeeded and the evaluation executed on its efficiency offered an extremely rich empirical basis (Mamede-Neves, 2004).

Another investigative process is aggregated to this aforementioned process, which is also very significant to me: my effective participation in the implementation and development Central Coordination for Distance Learning (CCEAD) at Catholic University of Rio de Janeiro (PUC-Rio). CCEAD PUC-Rio coordinates, supports, and promotes the activities of distance learning at the University, providing the growth of virtual learning communities with the same characteristics of excellence found in the practices and academic traditions of Catholic University-Rio. CCEAD's objectives are: accompany and give technological and pedagogical support to distance projects and courses developed by the Departments and Units of the Catholic University-Rio; promote research new format projects and instruments for distance learning; promote and develop courses and events of distance learning and establish contacts, agreements, and partnerships with companies and other institutions, aiming at distance learning.

From the experience originated from the evaluations carried out throughout the entire specialization course for teachers all over Brazil, regarding my participation as psychopedagogical coordinator at CCEAD PUC-Rio, I extract a significant range of empirical data which support the considerations I make in this text, not just concerning a change of paradigm in relation to the model of lesson, in other words, the transition of a teaching model where the teacher is physically present, to a course carried out long distance, as those considerations regarding the instruments used in e-learning and the importance of the symbolic universe of the Web.

Breaking the Barriers of the Physical Classroom: Reaching Cyberculture

When we say that what a student learns today is no longer almost exclusively what the teacher (once the absolute source of knowledge and sole responsible for the transfer of that knowledge) taught him, we surmount the limits of the physical classroom and place learning in other spaces, such as cyberspace. Put this way, it seems very simple, but it is not.

Such a progress advance involves, as an essential condition, a mentality shift on the part of parents and teachers, a change in curricula, as well as the appropriation of, and familiarity with, a new language, the digital language, and with new technologies. The so-called ICT, defined as computing, learning, and a range of activities in education, which include, for example, the use of CD-ROM as sources of information, electronic toys or games to develop different skills such as spatial awareness and psychomotor control, e-mail to support collaborative writing and sharing of resources, internet-based research, etc. Another complicating factor of such a stance is the inevitable passage from teaching based on the teacher's physical presence (which does not necessarily mean traditional teaching since these concepts should not and cannot be seen as synonymous) to teaching practices which rely on e-learning.[1]

These questions require taking some crucial points into consideration. Let us try to explain.

The possibility of building knowledge in a new cultural order, cyberspace, in which each individual or group is a node in a greater and expanding universe/ network and where concepts are formulated in such a way as to become difficult to unravel, has been greatly resisted in several teaching communities. Why so? To be sure, it seems that answering this question demands expanding the discussion and looking for reasons beyond the unawareness, on the part of teachers, of the use of these tools and the lack of appropriate teacher training. We need to understand what lies beneath this fear, this resistance, especially among teachers, to embrace this new pedagogical approach. Pscychopedagogy has been pointing out that deeper causes play a role here and that such fear is not limited to teachers—it affects every human being facing changes that can shake the paradigms that support them.

In the specific case of the evolution of media, here considered both as technologies and as mediation processes, that is, instruments that allow means to find, assure and communicate meanings, we notice that, cyclically, every time there is a qualitative leap in the world of media, there is always a certain suspicion that this new medium will produce a loss of his unit. This possibly happens because, since it is an innovation, it is interpreted as an intrusion into the constituted cultural scene, particularly into the pedagogical scene, seemingly meant to destabilize the status quo. This is what happened when the printed book, the radio, and television were invented, and it's been so since the start of the cybernetic revolution.

Actually, in order to explain this recurring attitude towards every novelty that comes to life, we have to ask ourselves on which structural bases human beings effectively operate in the world.

In my experience in e-learning, not only for the number of projects I have participated in, but also for the number of years in which these experiences developed, I had the opportunity to know and use a large portion of the mediation models and tools available at each time. It has become clear to me that each of the implemented innovations intended to bring advances, but this relation between innovation and advances, in terms of success in the use of ICT and e-learning, did not necessarily happened in the projects because, among other reasons, the most important was certainly the fact that it involved changes that were not always accepted or assimilated by the teachers and not effectively supported by the teaching institutions. As a matter of fact, regarding this point, it is necessary to take into account that what's implicit in the repercussion of an innovation about the standards of relationship, knowledge, and professionalism of the teachers that adopt it depend a lot on how this innovation got to them.

I understand that the innovations made in the e-learning field had to be externally induced, for inter-disciplinary reasons that impose, mainly among the field of Education and Technology. In other words, they demand an effort from the teachers to dominate the use of each new tool and understand the value of adopting it, which basically depends on the significance it will have on the everyday professional life of that particular teacher and the pragmatic value it provides, not taking into account that all the change also has to be taken by the institution that the teacher is in. I have always attested that the success of the innovation only occurred when there was some taskforce carried out for that purpose.

Actually, the relation between innovation and change, seen as re-significance of the practices (in which case, pedagogical practice) is not an easy relation. An innovation that has the purpose of determining modifications that involve, chiefly, the application of new technologies and consequently, new ways of acting based on new values, symbols, and procedures, is not built individually, nor does it occur through imposition. It must be anchored on pedagogical initiatives that go beyond individual efforts and, certainly, imply two tasks: overcome idea of hyper-responsibility of the teacher for the teaching quality that he is offering, grant him the position of product and producer of living experiences in the context he is in, which determines potentialities, circumstances, and limitations. In that sense, changing the pedagogical field requires a change of attitude, a renovation of the pedagogical practices, a theoretical/practical transformation. It is a cooperative action, built on interaction, on the everyday and collective exchanges that happen in the teaching-learning environment, from concrete actions developed by professionals. It is in that "environment" that the game of changes is played (Farias, 2003, 2002).[2]

We believe that man exists in a society, in groups and institutions, which represent a safe haven and that there is a tendency for society to defend and maintain what already exists and to avoid possible changes, thus keeping a convenient repetition as a guarantee of the sought-after balance, which, in the history of man, always proves to be ruptured. A common truism in the history of human communication is that any innovation in mass media brings about social change (McLuhan, 2000, p. 60). As I have mentioned above, this is the time we are living in education, a time when it is necessary for teachers, in order to absorb all these changes and to relinquish this stifling sectarism which affects both teachers and learners, to be able to find another didactic paradigm to cope with this new pedagogical moment—e-learning. They need to take on new teaching and learning styles that will enable them to both enjoy the existing innovations in the pedagogical fields and critically assess them.

Learning Through the Use of ICT

The learning process today that is more and more carried out by means of communication instruments had its start in one of man's most primitive yearnings, which is to communicate. This communication always occurs in a direct or indirect way. Direct, when it uses a language with their peers, either by a set of gestures or a chain of articulated sounds; indirect, when it is done by drawn images or a set of written marks that, although not being present, allows it to leave a communication of what the person felt or thought. It is, therefore, in these languages that the relations, the encounters and failures to meet occur, for there is no society without communication.

Actually, the drawing activity is a power that has always wondered humanity and has been exerted by people since the most primitive times. It has been present since the first years of a child, which shows signs of great satisfaction when they leave their handprints on the sand, wet soil, or humid ground; when a child draws lines on a wall or humid car windows. From this pleasure that human beings have for drawing, a pleasure that follows these activities that records their emotions, their wishes, follows the pleasure to contemplate, to be able to leave for others what they have produced. There is therefore, in humanity, a very strong wish to communicate, for greeting a whole language that allows them to transmit their thoughts and for perpetuating their marks. The human being wanted that this communication could be established to beyond closer relations, covering distances and would extend to beyond their own lives. That is how humanity went from the paintings on rocks to the most developed arts, from papyrus to the printed book, invented the radio, the cinema, TV, the VCR, and the DVD, went from LP to CD, living, in the present, the apparent madness of the digital world. The world to which e-learning belongs.

There is no doubt that e-learning has at its disposal a very significant range of computational tools but, in order to be able to utilize their possibilities, it is necessary to take into account both the potentiality as well as the limitations of each tool. And most of all, not fall for the traps that the fascination for these new tools may inflict in the pedagogical setting, giving the illusion that, just by adopting it, we are in a new educational age. In fact, Blikstein, Cavallo (2003, 2002), Blikstein and Zuffo (2003), Cavallo and Blikstein (2004) very well analyze this point in various works.

We comment on some of these resources that are normally present in the online courses.

The digital book, mastered in CD, may be very interesting, as it allows the compiling of a very large range of information, with texts and images. However, even if it bring benefits with its adoption, it is only a resource that digits what could be printed and, many times, obliges the student to spend time and money with its printing, or because he does not have the habit of reading from a computer screen, and especially because, in the cases of deeper studies, he will need to have it in printing, to better compare it with other texts and develop better critical analysis. Therefore, its adoption does not mean to be using new didactics. It is like dressing the old ways with an illusory outfit that changes nothing in essence.

The use of multimedia such as CD-ROM for the development of a long-distance course, certainly bring better pedagogical resources, because it is a tool that contains, besides the texts, illustrated images and schemes in slides that are presented in synchronization with audio explanations; it may contain illustrated videos and self evaluations, all that presented in a related way, chiefly, if your plan follow the hypertext model. There is also the advantage of easy transportation and can be used in any machine that complies with the conditions of its resolution. However, the CD-ROM has the great disadvantage of being a limited, closed, and a dated tool, not allowing updates, it is replaced, which constitutes an additional cost.

In my own experience with long-distance courses in terms of Brazil, with students from all kinds of social/financial situations, with many of them not owning a computer and with the necessity to use the existing ones in their working places or at the house of family and friends, this option has proven extremely appropriate. I am referring to a complete course I assembled in CD-ROM about learning psychology (Mamede-Neves, 2002) for graduates, in which, besides all the other possible resources in this tool, I presented each theme in a small video lesson, with a bigger presentation screen than usual. That occurred not only because in the evaluation made by the students of previous courses, they argued that they lacked seeing and hearing from the teacher who was responsible for the course, but also because in an investigation I made about the dimensions and adjustments of the teacher's image in a video. The outcome showed that the area needed to be larger than the one normally used in order to avoid tiredness in the ones who watched it. The results of that experience, except for the impairments already pointed out, proved to be very positive.

We now get to interactive with networks such as the Internet and the resources it offers to e-learning. Disregarding the technological conditions that are crucial so that there is the necessary maintenance of the network that supports an online course, I state here a few considerations about the tools that these courses may have available.

Nowadays, the e-mails substitute, most of the time, the letters of conventional mail. Undeniably, e-mails are a very strong possibility for quick intercommunication and more and more democratically used, since free providers give a large group of people of lower social classes the opportunity to use it. Thus, with the increasing possibility to carry messages with larger attachments, we observe in the world of Internet users, the increasingly systematic exchange of news, the sending of information that involves pictures, images, small videos, etc. Since there is no need for this to occur in real time, I have no doubts that it constitutes an important resource in long-distance teaching, especially in the support for the live-teacher teaching, in the development of the discussion forums, which certainly are one of the best instruments for the construction of cooperative learning.

As for the chat rooms, as much as they are viewed as an opportunity for meeting between people in real time and that they are the Internet's greatest attraction especially for teenagers, it has been shown that in e-learning, they can only be affectively used by small groups and, even then, if there is not a theme that restricts the conversation, requiring a certain discipline among the participants and, many times, the need of interference of a coordinator that manages the discussion. Without those conditions, it becomes some kind of "Tower of Babel" where everyone speaks to each other, but very little is absorbed in terms of learning because they spread out in multiple insights that are loose and without the due correlation.

In fact, the presence of a group of tutors that are conveniently prepared to really work in a cooperative way with their group of students and that is in direct tuning with the team that is responsible for the course is very important for the success of an online course. At this point, it is essential for the teaching team to have experience in e-learning environment, not only in the content of the course but mainly, in the field of psychopedagogy, regarding the functioning of any group and the functionality that can be developed intra-group; regarding the establishment of collaborations and adequate partnerships; and regarding the strengthening of bonds among the participants.

What psychopedagogy normally recommends for live-teacher study group dynamics becomes much more necessary when it refers to online groups, because in that case we are fighting against distances and the fact that we cannot count on the non-verbal language. What has been written is always more difficult to be understood because it comes along with nuances of the voice, gesture, and in short, all the structures that the live presence certainly allows.

The videoconference is a resource that has come to us with great emphasis. However, after the first moment of excitement, we detected that it also needed to be observed and evaluated. In my experience at CCEAD PUC-Rio, I notice that it is necessary to incorporate the experience of who does TV when producing a videoconference. We cannot simply place a teacher in front of a camera and expect him or her to develop the theme in the same time length he or she would in a live-teacher lesson, even if he or she is a good communicator. The videoconference's chronometric time needs to be more reduced than the one of a live-teacher lesson, because it is necessary to take into account the fact that the student is distant, in another environment, even though the technology was being used allows the possibility of interaction with the teacher. This interaction is somewhat artificial, even if we make an effort. Therefore, the videoconference has to be carefully used, or else it will end up becoming a strong element of no interest by the student.

Let us talk now about simulations. According to Billiard (2004, p. 1) "all too often, interactive screenshot walkthroughs of applications and courses with multiple-choice assessments are called simulations, even though they do not create a simulated environment. Such training applications have their place in corporate training, but they don't allow learners to engage actively and learn from their own mistakes in a simulated environment." Actually, despite the potential risk that a simulation may have, online simulations are not frequently used and that leads us to believe that the greatest obstacle for its adoption lies on how to develop them and incorporate them effectively. On the other hand, when analyzing some of the simulations that are presented in the e-learning environment, we notice that they are not a real simulation because they are restricted to just repeating the use of strategies. In a true simulation, the users make choices that lead them to different paths that, in turn, lead to different results and, therefore, give users power of decision in the solution of the proposed problem, with the risk and consequences of their decision. In the processes of a real simulation, the inherent motivation is present, in other words, that in which the development of the task itself is rewarding and satisfactory, and mainly because the feedback of the actions taken reconstructs the possibility to reach the solution for the proposed problem.

Last, in relation to the teaching platforms that aggregate the aforementioned devices, we know that the environment for the creation and maintenance of courses that they carry out may be used both for totally long-distance courses and for back up for the live-teacher courses. In fact, at CCEAD PUC-Rio, that show support to live-teaching courses has been given with more regularity, which I consider, with Blikstein (2002), a very positive point, since it gradually introduces and incorporates the innovations making the effective intended changes. These platforms generally allow great interactivity, obviously if effi-ciently managed by the group of teachers and with a well-prepared tutorial system; many of them do not require a technical knowledge of the Internet by the teacher, that is, many are user friendly. On the other hand, they allow the importation of existing files in available software and, like in the live-teacher classroom space, besides what has been said, they allow conventional teaching material (texts, additional comments, demonstrations, evaluations, references) to be stored, student's personal writings, writings in collaboration and possibilities of research.

The Web and Pedagogical Practice

Lévy (1999), in the Introduction to his book *Cyberculture*, refers to the current barrage of information as the "second deluge." This is no doubt a very pertinent expression if we consider that nowadays we have at our disposal Net browsing which surprises us at every node, opening up new links and offering us a huge amount of information which multiplies at an uncontrollable speed in data banks, in hypertext, in networks.

In effect, we are witnessing an actual deluge of data which floods our search for new knowledge in a pluralistic and, at the same time, fragmented way and renders us unable to discriminate between what is relevant to the effective construction of our knowledge and what we should discard in this sea of records found in communication networks. Added to this we find a proliferation of images and sounds in the media, the constant hammering of Spam in the Web. We live, then, drowned in chaos of data and in crossfire of images.

However, if we think that, still based on the ideas of Pierre Lévy, the metaphor of a deluge involves Noah's Ark representing a well constituted small world, with the express goal of preserving organization and transmission in the midst of chaos. The ark is, in itself, the counterpart of whatever is in disarray; it is order per se. It is the balanced life within a life that is changing.

In this way, we preserve our differences, our singularities in relation to other arks. At the same time we maintain our differentiation, we exchange messages and surf the Net, in a permanent cross-fertilization. Only the deluge is universal.

As Lévy puts it (1999, p. 119), cyberspace does not engender a universal culture because it is everywhere, but rather because its form and main idea imply the collectivity of human beings, a universal novelty which brings the co-existence of images back to its original context, however at another level, on a completely different orbit. The new universality is built by the interconnection of messages themselves. In this sense, interactive networks, such as the Internet, are nothing but an intricate network of connecting devices and computers of different kinds, submarine cables, and satellite channels among other means of telecommunications, which facilitate communication and enable a planetary conversation. Technical advances certainly empower us, but they also leave to us the choice of what to transmit through them. Therefore, these advances are neither the perdition nor the salvation of human communication. We should not fool ourselves.

We are then back to the starting point, the fact that several teachers are not comfortable with e-learning. Could it be that, in the advent of cyberculture, lies the death of dialoguing? It does not seem so. However, how is the human being supposed to articulate these two different orders, such as the culture of printed materials and of teachers' physical presence and cyberculture? For that to happen, there needs to be a mentality shift allowing the incorporation of innovations into the pedagogical setting without cannibalizing it. Applying these considerations to the problem at hand, that is, the way the teacher uses both cultures, there will only be a balance between them if the teacher can see them as subject to an interrelationship in which their conditions interact without threatening one another and form a new integrated system. The teacher's internal flexibility in building his or her course within this different paradigm, as well as the knowledge that it will be no easy task, is therefore essential. It demands a change in curricula; inner changes in the teacher, mostly in his or her affective, rather than cognitive dimension; time for preparation and specific knowledge of how to work with materials in e-learning, a competency that cannot be acquired without proper guidance and experimentation. It is not something intuitive!

The Symbolic Universe of the Web's Virtual Reality

Why is the Web, as a symbolic universe, so appealing to teenagers? Why is the Internet so well accepted by them, keeping them hooked, immersed in it for such a long time, while many adults, especially teachers, underestimate and despise it? Let us think for a while about the characteristics of adolescence. It is commonly defined as a period situated within mobile boundaries, with childhood on one side and the promise of autonomy in adult life at the other extreme. It is a time of searching and of uncertainty, of establishing new relationships, and of manifestations resulting from new feelings, ways of thinking and behaving. A time of choices and projects built more on desires and fantasy than on reality, but which are the basic ingredients of consolidating their identity and building their knowledge. Considering this scenario, we may draw hypothesis, using the contribution of psychoanalysis, that the Web is an environment in which the illusion of user is always present. We know that what remains in the psychic space is the wish to reencounter what has been lived and what has been experienced and it is, therefore, a representation that replaces the absences. Only that, in that space the absence is not felt as a demand, as a strength that forces one to keep searching, in the case of the Web, the links keep unfolding in an adventure that gives the illusion of infinite (Lombard, 2004ab, 2003; Turkle & Whither, 2002).

In reality, we must admit that the computer, with its programs which accept mistakes and allow redoing, erasing without shame or scruples, and the Web, which never gets tired, seems to always be available, and repeats as many times as necessary without complaining, both allow their users to have pleasure, creating the illusion that there is affection in their icons and links. Receptivity and unlimited patience are their trademarks; qualities we believe do not always exist in teachers in physical settings. In the development of cyberculture, the spread of knowledge expands, as well as a mode of conversation in which respect, attention, kindness, generosity, and a gambling spirit are trademarks of asynchronous communication, although this has been structured, developed, and adopted in this way in an attempt to lessen the harshness of messages which are basically written, voiceless, and with no touch or smell.

When this happens, the representation of both the computer and the Internet are connected to an experience of satisfaction through which a condition of agreeability is conferred on them.

Knowledge requires a series of trials, not just contemplating from afar. Young people are not afraid of trying, and the changes that happen on the screen when they drag the mouse and click, the paths they take on the Internet, the discoveries they make on search engines, all this gives them the illusion of exerting their autonomy because they feel as if they were walking with their own feet, which deletes the idea that behind all of these available possibilities lies an entire cultural and technological construction. They become fascinated, just like the infant who sees the object of desire when it hears us babble something meaningless but magical where these young people's wishes are understood and where they feel protected as to their real image and identity, since they are operating in the fluidity of virtual reality.

The Web as a Space for Virtual Social Production

The new virtual cultures refer to new ways of being together, which result from extremely fast processes related to the collective imaginary of a modernity identified with the speed of the flow of information and with the fragmentariness of information languages. The virtual town is a fact today and it is located in the virtual space of telematic networks. Its topography has to do with the logic behind the paths in hypertext and in information networks. The analogy to personal relations in a physical setting can encompass parts and circuits shared by different attendees, even simulating face-to-face encounters with Web cams and promoting synchronous conversations (Johnson, 2003; Martín-Barbero, 2002).

The neighbors and fellow countrymen from the cybertowns are no longer the ones anchored to the same physical space or born in the same land, but those who have become members of groups which revolve around common interests or areas organized by people with some affinity—those to be found in discussion forums or news groups. Despite being geographically apart, a group can establish itself as a virtual neighborhood, which will be determined by what is said in forums, exchanged in chats, thus having several ways of becoming closer (Aranha Filho, 1998).

We are then dealing with the existence of two worlds—one off-line, the other online—just like Rocha has suggested since 1995, with the idea of two societies in the mass media, the society within and the society without, coexisting in an interrelationship. The society within, besides conditioning and being conditioned by the society without, is in itself symbolic material in the same way as the information available in the telematic networks. The latter, a bit different from other mass media such as television or the press, make the production of individuals, social actors who interact with one another, available worldwide thanks to vast multimedia resources.

Conclusion and Recommendations

If we return to the above-mentioned metaphors of the deluge and Noah's Ark, we'll notice that cyberculture is built and expanded through the interconnection of messages that each ark exchanges with others, in such a way that each ark remains, at once, permanently linked and permanently differentiated. In this case, we verify that both cultures—the one based on a physical setting and cyberculture—are necessary and permanently responsive.

Thus, I defend the necessity, mostly in the pedagogical environment, to avoid the basis of two extreme opposite ideas that do not allow the inter-relation between two cultures. I consider that we have utilize technology in a more humane manner, which implicates two questions: the political question, for which we must maintain the ethical use of certain technologies; and the psychopedagogical question, in the sense of forming more critical and creative users, who may make their own opinions about the technologies, not always in accordance with the marketing that is made of them. I also defend the fact that the teacher needs not just training that enables him to use the ICT, but most importantly, that the conditions for an effective change of mentality must be given to him, in order for him to truly incorporate the innovations.

I believe that the mere inclusion of ICT does not guarantee the establishment of a new posture in pedagogical practice, since the use of these technologies may still leave room for contributions from so-called traditional teaching or for a didactic model deemed outmoded or proven less cutting edge in terms of knowledge building. In other words: the fact that the content is wrapped in multimedia does not ensure that it is adapted to didactic and methodological advances and to new pedagogical practices.

I defend that the teaching-learning process in e-learning must be structured as a bi-directional relation, with the use of several mediation processes, utilizing for such, many pedagogical procedures with the purpose of enabling the teaching practices using self-learning material, means of communication, great emphasis in tutoring and, most of all, in creating friendly relationship that assure to the community the possibility for its members not to feel lonely in their study process, enabling the formation of learning cooperative groups.

Last, I insist that it is necessary to invest in the use of e-learning based on the teaching institutions and not on students individually, so that the school system takes advantage of that formation, go through a positive pedagogical restructuring, regarding the approaches related to the building of knowledge and the adequate use of the media interfaces, reflecting, in turn, in the formation of more conscious citizens to deal with this innovation in the contemporary context. It is my belief that without these precautions, the educational situation, in spite of all the available technological advances, will not change.

References

Aranha, J. T. (1998). *Eletrônicas: Usos costumes Anais do Seminário preparatório sobre aspectos sócio-culturais da Internet no Brasil.* Retrieved February 20, 2005, from http://www.alternex.com.br/~esocius/t-jayme.html

Ardizzone, P., & Rivoltella, P.C. (2003). *Didattiche per l'e-learning.* Roma: Carocci.

Billiard, B. (2005). *The promise of online simulations.* Retrieved March 20, 2005, from http://www.clomedia.com/content/templates/clo_feature.asp?articleid=382&zoneid=29

Blikstein, P., & Cavallo, D. (2002). Technology as a Trojan Horse in school environments: The emergence of the learning atmosphere (II). In *Proceedings of the Interactive Computer Aided Learning International Workshop.* Villach, Austria: Carinthia Technology Institute.

Blikstein, P., & Cavallo, D. (2003). God hides in the details: Design and implementation of technology-enabled learning environments in public education. In *Proceedings from Eurologo,* Porto, Portugal.

Blikstein, P., & Zuffo, M. K. (2003). As sereias do ensino eletrônico. In M. Silva (Ed.), *Online education: Theory, practice, legislation, and corporate training.* Rio de Janeiro: Ed. Loyola. (Title in Portuguese: As Sereias do Ensino Eletrônico *in* Educação Online: Teoria, Prática, Legislação e Formação Corporativa).

Carvalho, E. A., & Mendonça, T. (2003). *Ensaios de complexidade 2.* Porto Alegre: Sulina.

Cavallo, D., Blikstein, P., et al. (2004, September). The city that we want: Generative themes, constructionist technologies and school/social change. In *Proceedings from the IEEE International Conference on Advanced Learning Technologies,* Finland.

Elias, N. (1994). *O processo civilizador* (vol. 2). Rio de Janeiro: Jorge Zahar.

Farias, I. M. S. (2002). *Inovação e mudança: Implicações sobre a cultura dos professors.* Fortaleza: Universidade Federal do Ceará. Retrieved from http://kurzweilai.net/articles/art0529.html?printable=1

Farias, I. M. S. (2003). Os professores e as tecnologias em escola: Limites e perspectivas da inovação. *Revista brasileira de tecnologia de educação,* 159-160.

Johnson, S. (2003). *Emergência: A vida integrada de formigas, cérebros, cidades e softwares.* Rio de Janeiro: Jorge Zahar.

Lévy, P. (1999). *Cibercultura*. São Paulo: Ed.34.

Lombard, G. (2003). *Winnicott et la Web*. Retrieved March 19, 2005, from http://inconscient.net/winnicott.html

Lombard, G. (2004a). Psychanalyse et technologie: Role of reference elements. In Favez-Boutoniez, & S. Turkle (Eds.), *Psychanalyse et technologie*. Lectures Croisées 1, *Le Nouvel Observateur*. Retrieved March 20, 2005, from http://inconscient.net/ psychanalyse et technologie.html

Lombard, G. (2004b). Psychanalyse du net. Role of reference elements. In M. Civin (Ed.), *Psychanalyse du net*. Paris: Hachette (w/d). Retrieved March 20, 2005, from http://inconscient.net/civin.html

Mamede-Neves, M. A. C. (2002). *Aprendendo aprendizagem* (2nd ed.). Rio de Janeiro: PUC-Rio. CD- ROM.

Mamede-Neves, M. A. C. (2004). *Currículo e prática ducativa*. Rio de Janeiro: CCEAD PUC-Rio. Relatório técnico.

Martín-Barbero, J. (2002). Identidades: Tradiciones y nuevas comunidades. *Comunicação & Política, 9*(1), 165-189.

McLuhan, M. (2000). Visão, Som e Fúria. In Costa Lima, L. (org), *Teoria da cultura de massa*. São Paulo: Paz e Terra.

Rivoltella, P. C. (2003). *Costruttivismo e pragmatica della comunicazione online: Socialitá e didattica in Internet*. Trento: Erickson.

Rocha, E. (1995). *A sociedade do Sonho: Comunicação, cultura e consumo*. Rio de Janeiro: Mauad.

Santos, A. (2003). *Leitura de nós: Ciberespaço e literature*. São Paulo: Itaú Cultural.

Sipitakiat, A., Blikstein, P., & Cavallo, D. (2004). GoGo board: Augmenting programmable bricks for economically challenged audiences. In *Proceedings of the International Conference of the Learning Sciences*, Los Angeles, CA.

Turkle, S., & Whither. (2002, May 6). *Psychoanalysis in a computer culture*. Conference in Sigmund Freud Society.

Endnotes

[1]   The critical analysis developed by Blikstein, in different personal work or in collaboration (2004, 2003, 2002) about the irrestricted adoption of e-learning is in total agreement with what my experience on this field has shown.

[2]   Rivoltella (2003) and Ardizzone and Rivoltella (2003) also make valuable considerations on this subject.

Chapter III

ICT, Knowledge Construction, and Evolution:
Subject, Community, and Society

Antonio Cartelli
University of Cassino, Italy

Abstract

After a short introduction on the hypotheses scholars developed for explaining knowledge construction and evolution in mankind, the role that ICT is playing on this phenomenon is described. From the results of many studies and from the separation today well settled between human knowledge and corporate knowledge, the idea of a tri-partition of knowledge contexts arises and is developed and analyzed. The idea of three different kinds of knowledge receives good support from the observation of the effects of ICT on individuals, communities/organizations, and society; it sounds as the confirmation for the three different contexts of knowledge construction and evolution the author hypothesizes. The experiences described in this chapter show how ICT, while playing a relevant role in each of the above environments, influences all the others and determines a continuous evolution of knowledge in the three contexts. The hypothesized perspective opens to new interpretations for knowledge phenomena, leads to the overcoming of misleading learning explanations, and gives a strong impulse to the planning of projects for the introduction of ICT in education.

Introduction

The 20th century has marked the transformation of the philosophical definition and explanation of knowledge into a different one, mostly depending on the ideas emerging from human disciplines like psychology, pedagogy, anthropology, sociology, etc. (i.e., many contributions are also due to biology, neurophysiology and cybernetics). Two main ways for interpreting knowledge construction and evolution affirmed during last decades: the former one mostly looking at the individual, the latter one emerging from corporate and organization studies.

In what follows the above perspectives are analyzed and the role IT and ICT had in explaining knowledge construction are recalled.

Theories for Knowledge Development in Individuals

J. Piaget and D. P. Ausubel were among the first scientists stating the importance of subjects' mental actions in cognitive processes. They assigned a great role to subject-reality interaction for the explanation of knowledge development and evolution; for this reason they are also considered cognitivists and precursors of constructivism; the same scholars, on another hand, assign a little or no role to social and cultural interactions in knowledge construction.

J. Piaget hypothesized different stages in cognitive development, for example, he stated that the evolution of knowledge in a subject is marked by the transition from a first stage to the following one; this process is the result of the interaction between the individual and the environment and is based on adaptation processes marked by the assimilation of new stimuli in old mental schemes and by the accommodation of old mental schemes into new ones (Piaget, 1971, 1973). He also hypothesized the existence of a genetic epistemology to explain the genesis of knowledge in mankind, for example, the individual cognitive development runs parallel to history of science and the analysis of pupils' ideas can be used to explain the origin of scientific concepts.

D. P. Ausubel, on another hand, accepted and developed the idea of knowledge construction emerging from the addition of new knowledge to pre-existing knowledge (formerly proposed by Gagné); the bases of his theory can be found on the following three elements:

1.   The internal coherence of the topic to be learned
2.   The existence of a net of pre-existing concepts the new topic has to connect to
3.   The subject's bent to receive and accept the new topic

He also hypothesizes the distinction between meaningful learning and mechanical learning and states that the difference between them rests on the existence of subsumers (special units of previous knowledge making the construction of new knowledge easier), which have great influence on the insertion of new information units into pre-existing knowledge (Ausubel, 1990).

The ideas of J. Piaget and D. P. Ausubel have been verified, integrated and, sometimes, contradicted from further scientists but have retained all their importance for the role they assigned to individuals in knowledge management and development. A different basis moved D. H. Jonassen (1994), who founded the project of learning environments on the following statements:

1.   Knowledge construction is based on individual and social influences.
2.   Meaningful contexts support problem solving skills (which have to be derived from real situations).
3.   Cooperation between student and teacher and among peers is at the basis of learning processes.

Further studies introduced the concepts of multiple intelligence (Gardner, 1993), learning styles (McLellan, 1996), and cognitive flexibility (Spiro & Jehng, 1990) to consider the complexity of the cognitive phenomenon into individuals.

The importance of context and social effects on individuals' knowledge development has been stated in many recent studies, often under the influence of Vygotskij and Leont'ev hypotheses (Varisco, 2002). Most relevant results of these studies concern two specific models of the knowledge transition from the concrete to the abstract: (a) the cognitive apprenticeship, and (b) the expert practical thinking. The former hypothesis rediscovers the well known apprenticeship properties (i.e., modeling, coaching, scaffolding, and fading properties of training in Renaissance studios), and integrates them with the following new principles: articulation, reflection, and exploration. The latter one, mostly due to S. Scribner research (1997), evidences the properties of the expert thinking in a given context with respect to the novice one; main traits of the expert thinking are:

1.   Use of the context's elements concerning the problem to be solved
2.   Use of economic strategies in the finding of solutions
3.   Use of well settled knowledge units and skills in the definition of problem solving strategies

The most comprehensive theory about the influence of social phenomena on human knowledge and learning is the E. Wenger's social learning theory (1998). This theory has at its bases the following principles:

1.   Individuals are social beings and are the focus of the learning action.
2.   Knowledge is a specific aspect of competence.
3.   Knowledge is the expression of the participation.
4.   Meaning is the product of learning.

If the above ideas are mostly concerned with the effects of learning actions on individuals it has to be noted that E. Wenger looks at communities as autonomous realities and, for him, communities of practice coincide with learning communities.

Corporate and Organization Knowledge Theories

While starting from Wenger's research on communities of practice recent studies analyze knowledge construction in those communities for the importance they have in corporate and organizations. In other words, a theory of knowledge construction and development in communities has been developed, autonomously from the hypotheses on individuals reported in the above paragraph.

Among the starting points for these studies there are Wenger's (2004) basic elements marking a community of practice:

1.   **Shared Identity Domain:** Where membership implies a commitment to the domain, and therefore a shared competence that distinguishes members from other people.

2. **Community:** Because in pursuing their interest in the domain, members engage in joint activities and discussions, help each other, and share information; for example, they build relationships enabling them to learn from each other.

3. **Practice:** Because members of a community of practice are practitioners; they develop a shared repertoire of resources for example, experiences, stories, tools, ways of addressing recurring problems (in short a shared practice).

Furthermore, the analysis of knowledge development in communities of practice inside organizations and the study of corporate knowledge construction and transmission led some authors to state the basic principles for knowledge management. S. Denning (2000), for example, proposed the following remarks (usually known as knowledge management laws):

1. Knowledge is the key factor for the organization surviving

2. Communities of practice (CoPs) are the core of any knowledge sharing program

3. Virtual communities need presence interaction

4. Professional enthusiasm sways CoPs

5. Knowledge management activates bi-directional and dynamic information flows inwards and outwards organization

6. Experience and story telling animate and strengthen knowledge sharing

With respect to studies on individuals' knowledge development, new hypotheses were now developed to explain knowledge features and structure within communities and organizations. I. Nonaka and N. Konno (1999), for example, based their ideas on the definition of two different kinds of knowledge: (a) tacit knowledge, which is deeply-rooted in actions and experiences of community's members and can be only difficultly codified, transmitted and shared; (i.e., it is the individuals' know how marking the skills of the community), and (b) explicit knowledge, which is the community's knowledge and can be easily formalized, represented, transmitted and shared.

In regards to learning organizations (i.e., organizations continuously developing new knowledge), I. Nonaka and H. Takeuchi (1995) developed a model for knowledge construction and evolution strongly based on the tacit and explicit knowledge transformations. This model is made by four phases (which initials give the name SECI to it):

1. **Socialization:** It is the informal process of letting tacit knowledge be shared (often in a non-verbal way). It has features very similar to the modeling phase of apprenticeship and to the on-the-job-training used in many organizational contexts.

2. **Externalization:** It transforms tacit knowledge in explicit concepts and is the crucial phase of knowledge construction. Formal language, metaphors, and analogies play an important role in helping people making explicit their know how.

3. **Combination:** It inserts the newly built concepts into organization's knowledge and connects them to previous knowledge, so increasing the knowledge of the community and of the organization.

4. **Internalization:** It closes the cycle by making internal the explicit knowledge and transforms it into know how for the organization. The cycle is now ready for starting again with socialization of tacit knowledge, etc. and the model describing the knowledge evolution process is reported in Figure 1.

The Role of IT and ICT on Knowledge Construction and Evolution

In regards to the influence of IT and ICT on individual teaching-learning processes, it can be useful to remember here the contributions of R. Taylor and L. Galliani. The former one proposed three metaphors for computer use in education: tutor, tool, and tutee (Taylor, 1980), the latter one extended these metaphors while considering the great deal of software tools developed in last decades (Galliani, Costa, Amplatz, & Varisco, 1999). At the end of such an integration, tutor appellation describes the experiences people can make under

Figure 1. SECI cycle for learning organizations

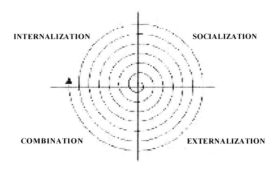

behaviorist and cognitivist influence with the help of special programs like CAI, CAE, and CAL tools, or with the help of Artificial Intelligence software like ICAI and ITS. Tool metaphor includes special software for analyzing large amounts of data and browsing specific contexts (usually provided with authoring and co-authoring functions). Tutee metaphor mainly includes programs for the creation of special developmental environments, such as micro-worlds made by Papert with LOGO. Together with computer metaphors, meta-cognitive ideas must be remembered. Strictly speaking, they suggest that computer use stimulates functions' development more than learning topics so that meta-cognitive atti-tudes and learning are better developed in students systematically working at the computer (Cornoldi & Caponi, 1991).

Furthermore, ICT influence on individuals' knowledge development can be summarized in the following ideas:

1.   H. Rheingold (1994) introduced the definition of virtual communities to describe the set of individuals who use the Net for interpersonal commu-nication and knowledge construction.

2.   D. de Kerckhove (2000) defined connective intelligence as the set of strategies and cognitive skills developed from individuals contextually to ICT use.

3.   P. Lévy (1996) stated that collective intelligences well characterize the situation emerging from the increase in the individuals' communication speed due to the Net and from the great amount of information freely available in it.

4.   A. Calvani and M. Rotta (1999) suggest that ICT introduce hypertext and multimedia features in the knowledge structure while the Net extends the social negotiation aspects of knowledge.

On another hand, the impact of ICT on learning environments is mostly due to the role it can play in educational contexts:

1.   Repository for information and documents of every kind (CMS—Content Management System)

2.   System for the management of Learning Objects (LMS—Learning Man-agement System)

3.   Virtual environment letting individuals interact and build communities of learners (CSCLS—Computer Supported Collaborative Learning System)

In communities and especially corporate and organizations, knowledge management has seen a great application and use of ICT for the collection, organization, sharing and analysis of community knowledge. The tools adopted as instruments for the application of knowledge management principles are devoted to knowledge discovery, and knowledge audit (usually based on knowledge mapping) together with the planning and carrying out of knowledge networks.

G. Trentin (2004) hypothesizes for networks, and especially for the Internet, the role of technical infrastructure letting communities build a shared memory (i.e., shared knowledge basis supporting professional CoPs).

Towards New Models for Knowledge Construction and Evolution

At this point of the discussion two main kinds of knowledge can be recognized: the individual and the community ones. They are also marked from different hypotheses concerning the ways they are built up and the involvement of ICT in their management. In the author's opinion, the above separation is still inappropriate to describe today's knowledge phenomenon and a tri-partition of knowledge definitions and environments can be proposed: individual knowledge, community knowledge, and social (scientific) knowledge. In what follows, the reasons for the above hypotheses are reported but the need for a reconciliation of methods and results coming from the different knowledge structures and environments is also evidenced.

First of all, the results on misconceptions and mental schemes are reported to explain the separation between individual and social knowledge (this last one being considered equivalent to scientific knowledge). Soon after the results of the studies concerning a special community of students are analyzed and last, the interaction among all above knowledge environments is described and the positive effects individuals, communities and science, derived each other from that experiences is discussed.

Individual, Community, and Social Knowledge

Theories reported in the introduction for the analysis and explanation of knowledge management in individuals have at their basis the identification of the knowledge naturally built by subjects (either autonomously or under the effect of an educational program), with scientific and disciplinary knowledge.

During the past decades, the amount of discoveries in all fields of human knowledge produced an exponential growth in the number of sciences analyzing phenomena and many new disciplines were born. Teachers and professors, while submitting new topics to their students, often adopted and still use a different perspective with respect to Piaget's genetic epistemology, they usually start from the history of disciplines to build school curricula and create learning paths for education (i.e., discipline logic structure is proposed as a natural scheme for knowledge construction in individuals).

The positivistic hypothesis that an increase in the number of topics to be taught and the introduction at earlier stages of education of many concepts could help mankind in reaching new and more advanced frontiers of knowledge, showed very soon all its limits. Many studies on misconceptions and mental schemes evidenced, in fact, how difficultly subjects build the right scientific concepts (MLRG, 2005). The same studies evidenced the presence of wrong ideas in differently aged and skilled people (including teachers) and how difficult can be the finding of the right strategies for helping people in overcoming the difficulties they meet in the study of sciences or in interpreting phenomena.

Three main aspects clearly emerge from the above studies (Cartelli, 2002):

1. Wrong ideas involve all domains of human knowledge; the investigated fields concern in fact scientific topics pertaining mathematics, physics, statistics, computer science, chemistry, biology, natural sciences, cosmology, etc. but there is (and is still growing) the number of studies investigating the wrong ideas the students show with language, literature, history, and many other human sciences.

2. Wrong ideas can be found in people all over the world and no relevant differences can be detected while passing from East to West or from North to South.

3. Two main approaches can be recognized in the above studies: a former one called ideographic or naturalistic, which analyzes pupils' reasoning and the ideas people show when explaining phenomena, with no dependence from scientific paradigms (i.e., only the internal coherence of people's concepts and ideas is evaluated and the name of natural mental schemes is adopted for them); the latter one, involving people who already approached scientific topics (or were beginners), which evaluates the correctness of people's ideas with respect to scientifically accepted ones (the name of preconceptions and misconceptions is now adopted for wrong ideas).

Two experiences the author made during the past years with High School and University students confirm what has been stated until now and give support to the idea of a separation between individual knowledge and social knowledge (this last one being identified with science and discipline knowledge) (Cartelli, 2005). In other words, individuals' knowledge can never be identified with scientific knowledge, because:

a.   Only a few subjects can be considered really skilled in a scientific domain.

b.   Only little segments of scientific knowledge can be shared within the members of a given community.

c.   When students in a class correctly build scientific knowledge in a given domain (with the help of constructivist strategies and technological environments) special ambiguous situations can lead to the detection of misconceptions and wrong ideas in their knowledge.

In other words, the high specialization of knowledge in every discipline, the very large amount of elements marking scientific knowledge and the presence of preconceptions, misconceptions, and mental schemes in individuals, all play a relevant role in stating that scientific knowledge (i.e., knowledge certificated and validated from scientific community) is the knowledge of mankind (i.e., a construction of mankind continuously evolving and growing like any human artifact or technology) and not the knowledge of a single individual. Subjects can use scientific knowledge to explain phenomena, and usually do so by adopting the paradigms that the scientific community developed and accepted for that phenomenon (in a given context and time and until new paradigms appear more suitable for the explanation of the same phenomenon); but it has to be noted that the use of such knowledge has very little, if any, element in common with the developmental and evolutionary process of individual knowledge. All the above arguments lead, in the author's opinion, to the following conclusion: individual and scientific knowledge are very different and scientific knowledge is better defined as social knowledge (if we identify mankind with society and look at the contribution to scientific knowledge development from individuals and communities with the time).

The draft in Figure 2 synthesizes individual and social-scientific knowledge and the dependencies between them. They surely have common parts but don't superpose each other and have elements pertaining specifically to each of them (individual and society-science).

If the above scheme correctly describes knowledge inter-dependencies while looking at individual and society, (mankind) it is certainly inappropriate for the explanation of knowledge phenomena if corporate and organizations' experiences and theories are considered (i.e., the results from studies on communities of practice don't benefit from the above hypothesis). This difficulty disappears

Figure 2. Separation between individual and social knowledge

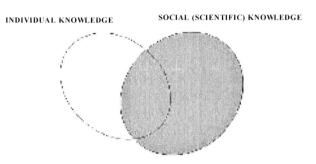

if autonomous community knowledge for each CoP a subject belongs to is hypothesized; in such a case, in fact, together with the rules governing individual and social knowledge management, the rules reported in the first paragraph for CoPs can be adopted to explain community knowledge phenomena. A new scheme for the description of the different kinds of knowledge can then be drawn and within it one or more community knowledge find their right place. Figure 3 drafts the author's hypothesized tri-partition among individual, community, and society/scientific knowledge.

The tri-partition in Figure 3, where multiple communities are reported, finds an explication in the rules governing community knowledge: For example, an individual can belong to different CoPs and can contribute in developing different knowledge in each of them, but the rules governing each CoP and knowledge construction and development within it are just the same (and are derived from Wenger's characterization of a CoP).

Figure 3. Distribution among subject, communities and society of the components of human knowledge

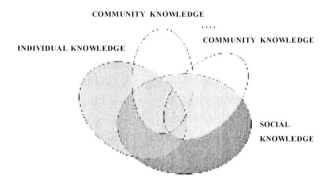

The above tri-partition has a relevant influence on further studies concerning knowledge construction and evolution because it states the existence of different fields and methods of investigation for the research in each of the three environments. Furthermore, it implies a great attention to possible results from the same research, for the effects the results obtained in a field can have on all the others. In other words scholars and scientists can now concentrate their efforts on the different ways knowledge (individual, community, and social/scientific) is built and evolves, without forgetting the consequences the results they obtain in one of the above fields can have on all the others. A question poses suddenly: what role does ICT play in this way of looking at the knowledge phenomenon? Does it operate across all knowledge specifications (individual, community, and society) or pertain especially to one or more of them? It is perhaps too early to give a definite answer to these questions but in what follows the experience the author made with some students is reported and an attempt for answering to the above questions is made.

Students' Communities and ICT: The Case of Paleography

What is reported below is the result of the author's work at the Faculty of Humanities of the University of Cassino-Italy, while cooperating with M. Palma, professor of Latin paleography. The cooperation between a researcher in education technologies and a scholar in paleography can seem, and perhaps is, unusual but is the result of the common persuasion that Internet, and ICT more in general, changed the well settled connection and temporal dependency between research and teaching. Before the Internet, in fact, there were separated times and spaces for research and didactics, now they can be contemporary and can reinforce each other.

The experiences the author made and is still carrying out mostly concern the planning and carrying out of special information systems (mostly based on Web sites) both for researching and teaching.

Among them, the most relevant ones and those which have a greatest relevance for their consequences on the hypothesized knowledge tri-partition are: (1) *Bibliography of Beneventan Manuscripts* (BMB), an information system hosting the bibliography of manuscripts written in the South Italy national script during the Middle Ages and (2) *Women Copyists and Written Culture in the Middle Age*, a dynamic Web site interfaced with a database containing women and manuscripts' data.

The Bibliography of Beneventan Manuscripts

The BMB experience (*Bibliografia dei Manoscritti Beneventani*—Bibliography of Beneventan Manuscripts http://edu.let.unicas.it/bmb/) started in 1992 with the main aim of collecting the quotations of Beneventan manuscripts (i.e., medieval books written in the South Italy national script) by means of a MS-DOS program called BIBMAN. In 1997 a first Web site was developed to make it faster and easier for scholars to download new bibliographical data (nearly monthly).

Recently many problems depending on the BIBMAN program induced to plan and carry out a new Web site: the *BMB online* (Cartelli & Palma, 2004). It is an information system where differently allowed people can store the quotations of Beneventan manuscripts, so that it can be freely queried by general users.

Persons entrusted with the task of collecting the quotations of Beneventan manuscripts are grouped into three categories:

1. **Contributors:** Who can access a special Web area where they can write, modify, and delete bibliographical data for the materials assigned to them
2. **Scientific Administrators:** Who can manage all data and write, modify, and certify bibliographical materials, this last operation being done only once because certified records cannot be subsequently accessed for revision
3. **System Administrator:** Who is allowed to do all operations including the modification or deletion of certified data

The access to certified bibliographic materials is possible according to different query pages: (a) by author's name, (b) by manuscript, (c) by contributor, or (d) by one or more words or part of them concerning title, location, or bibliographical abstract of a given publication.

It has to be noted that the following are implemented in the system also: (1) a closed communication subsystem made by an electronic blackboard letting contributors involved in the collection of bibliographical data exchange messages and texts among themselves, (2) some special functions, available only to system administrator, for the production of the printed version of the data yearly collected.

The Web Site "Women and Written Culture in the Middle Ages"

Main aim of the dynamic Web site on women copyists (http://edu.let.unicas.it/womediev/) was to systematize the data emerging from former research while leading to an instrument which could help scholars finding new elements for further studies (Cartelli, Miglio, & Palma, 2001).

Data appearing relevant to the scientific community were:

1. **For every scribe:** (a) the name of the woman as it appears in manuscripts, (b) her qualification (i.e., if it is known, whether she was a nun or a lay), and (c) the date or the period she belonged to (up to the 15th century)

2. **For the manuscripts:** (a) their shelf mark (i.e., town, library, and number of the manuscript), (b) the place and the country where they were written, (c) the date or the period they belong to, (d) the authors and titles of the texts, and (e) the bibliography or its source of information

Furthermore, it appeared important to show for each woman, the manuscript/s she wrote and vice-versa and, if possible and available, at least an image of the copyist's hand. The site has not produced until now any printed bulletin or other periodical printed matter and is made of two separated sections: the former one being operated only by editors, who access it by a personal ID and a password (to insert, modify, and delete the data stored in the database), thus ensuring the scientific validity of the information reported there; the latter one at everyone's disposal to obtain the list of all women and manuscripts in the database, or to make queries concerning women and manuscripts with specific qualifications.

Results from Researching and Teaching with ICT in Paleography

The systems and Web sites described above were carried out from the author in different times but they were suddenly introduced in everyday teaching and researching work. The number of students participating each time in the experiences described below was very little (in the best case there were 19) so that students' features, performances, and behaviors could be carefully analyzed each time. Main activities the students were involved in have been:

1. After having attended the basic courses on cataloguing, they were asked to become contributors for *BMB online* and to produce bibliographical materials. The discussions they had with administrators, professors, and among themselves, the use they made of the electronic blackboard and of the e-mail services for the exchange of messages and, last but not least, the chance of working in little groups on the same problems helped them very much in acquiring the knowledge and in developing the skills they would need (as paleographers) in their everyday work.

2. They not only used the materials reported in the *Women Copyists* Web site for their study, but were also charged of the description of manuscripts and of the collection/digitization of plates reproducing texts written from women (i.e., they learned to distinguish the different hands of women copyists and their way of writing manuscripts while practically working on the manuscripts and translating them in digital documents). Furthermore, the number of bibliographic notes coming from scholars all over the world has grown with time; main consequence of this unexpected interest for women copyists has been the need for the planning of a new information system (still under development) helping the virtual community born around this theme to continue the study of women copyists (it has to be noted that the system has already been modified since its origin).

The effects produced from above activities on the teaching-learning processes will be analyzed in what follows looking at the three different components of knowledge described above: the individual, the community, and the social (scientific) ones.

1. In regards to single students, and especially the knowledge and skills each of them developed while attending paleography course, it can be stated that ICT, and especially Web technologies and information systems, contributed to creating constructivist learning environments which helped them very much. Furthermore, the careful analysis of students' behaviors during lessons, exercises, laboratory activities, and examinations led the author to deduce that the following skills, never observed before in a paleography's course, could be detected: talent in working in a group (in traditional courses it was a very rare experience), easier facing of complex tasks (thanks to the help each student could have from colleagues) and raising of the individuals' peculiarities within the community. In other words, the results of the studies by A. L. Brown and J. Campione (1994) and J. Lave and E. Wenger (1991) on communities of learners (CoLs) were fully confirmed.

2. In regards to communities of practice (CoPs) and especially learning organizations, a new model for knowledge development emerged. First of

all, it has to be noted that each class or group of students involved in the above experiences was a real CoP (the three elements marking for Wenger a community of practice were in fact observed). Furthermore, the information systems described above had two main features: (a) they helped students and scholars in their everyday research work, and (b) they implemented the best practices researchers developed while accomplishing their studies and obliged students to respect times and procedures in those practices. To better understand the meaning of the above assertions, the BMB online case is analyzed (Cartelli, 2004) in a greater detail: when a student/contributor aims at writing a bibliographic card he or she has to follow the procedure implemented into the system. For example:

(a)   He or she has to be authorized to analyze the documents (books, papers, magazines, Web sites, etc.) probably containing the citations of Beneventan manuscripts.

(b)   Once scientific administrators attribute documents for the analysis, contributors can compile bibliographic card/s.

(c)   Compiled card/s must be reviewed and approved from BMB scientific administrators.

(d)   Approved card/s can finally be accessed from general users querying the data base.

The above steps can be seen as the formalization and implementation into the information system of the practices BMB editors adopted before the creation of the Web site (also if, at that time, they used a MS-DOS software for the management of bibliographies) and let us state they help community in covering and completing the SECI cycle. In other words, the *BMB online* system makes the socialization, externalization, combination, and internalization of community knowledge easier, and, what is more, it implements the community practices, (i.e., the processes leading to the creation of the bibliography shared by people working on Beneventan manuscripts). It also has to be noted that if BMB editors cannot be considered a learning organization at all (i.e., they are not continuously developing new knowledge/practices to share among the members of the community), the elements of at least a cycle of the Nonaka and Takeuchi's SECI model can be recognized in the development of community knowledge and a new element can be added to the former ones: the implementation of communities' practices by means of ICT.

If the *BMB online* experience can be only partially compared with Nonaka & Takeuchi's SECI model, as applied to paleographers' community, what happened with the site *Women and written culture in the Middle Ages* (i.e., the changes in its structure following one another with the time), better support the idea of a new model for the cyclic structure describing knowledge evolution in organizations (at least in the special case under analysis). The Women copyists Web site was modified accordingly to the database structure at least two times:

1. When it was made the first time it had only one table containing data concerning both women and manuscripts, as it was explicitly asked from the paleographers who commissioned its planning and carrying out (paleographers liked a system letting them make their everyday operations easier and faster and asked for a system implementing only and exclusively their knowledge/practices). After the introduction of some information in the system and after the analysis of the stored data, the need for a revision of the structure of that system became evident (i.e., the first SECI cycle came to its end, after socialization, externalization, combination, and internalization of knowledge/practices).

2. The end of the first SECI cycle showed the limits of the system (which were also the limits of former practices) and required changes in the database structure: it had to be split into three tables, former data had to be translated into the new structure and new FORMS had to be made for managing data and for querying the system (i.e., new data structures were needed, new practices emerged and their implementation by means of ICT in the new system was asked, to let a new SECI cycle start).

Once ready, the new system has been used by editors for managing women and manuscripts data and now, while it is coming to the end of the second SECI cycle, the need for further changes in the structure of the system is emerging; i.e., it difficultly manages external contributions, like the ones coming from scientists and scholars who don't belong to the community.

As a conclusion, at least in the paleographic community (but there is no reason for limiting the above idea to this unique case), the above remarks suggest that the cycle marking the evolution of the community knowledge must be based on a further element with respect to the four initially stated. The new structure of a model inheriting the basic elements of I. Nonaka and H. Takeuchi hypothesis lays, as suggested above, on the following elements: Implementation of communities' practices by means of ICT, Socialization, Externalization, Combination, and Internalization (as reported in Figure 4).

In regard to social (scientific) knowledge and the influence the above information systems had on it, only a remark is needed. The above information systems are not static in their content and continuously evolve by addition of new information, with the support of individuals and communities involved in their management;

Figure 4. New model for knowledge evolution in CoPs

the validation of the information stored within them by scientific committees lets us state that they represent a source of scientific knowledge freely available on the Net for students, scholars, and everyone interested in them. As reported above, in fact, both *BMB online* and *Women and written culture in the Middle Ages* sites have a public section letting general users freely access data stored in their databases and retrieve them. In other words, they contribute in the construction and diffusion of scientific knowledge concerning manuscripts and the disciplines studying them.

Conclusion and Future Trends

It is probably too early to say if the new model hypothesized from the author for knowledge development in organizations can be applied to every kind of community of practice and learning organization as it is, but some conclusions can be drawn.

First of all, it has to be noted that the implications of this study concern all elements involved in the knowledge phenomenon: subjects, communities, and society (science). Subjects' knowledge and skills evolve due to the individuals' belonging to community and society, but they give a valid contribution to community and society (scientific) knowledge evolution too. In regard to communities, a special attention must be devoted to CoPs, CoLs, and virtual communities for the influence each of them can have on the others:

1.   Communities of practice can be virtual. Subjects with special interests in the community's work/practice can, in fact, become members of the

community by means of ICT without physically knowing the members of the community. The only requirement seems the level of their basic skills, which must be adequate to those of the community, to guarantee their entrance and permanence in the community.

2.   Implementation of practices by means of ICT can help teachers/professors in the creation of new constructivist learning environments and can help students in developing meaningful learning of discipline topics and new skills (very common in CSCLS).

3.   Studies on CoPs and CoLs until now, carried out separately, can cooperate and integrate themselves in explaining knowledge phenomena in the two different contexts: corporate and school/university.

At last, the creation of systems letting students freely access scientific knowledge in efficient ways gains new importance so that Semantic Web, ontologies, and learning management systems appear a real need more than an academic exercise. Undoubtedly advanced education (university courses) and lifelong learning can take great advantage from instruments similar to the ones adopted in the author's experiences and the results of paleography students can be obtained also in other contexts. Perhaps the simple transfer of the experiences will not be enough to guarantee the success of the educational process and a reorganization of teaching, new planning strategies for didactics and new functions and meanings for teachers' work will be needed.

References

Ausubel, D. P. (1990). *Educazione e processi cognitivi*. Milan: Franco Angeli.

Brown, A. L., & Campione, J. C. (1994). Guided discovery in a community of learners. In K. Mc Gilly (Ed.), *Classroom lessons: Integrating cognitive theory and classroom practice* (pp. 229-270). Cambridge, MA: MIT Press.

Calvani, A., & Rotta, M. (1999). *Comunicazione ed apprendimento in Internet, didattica Costruttivistica in rete*. Trento: Erickson.

Cartelli, A. (2002, June 17-19). Web technologies and sciences epistemologies. In E. Cohen & E. Boyd (Eds.), *Proceedings of IS and IT education 2002 Conference*, Cork, Ireland. Retrieved August 16, 2004, from http://ecommerce.lebow.drexel.edu/eli/2002Proceedings/papers/Carte203Webte.pdf

Cartelli, A. (2004). Open source software and information management: The case of BMB online. In M. Khosrow-Pour (Ed.), *Proceedings of IRMA*

2004 International Conference: Innovations through information technology (pp. 1023-1024). Hershey, PA: Idea Group Publishing.

Cartelli, A. (2005). Computing and ICT literacy: From students' misconceptions and mental schemes to the monitoring of the teaching-learning process. In D. Carbonara (Ed.), *Technology literacy applications in learning environments* (pp. 37-48). Hershey, PA: Idea Group Publishing.

Cartelli, A., Miglio, L., & Palma, M. (2001). New technologies and new paradigms in historical research. *Informing Science (The International Journal of an Emerging Discipline), 4*(2), 61-66.

Cartelli, A., & Palma, M. (2004). BMB online: An information system for paleographic and didactic research. In M. Khosrow-Pour (Ed.), *Proceedings of the IRMA 2004 Conference: Innovations through information technology* (pp. 45-47). Hershey, PA: Idea Group Publishing.

Cornoldi, C., & Caponi, B. (1991). *Memoria e metacognizione.* Trento: Erickson.

de Kerckhove, D. (2000). *La pelle della cultura.* Rome: Editori Riuniti.

Denning, S. (2000). *The springboard: How storytelling ignites action in knowledge-era organizations.* Boston: Butterworth-Heinemann.

Galliani, L., Costa, R., Amplatz, C., & Varisco, B. M. (1999). *Le tecnologie didattiche.* Lecce: Pensa Multimedia.

Gardner, H. (1993). *Multiple intelligences: The theory in practice.* New York: Basic Books.

Jonassen, D. H. (1994). Thinking technology: Towards a constructivist design model. *Educational Technology, 34*(4), 34-37.

Lave, J., & Wenger, E. (1991). *Situated learning: Legitimate peripheral participation.* Cambridge: Cambridge University Press.

Lévy, P. (1996). *L'intelligenza collettiva: Per un'antropologia del cyberspazio.* Milan: Feltrinelli.

McLellan, H. (1996). Being digital: Implications for education. *Educational Technology, 36*(6), 5-20.

Meaningful Learning Research Group (MLRG). (2005). Abstracts, lists of works presented in four different international conferences. Retrieved December 27, 2004, from http://www.mlrg.org

Nonaka, I., & Konno, N. (1999). The concept of Ba: Building a foundation for knowledge creation. In J. W. Cortada & J. A. Woods (Eds.), *The knowledge management book 1999-2000.* Boston: Butterworth-Heinemann.

Nonaka, I., & Takeuchi, H. (1995). *The knowledge-creating company: How Japanese companies create the dynamics of innovation.* New York: Oxford University Press.

Piaget, J. (1971). *L'epistemologia genetica.* Bari: Laterza.

Piaget, J. (1973). *La costruzione del reale nel bambino.* Florence: La Nuova Italia.

Rheingold, H. (1994). *Comunità virtuali: Parlare, incontrarsi, vivere nel cyberspazio.* Milan: Sperling & Kupfer.

Scribner, S. (1997). Head and hand: An action approach to thinking. In E. Tobach et al. (Eds.), *Mind and social practice: Selected writings of Sylvia Scribner.* Cambridge: Cambridge University Press.

Spiro R. J., & Jehng I. C. (1990). Cognitive flexibility and hypertext: Theory and technology for the nonlinear and multidimensional transversal of complex subject matter. In D. Nix & R. Spiro (Eds.), *Cognition, education, and multimedia: Exploring ideas in high technology* (pp. 163-205). Hillsdale, NJ: Lawrence Erlbaum.

Taylor, R. (1980). *The computer in the school: Tutor, tool, and tutee.* New York: Teachers College Press.

Trentin, G. (2004). *Apprendimento in rete e condivisione delle conoscenze.* Milan: Franco Angeli.

Varisco, B. M. (2002). *Costruttivismo socio-culturale: Genesi filosofiche, sviluppi psico-pedagogici, applicazioni didattiche.* Rome: Carocci.

Wenger, E. (1998). *Communities of practice: Learning, meaning, and identity.* Cambridge: Cambridge University Press.

Wenger, E. (2004). *Communities of practice: A brief introduction.* Retrieved December 27, 2004, from http://www.ewenger.com/theory/index.htm.

Chapter IV

Education and Organization:
ICT, Assets, and Values

Pier Cesare Rivoltella
Catholic University of Milan, Italy

Abstract

The goal of this chapter is to define the problems a school can have when it implements technology in education. This phenomenon is explained according to theory of organization, and especially Norman's perspective. Norman's theory stated, in fact, that organizations passed from fordist and tayloristic structures to the service management paradigm; finally, nowadays, they build values together with consumers. We try to show how this transition is also present in schools' implementation of ICT. In doing this we criticize the deterministic solution (which says that implementing technology changes everything and produces innovation) and adopt a systemic vision with the characteristics of presumption, community, and value constellation.

The Information Society and the School

The information society today is one of the scenarios most frequently described by media. They speak about it as the great new revolution, after the revolutions of the alphabet and the press. The essential part of this revolution is technological and relates to new and original ways of elaborating and transmitting information. We can describe it according to three indications (Rivoltella, 2003a):

1. The management and transfer of large quantities of data (with the problem of finding a selection method for discriminating between useful and useless information).

2. The irrelevance of the place in communication, because of the real time interaction made possible by the Internet (i.e., videoconferencing allows speakers to communicate with each other without being in the same place).

3. The great speed of processes, whose acceleration is one of the basic categories for understanding our socio-cultural environment (Virilio, 1995).

In school, the main importance of this revolution is its effectiveness; that is, its capacity to impact school systems that brings a deep change in their configuration. The most common words describing this process are: modernization, integration, innovation, and extension. In other words technologies can aid systems to renovate teaching and learning practices (modernization), build up networking systems among different schools (integration), actualize structures and processes (innovation), and also make the personalization of learning possible outside the school building and school hours (extension). We can imagine a great future where technologies can lead schools to become better.

Into this quite optimistic scenario it is possible otherwise to highlight almost two important problems. Firstly we can discuss the nature of this revolution (Wolton, 1999, 1986). But is this true? Is it enough to introduce technologies in the school to automatically have innovation and modernization in teaching? Isn't there, under this idea, a homeopathic conceptualization of technology (that is, to think that technology is able to transform all processes in which it is implemented)? This is the case the sociologists named the "auto-coming true prophecy" (Merton, 1949); that is, to think that ideas frequently presented as possibilities of the future will come true.

Under this "prophecy," there are two possible risks (Rivoltella, 2003b):

1. The risk of technological determinism[1]; that is, the consideration of technology outside its use and context.

2.   The risk of changing all for changing nothing, as Negroponte (1996) says, citing (perhaps without knowing it) a famous scene of *Il gattopardo*, a novel by Filippo Tomasi di Lampedusa (from which Luchino Visconti made a memorable movie).

The second problem is the same idea of impact. The European Council, in 1998, in Strasbourg, devoted an international seminar to this theme: *The Impact of New Information Technologies on Schools: Issues and Problems.* Here, the idea is that technology runs throughout schools: a natural process, perhaps one that is out of managers' and educators' control. The author does not agree with this last assertion and reports the following example: the invention of stirrups was surely important in the Middle Age, and probably without it we wouldn't have the Cavalry; but, according to Levy's (2001, p. 29) ideas, Cavalry that did not depend exclusively on stirrup's invention. Technology is surely important, but it needs to be related with other developmental factors and driven by an organizational perspective. So, more than impact, we can talk about a systemic relationship among technologies, individuals, and context variables.

According to this systemic point of view, the aim of this chapter is to propose to educators a tool by which they can think about the evolution of organizational models the schools can adopt to drive technological innovation. I found this tool in the theory of organization, particularly into the theory of the Swedish economist Richard Norman (2001). Developing my reflections I hope to not respond to school managers and educators, but only to make a critical review of consolidated practices and possible solutions.

Models of Organization: An Evolutionary Perspective

According to Norman, we can understand the evolution of organizations with three main paradigms: the industrial paradigm, the service management paradigm, and the systems reconfiguration paradigm.

The industrial paradigm—from the end of the 19th century to the '60s of the 20th century—is based on Fordism and Taylorism. The principles include a great confidence in rationality and technologies' possibilities (Fordism) and adopting a production system made by division of labor, task specialization and optimization of time and methods (Taylorism). These features produced a special (really particular) way of driving value that Norman calls Macdonaldization, because of its resemblance to the famous fast-food organization model. The focus of this system is the product, with its specificities; the critical competence of the system is the production, (i.e., to be able to produce a certain kind of goods); finally, the customer is thought in terms of capital, an abstract and passive object having a little or no importance in the economical process.

Starting from 1960, things changed according to three main factors. Firstly, consumers became more demanding and asked for a major care of their needs and satisfaction. At the same time, the growth of the Japanese economy produced an overload of circulating goods with very competitive prices: this phenomenon produced the first relevant crisis of Fordist economy whose core-part production isn't sufficient to contrast a more aggressive market situation. The gasoline crisis completed this scenario producing effects predominantly on the Fordist economy upon which it was built. These factors bring organizations to rethink what makes up their driving value. The focus of the system is no longer based on the product, but on the customer; the critical competence is now becoming the capacity of systems in managing customer relationship; that is, to develop relational marketing, to take care of quality, to create techniques to obtain customer loyalty. Naturally, the idea of the customer is also changing; they are no longer thought of as an undifferentiated target, but become the principal source of system production. In the industrial paradigm the customer is only the conclusion of production, in this new model of organization it is the starting point of the whole production process. The change is from production to services; service management is the real focus of this new perspective.

According to Norman this situation is changing again. The new perspective is now that of a reconfiguration of value creation systems. It means that the way in which value is driven is no longer production nor customer care, but a new sort of collaboration between industry and its clients. Once again we assist in a transformation of the core elements of the system: the focus of the system is now co-construction of value, where actors of this co-construction are producers and consumers (the exemplar case history, according to Norman, is IKEA, the famous Swedish producer of furniture who first proposed to the customer to be the co-producer of their own furniture, transporting it from the store to the home and assembling it with simple instructions); the critical competence of industry is its managing capacity in value creation; finally, the customer is really a co-designer and co-producer of value. In this organizational model both the roles of producer and customer are changed: a producer is no longer someone who can do anything well, but a person whose soft skills concern the ways through which he or she can collaborate with the customer in value production; on the other hand, a customer is no longer a passive conclusion of goods production, but someone who actively collaborates in production itself.

Figure 1. Models of organization evolution (Norman, 2001)

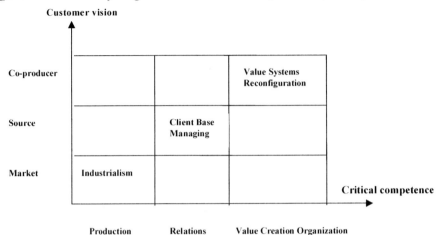

School and Organization

The three models of organization (in Figure 1) are the same models by which ICT in schools is organized. We will try to prove this with reference to the Italian school system (but we can extend these considerations to other European school systems and perhaps to American ones as well).

The industrial paradigm operates in education each time the Ministry tries to make a general change in the school system. In Italy, this happened in 1997 with the introduction of a Plan for Educational Technologies Development (*Piano di Sviluppo delle Tecnologie Didattiche*, PSTD). The problem here consisted in the production of a huge change in the schools. In fact, before PSTD, Italian Schools had neither technologies (computers, net-connection, LANs, etc.), nor the competencies to use them in education. So the Ministry of Education made a choice of general transformation of the system putting computers into the schools and organizing courses that provided training for teachers in Education Technology.

In these choices we can recognize some aspects already talked about: the confidence in rationality and technology (Fordism) and the orientation to a specialized approach to the problems (Taylorism). Both of these drive school systems to be built on errors.

Experts have called the first error "technological fallacy." This means to conceptualize the relationship between school and technology according to a linear and mechanical model; we already discussed this model and its metaphor of "impact" with which it explains the relationship between technology and organizations. Using this perspective it seems it would be enough to introduce technology in schools to change their organizational model. This is a deterministic point of view, too optimistic towards technological possibilities and unable to consider all the other complex factors that condition technology implementation and appropriation in every context.

This idea is often pursued through a Tayloristic organization of the schools. In Italy, this kind of organization is part of a global approach to teaching with technologies. The elements of this approach are:

1.   The conception of professional figures whose task is to manage technolo-gies, to provide a technological help-desk for teachers, and to help teachers in training and teaching. These figures are called by different names (*figure di sistema, funzioni obiettivo, funzioni strumentali*). Whichever name is used they must be discussed, keeping in mind the following questions: Should they be teachers inside the schools or consultants who are outside? If they are teachers, who should decide which criteria to use to select them from their colleagues? What kind of formation do they need? They could simplify work in the school, but also complicate it: what allows us to discriminate when and how they work? Then, it is important to consider that these figures must be paid and recognized in different ways than standard teachers.

2.   The equipment of classrooms with computers and Internet. In Italy, most of these classrooms have a structure in which computers face the teacher's desk; this disposition suggests a utilization of machines that does not allow collaborative work but only a repetition of the lesson *sub specie technologica*.

3.   The individualization of a place where technology is stored (a computer classroom) suggests that education technology is an unusual didactic moment and not, as it should be, simply a part of everyday school activity. In Italy, technology in education was, and is, often organized by special projects. This means that interest and enthusiasm is produced around technology, but also that it cannot have a real impact over teachers' practices and schools' standards. When the project is finished, people return to their normal routines.

4.   Finally, in Italy, these projects were identified with multimedia production (and now with Web activities) in the school. From a media education perspective, this means by-passing traditional media and reducing technol-ogy to new media. Often this choice overlooks that the aim of education, even when we educate with technologies, is not only to provide them with technical abilities, but also to improve pupils' critical thinking. From this

point of view, the Tayloristic model in schools is not able to pursue information literacy but only to provide information training.

The change to the Service Management Model began in Italy in 1999 when a new law gave a new *status* to schools. They are now no longer considered as a terminal of public administration, but as autonomous realities from several points of view: financing, didactic, marketing, fundraising, and projecting (Perrone, 2000). This change forces schools to be more active and to consider their customers' needs as the new focus of their actions. Therefore, the new key words of school organization are becoming "quality" and "educational marketing." In a system where customers are no longer taken for granted but need to be sought out, schools must use whatever quality criteria will make parents and children choose it over other schools. Technology becomes one of these criteria. Informatics, the Internet, and the use of ICT in education are all elements that, from a marketing perspective, can help systems give the impression of modernity and of having the capacity to prepare pupils for the future. Unfortunately, the risk here is to consider all these elements only as gadgets and not really as quality factors: new change is needed from a more serious perspective. This is the case of what Norman says about cooperation between organization and its customers.

Thinking of cooperation between the organization and its customers in schools means:

1.   To think about the ways with which customers (pupils and theirs parents) can collaborate with schools in enhancing value (prosumption)

2.   To promote ways of cooperation among customers themselves (community)

3.   To identify the actors that put them together with new modalities (constellation of values)

Norman (2001) gives the example of EF Education, a Swedish enterprise that, in the '60s, tried to find a new way of teaching foreign languages by democratizing the traditional choice of sending pupils to an English College. The idea according to which they created this new approach was by re-combining previously unrelated resources with their needs:

1.   Children, with their need to learn, have long summer holidays to have new experiences

2.   Teachers, with their need to practice, have long summer holidays to have good didactic results

3.   English schools, with their empty classrooms in the summer

4.   English families, with their desire to have new experiences and communicate their own culture—free rooms and a chance of socialization for their children in the summer months

5.   Parents, with their interest for their children's culture

I think that this kind of analysis is precisely what schools need to do when they think about the implementation of ICT.

Conclusion: Operative Suggestions

In this chapter we adopted an organizational perspective (by Richard Norman) for analyzing the presence of ICT in the schools. The main idea we've proposed is the necessity to abandon tayloristic models. According to those models, in fact, innovation is strictly dependent upon implementation of technology. This deterministic idea doesn't explain the real situation of the schools, whose real problem in ICT is not a technological but a cultural problem. So, what can the schools do to promote innovation in ICT and introduce education technologies in teachers' and pupils' practices? We must try to implement Norman's suggestions.

Firstly: prosumption. To involve pupils and parents means to allow them to be actors and not only receivers. Can technologies facilitate this change? The answer is yes, only if they allow:

1.   **Empowerment of learning:** that is, the chance that technologies of education give of developing a learner-centered system alternative to the traditional teacher-centered system, and

2.   **Individualization and personalization of teaching:** that is, the possibility for the teacher to be more present and responsive according to the needs of learners (individualization) and for the pupil to appropriate cultural issues in a more personal way (personalization). With these two focuses schools can work with parents and pupils to grant them the skills needed in an information society: "Employees need to be able to access and comprehend information presented on computer screens, analyze the use and reliability of information, and solve problems" (Pachler, 2001, p. 25).

Secondly: community. It is important that schools make an environment available in which teachers, students, and parents can develop communities. For teachers there should be communities of practice where they can develop their own professional identity, share procedures, find teaching tools, learn together, and perform collaborative problem solving. Students can develop communities as well, with different goals: free communities, for chatting and hobbies, help communities, for asking questions, sharing personal notes about lessons, managing didactic materials, and building communities, whose goal can be to develop projects and work together to enhance knowledge. Parents, on the other hand, can use a community for finding out information about school (curricula, events, and so on) and their children, and exchanging opinions and ideas. The most important thing is the possibility of making transversal participation available in all these communities, allowing their members to meet and work together (teachers and parents, for example, can develop a community where professional competencies of parents may be useful for curriculum implementation).

Thirdly: constellation of value. Community implementation can facilitate what Norman describes when he talks about the necessity of the organization and knowledge of the needs and desires of its clients. This kind of needs analysis and social relationship building will allow a new configuration of the school and its relationship with ICT. Otherwise, we run the risk of implementing technology without changing anything in the traditional organization of the school. As Papert (1996, p. 18) once said, "the important question is not simply about changes in curricula but changes in the human relationships most closely related to learning: relationships between generations in families, relationships between teachers and learners, and relationships between peers with common interests."

References

Leask, M. (2001). *Issues in teaching using ICT.* London: New York: Routledge.

Levy, P. (2001). *Cyberculture.* Minneapolis: University of Minnesota Press.

Merton, R. K. (1949). *Social theory and social structure.* New York: The Free Press.

Negroponte, N. (1996). Impariamo a imparare come si impara. *Télema, 3*(1), 80-81. Retrieved from http://fub.it/telema

Norman, D. (2001). *Reframing business: When the map changes the landscape.* Chichester, UK: John Wiley & Sons.

Pachler, N. (2001). Connecting schools and pupils: To what end? In M. Leask (Ed.), *Issues in teaching using ICT* (pp. 15-30). London, New York: Routledge.

Papert, S. (1996). *The connecting family: Bridging the digital generation gap.* Atlanta, GA: Longstreet Press.

Perrone, A. (2000). *L'educazione multimediale nella scuola dell'autonomia.* Rome: Quaderni FIDAE.

Rivoltella, P. C. (2003a). From the information society to that of knowledge. *Personae, 7*(2), 10-15.

Rivoltella, P. C. (2003b). *Scuole in Rete e Reti di scuole: Temi, modelli, esperienze.* Milano: ETAS Libri.

Virilio, P. (1995). Speed and information: CTheory. *Theory, Technology and Culture, 3*(18). Retrieved from http://www.nicoladoering.net/Hogrefe/virilio.htm

Wolton, D. (1999). *Internet et après: Une théorie critique des nouveaux medias.* Paris: Flammarion.

Endnote

[1] It is possible to talk about the technological determinism such as Papert (1996, pp. 50-54) does highlighting on how it can develop three objectionable features: (1) it gives agency to machine, not to child, (2) it is deceptive and proud of it, and (3) it favors quick reactions over long-term thinking. All becomes mechanical, child is conceptualized like an answering machine, and finally it seems that critical evaluation becomes less important, as educational objective, than technology implementation and skills acquisition.

Chapter V

Some Insights into the Impact of ICTs on Learning Agency and Seamless Learning

Hitendra Pillay
Queensland University of Technology, Australia

John A. Clarke
Queensland University of Technology, Australia

Peter G. Taylor
Queensland University of Technology, Australia

Abstract

The learning capacity of individuals is becoming recognised as the most valued commodity in a knowledge and information society and this has fostered an increased attention on the innovation, transfer, and management of knowledge. To explain these processes, it is necessary to move beyond what has traditionally been conceived of as a learning environment and to develop alternative models that acknowledge and accommodate the learning competencies required to successfully engage with a contingent and dynamic learning culture, the changing nature of knowledge, and the influence of the cultural background of learners. Such models need to explain the lifelong and continuous nature of learning as learners move seamlessly among a range of diverse learning environments. This chapter proposes the concept of learning agency which incorporates the intelligence inherent in learning environments as a mechanism to explain seamless learning within and across environments, particularly those that are rich in technology.

Introduction

The rapidly changing international social, economic, and political order has fostered an increased attention on innovation, transfer, and management of knowledge. While many believe that the emergence of the centrality of knowledge to society's growth is a consequence of economic reform and the proliferation of communication technology (Jentzsch, 2001), others argue that it is also an outcome of a gradual evolution of our social, political, and economic models (Lankshear, 1997). Irrespective of what might have triggered the focus on learning and knowledge creation, both the above assumptions imply that a very diverse and complex mix of concepts, principles, and variables may influence what constitutes knowledge, information technology, learning context and processes, learner motives, and social and political imperatives. This diversity and complexity challenges us to re-conceptualise learning and teaching.

As a consequence of the above complexity and the contingent nature of our society, the learning capacity of individuals is increasingly being recognised as the most valued commodity in a knowledge and information society (Department for Education and Employment, 1998; Hargreaves, 2003). The search for models to support contingent yet sustainable learning, accelerated deep approaches to learning and the development of an understanding of the distributed and complex nature of learning has resulted in intensive research focussing on understanding human cognition and the meaning-making processes (e.g., Collin & Tynjälä, 2003; Lave & Wenger, 1991). This increased research activity, while contributing new insights, has tended to be narrowly defined and focussed on specific aspects of problems rather than investigating how the various aspects complement and/or hinder each other. For example, despite the development of the actor-network theory and its application in research (Latour, 1988, 1993; Somerville, 1999), it has not been used to explore the relationships between learners' motives, beliefs and values, and their engagement with the various aspects of the actor-network systems. Similarly, the acknowledgement that learning permeates all aspects of our lives has resulted in the emergence of constructs such as "learning society" (Nonaka & Teece, 2001), "knowledge workers" (Maxwell, 2003; Rifkin, 2000), and "learning communities" (Shapiro & Levine, 1999). These constructs challenge the traditional conception of learning environments as they are all underpinned by principles of lifelong learning and continuous learning—principles that assume learning occurs seamlessly throughout individuals' lives and types of learning environments, as they negotiate their way within and among different contexts, contents, strategies, tools, and artefacts.

Against this backdrop, we explore and revise the existing concept of what constitutes a learning environment and speculate on ideas that may assist in understanding how learners identify and engage with the diversity and complexity of those environments.

Reconceptualising Learning Environments

Most assumptions underpinning research into learning environments have emerged from models derived from the discipline of psychology. Such research has furthered our general understanding of learners' affective and cognitive needs in formal settings by identifying a number of influential psychosocial dimensions and also provided coherent models that can be satisfactorily adapted for teaching in specific versions of such environments. For a recent extensive review of this type of learning environment research, see Harington (2001).

Current literature on learning environments can be synthesised into a matrix comprised of environments, processes, and approaches. There are a number of different types of learning environments such as institutional, workplace, home, and social and community networks wherein a number of learning processes, such as face-to-face, distance learning, mentoring, experimentation, observation, and online learning can be utilised in a blend of independent and instructor supported approaches. Each of these combinations of learning environment, process, and approach presumably has their own peculiarities and unless researched, understood, and managed appropriately, may not produce their intended outcomes. For instance, motivation in a face-to-face learning environment is often created by the instructor's personality and ability to engage learners whereas in an on-line situation, it is more likely to be the user friendliness and types of interaction embedded in the design of the instruction. However, most of the research summarised in reviews such as Harington's (2001) tends to have a uni-dimensional focus. There is extensive research into online learning environments (Teh, 1999) most of which explore only the characteristics of the technological support and the technological capabilities of learners while ignoring cultural influences that may affect the differential engagement of learners with such a learning environment. They may vary in their methodology or the aspects of technology they pursue, but still have the focus on technology which is only a tool and thus may not have all the answers. Similarly, while the workplace is often considered a rich learning environment because of the authentic experience available to learners in such contexts (Beckett & Hagar, 2000), little is known about the impact of learner capabilities in workplaces to deal with online learning or learning more abstract principles that underpin practices (Edwards, 1998; Eraut, 2000).

An examination of the current approach to learning environment research suggests that it is based on two fundamental assumptions. First, it assumes learning environments to be isolated entities, "bounded" in nature. This has hindered rigorous research into investigating learner behaviours as and when they traverse boundaries of traditionally defined learning environments. The current convergence of the formal learning (school), informal learning (at home and on excursions) and social learning (sport and social events) challenges the perimeters of boundaries of learning, yet very little research is available that attempts to explain this emerging notion of seamless learning environments. An illustration of this "bounded" approach can be seen in Teh's (1999) comprehensive study on formal learning environments where the informal learning experiences are not given any consideration. Similarly, little is known about the mechanism of the transfer of learning skills and knowledge from one learning environment to another or how learners simultaneously deal with several learning environments. The shift of vocational education from institutions (formal) to workplaces (informal) generated considerable interest in transfer (Lave & Wenger, 1991) and as this change was very distinctive, it was relatively simple to study. But with the increasing overlap between the traditional learning environment and the choice options available to learners, attempting to map learning skills and knowledge has become much more complex and fluid. Further, the processes of learners negotiating and navigating through a range of learning environments will increasingly become common practice and will need to become the focus of serious research. Both the negotiation of and navigation among fluid learning environments are critical attributes needed by learners in a rapidly evolving knowledge society.

Secondly, learning environments are currently viewed as essentially homogenous entities with a lack of appreciation of the diversity and complexity contained within a specific environment. There is a need to explore the nature of the learning environments and their associated elements (Jamieson, Fisher, Gilding, Taylor, & Trevitt, 2000; Luppicini, 2003; Newhouse, 2001). Each environment has its own set of underlying ideologies, software and hardware (physical and human resources), optimum strategies, etc., and variables which can have a significant influence on how, when and why learners engage in learning. Investigating this issue, Pillay and his co-researchers (Pillay, in press;

Pillay & Elliott, 2002; Pillay & McCrindle, 2005) have proposed a distributed framework to conceptualise and deal with some of the significant variables in a holistic yet differentiated manner that recognises the different elements in an environment and allows them to exist as separate but connected systems. The framework has identified four key factors that the authors believe capture all significant sources of influence on learner engagement and subsequent prag-matic action: (1) socio-cultural and political dispositions and ideologies which provide a personal rationale for learners to appreciate why they need to engage with learning, (2) domain knowledge which is constantly evolving and being redefined. Understanding the functional and relational aspect of the evolutionary process and the content will encourage sustained engagement, (3) strategies and processes which provide learners with ways to optimise their learning outcomes. This is often referred to as the "software of learning systems," and (4) tools and artefacts which extend our capacity to research, access, and collect data, simulate activities to illustrate the effect of input variables and provide support for, and the enhancement of, learning. In this distributed framework, the attributes of each factor can have different sub-elements depending on the type of learning environment under scrutiny. Nevertheless, the key factors and sub-elements all may variously and simultaneously influence learner engagement in learning tasks in a reciprocal manner with the influence also extending to the motives and the choice of strategies adopted by students.

While this model provides a framework for thinking about ways in which some of these elements may interact, it is essentially descriptive and lacks any explicit reference to the energy that entices the learners to consciously reflect, reason, and perform the necessary learning activity. A possible way of conceptualising that energy is considered next.

Catering for Complexity and Diversity in Learning and Learning Environments

Acknowledging the complex mix of variables that influence learning, our current longitudinal research into e-learning (Taylor, Pillay, & Clarke, 2003, 2004a, 2004b) provides the basis for our theorising that the influence of learning environments on learning can be thought of as an outcome of the knowledge and/ or intelligence designed into that environment. In order to design the intelligence in the environment we need to consider the elements and the possible influence they might have on learner engagement. As an example, take one of the elements in the distributed learning model, variously referred to as tools, objects or artefacts (including ICTs). We are in agreement with Csikszentmihalyi and

Rochberg-Halton (1981) in that we argue that they have an epistemology of their own which together with the learner's own epistemological beliefs about learning, trigger a reciprocal engagement similar to Bandura's (1997) "triadic reciprocal causation" (p. 6) which in turn fosters subsequent pragmatic actions (Taylor et al., 2004a). To explain the energy that fosters this reciprocal engagement, we have introduced the term "learning agency" to represent the mediating reciprocity emerging from the environmental effects (Pillay, Clarke, & Taylor, 2006). The term "learning agency" is derived from the original Bandurian concept of "learner agency" (Bandura, 1997). We argue that Bandura's "triadic reciprocal causation," where the triad is the person, the environment, and behaviour is not only triggered by chance but can also be engineered by designing the environment in ways that may stimulate the reciprocity. Therefore, the influence of the knowledge designed into and available within a learning context can influence how learners engage in and with that environment. Considering the possibility of differentiating each of the triadic nodes in Bandura's model and investigating the reciprocal causal links may contribute to our understanding of the energy that entices learners to consciously reflect on the various elements in an environment, to reason and to perform the necessary learning activity (Pillay et al., 2006).

There is a need to move away from a homogenised model of learning environments as emphasised in Harington's (2001) review paper and to engage with and investigate the complexity and diversity in learning environments together with the elements and relationships contained in them. We are increasingly recognising that the optimum competencies required to successfully engage with a contingent and dynamic learning culture cannot be appreciated by viewing learning environments as bounded and learning processes as linear and unidirectional. In real life contexts, learners do not stay in bounded learning environments but frequently navigate through several environments, each of which may have several different learning elements. The motivation for learners to stay engaged also varies and oscillates between the traditional intrinsic and extrinsic values. In addition, increasing recognition is being given to *strategic* rather than exclusively *surface* or *deep* approaches to learning. Therefore, what is required is a framework that has the capacity to go beyond the boundaries of specific environments and redefine/expand some of the traditional constructs such as motivation, deep learning and transfer of skills and knowledge in order to explain the seamless and continuous nature of learning. As we see increasing diversification in what constitutes a learning environment, the challenge is not only to open the individual environments for deeper and closer scrutiny but also to explore bridges across new learning environments to ensure and support seamless learning. Thus we are challenged to seek alternative frameworks that have the capacity to explain the dynamic and temporal nature of learning culture which transcends specific learning environments, something that the traditional approach to researching learning environments cannot do as it is, by its very nature, "environment-bound."

The concept of *learning agency* provides a mechanism to represent these seamless learning environmental effects (Pillay et al., 2006). This notion of learning agency is consistent with the core concepts associated with actor-network theory (Law, 1992). Law uses the metaphor of "heterogenous networks" to suggest and recognise that society, including education systems and organisations, "are all effects generated in patterned networks of diverse (not simply human) materials." Further, actor-network approaches see "knowledge" as a product or an effect of those networks of heterogenous materials, rather than simply individual or social agents. For example, in our longitudinal study (Taylor et al., 2003, 2004a, 2004b), a large number of part-time students recognised themselves as not only knowledge learners but also knowledge creators for other students by drawing on their workplace experiences. They were able to move in and out of work environment (as consumers and creators) and the university environment (as learners and creators) experiencing seamless learning.

In our longitudinal study of e-learning at a university campus (Taylor et al., 2003, 2004a, 2004b), we asked students about their approaches to learning, perceptions of their learning environments, and epistemological reflections on themselves as learners. A counter-intuitive result of a mismatch between espoused learning motives and strategies emerged—students tended to have significantly lower surface strategies scores than surface motive scores; and students tended to have significantly higher deep strategies scores than deep motive scores. This meant that the students' behaviour (manifested in their learning strategies) could not be explained by their individual characteristics (learning motives). However, based on their perceptions of the learning environments and their epistemological reflections, the counter-intuitive finding was explained by the influences of the technology-rich learning environment which included the usual ICT tools and peer networks, suggesting that individuals' approach to learning arises from mutual interactions between individual and contextual agency (ICT tools plus peers) which we labelled learning agency.

Our proposed driver of learner engagement, learning agency, is the total of the inherited ideas, beliefs, values and knowledge which guides the pragmatic action in social, cultural and professional environments. Learning agency is seen as implicit rather than explicit knowledge—it is *experienced* rather than *taught*—which makes it all-pervasive and relatively resistant to change. In our attempt to make it explicit in a learning context, we see learning agency as providing a strong sense for the design of institutional structures and their functions which in turn can impact on learner engagement in learning activities.

Conclusion

While this theorising deals with the recognition of the complexity and influence of a learning environment, the emergence of a knowledge society (Takeuchi, 1998) has seen an increased diversification in what are regarded as learning environments. This is due in no small way to the proliferation of ICTs in teaching and learning which have provided the opportunity to expand the range of legitimate learning environments from the traditional face-to-face modes. In this chapter, we are extending our previous theorising to address the increasingly diverse types of learning environments such as on-line learning, computer-based learning, workplace learning, institutionalised learning and their hybrids. In particular, we have argued the limitations of current theorising and understanding of learning and learning environments interpreted in terms of the reciprocal influence of agency, usually confined to the individual in the form of learner agency (Bandura, 1997). This tends to give limited attention to the nature and influence of the environment and assumes that learning environments are isolated entities, bounded in nature. In real life contexts, learners do not stay in bounded learning environments but frequently navigate through several environments. Further, the notions of lifelong learning and seamless learning are central to a knowledge society and the extended theorising aims at accommodating these concepts.

The chapter offers a view that learning environments are a complex mix of teaching and learning tools or artefacts (ICTs), strategies (informal and formal individual and group learning), philosophy and ideology of learning (learning to learn, life long learning, seamless learning), the structural and functional aspects of discipline knowledge, and the physical design and furnishing of learning environments. The contradiction evidenced in the current public and private sector discourse towards promoting lifelong and continuous learning, both of which can presumably happen when working across several different learning environments, and at the same time encouraging a fragmented and highly contextualised approach to dealing with this complexity, needs to be challenged. Support for the above challenge can be seen in Winn's (2002) call that "educational researchers should…study which characteristics of these environments help or hinder learning" (p. 114). The notion of learning agency may provide a key to understanding the diversity and complexity of the seamless learning environments that are co-emerging with the knowledge-based society.

References

Bandura, A. (1997). *Self efficacy: The exercise of control.* New York: W. H. Freeman.

Beckett, D., & Hagar, P. (2000). Making judgments as the basis for workplace learning: Towards an epistemology of practice. *International Journal of Lifelong Education, 19*(4), 300-311.

Collin, K., & Tynjälä, P. (2003). Integrating theory and practice: Employees' and students' experiences of learning at work. *Journal of Workplace Learning, 15*(7/8), 338-344.

Csikszentmihalyi, M., & Rochberg-Halton, E. (1981). *The meaning of things: Domestic symbols and the self.* New York: Cambridge University Press.

Department for Education and Employment. (1998). *The learning age: A renaissance for a new Britain.* Retrieved July 5, 2002, from http://www.leeds.ac.uk/educol/documents/000000654.htm

Edwards, R. (1998). Flexibility, reflexivity, and reflection in the contemporary workplace. *International Journal of Lifelong Education, 17*(6), 377-388.

Eraut, M. (2000). Non-formal learning and tacit knowledge in professional work. *British Journal of Educational Psychology, 70,* 113-136.

Hargreaves, A. (2003). *Teaching in the knowledge society: Education in the age of insecurity.* New York: Teachers College Press.

Harington, D. G. (2001). *The development and validation of a learning environment instrument for CSIRO Science Education Centres.* Unpublished doctor of science education, Curtin University, Western Australia. Retrieved August 13, 2004, from http://adt.curtin.edu.au/theses/available/adt-WCU20031013.114200/

Jamieson, P., Fisher, K., Gilding, T., Taylor, P. G., & Trevitt, A. C. F. (2000). Place and space in the design of new learning environments. *Higher Education Research and Development, 19,* 221-236.

Jentzsch, N. (2001). *The new economy debate in the U.S.: A review of literature* (Working Paper No. 125/2001). Freie Universitat, Berlin: John F. Kennedy Institute.

Lankshear, C. (1997). Language and the new capitalism. *The International Journal of Inclusive Education, 1*(4), 309-321.

Latour, B. (1988). Mixing humans and nonhumans together: The sociology of a door-closer. *Social Problems, 35*(3), 298-310.

Latour, B. (1993). *We have never been modern*. Brighton, UK: Harvester Wheatsheaf.

Lave, J., & E. Wenger (1991). *Situated learning: Legitimate peripheral participation*. Cambridge, UK: Cambridge University Press.

Law, J. (1992). *Notes on the theory of the actor network: Ordering, strategy and heterogeneity*. Retrieved July 25, 2003, from http://www.comp.lancs.uk/sociology/soc054jl

Luppicini, R. (2003). Categories of virtual learning communities for educational design. *Quarterly Review of Distance Education, 4*(4), 409-417.

Maxwell, J. (2003). *Innovation is a social process*. Quebec, Statistics Canada. Retrieved December 10, 2003, from http://www.statcan.ca/cgi-bin/downpub/listpub.cgi?catno=88F0006XIE2003006

Newhouse, C. P. (2001). Development and use of an instrument for a computer supported learning environment. *Learning Environments Research, 4*(2), 115-138.

Nonaka, I., & Teece, D. (2001). *Managing industrial knowledge: Creation, transfer, and utilization*. London: Sage.

Pillay, H. (2006) *Distributed cognition: Understanding tensions embedded in workplace knowledge and skills* (Chapter 12). New York: Nova Science Publishing Inc.

Pillay, H., Clarke, J. A., & Taylor, P. G. (2006). Learning agency in new learning environments: An Australian case study of the influence of context. In A. D. de Figueiredo & A. P. Afonso (Eds), *Managing learning in virtual settings: The role of context* (pp. 231-246). Hershey, PA: Idea Group Publishing.

Pillay, H., & Elliott, R. G. (2002). Distributed learning: Understanding the emerging workplace knowledge. *Journal of Interactive Learning Research, 13*(1/2), 93-110.

Pillay, H., & McCrindle, A. (2005). Distributed and relative nature of professional expertise. *Studies in Continuing Education, 27*(1), 69-90.

Rifkin, J. (2000). *The age of access: The new culture of hypercapitalism*. New York: J.P. Tarcher/Putnam.

Shapiro, N. S., & Levine, J. H. (1999). *Creating learning communities: A practical guide to winning support, organizing for change, and implementing programs*. San Francisco: Jossey Bass.

Somerville, I. (1999). Agency versus identity: Actor-network theory meets public relations. *Corporate Communications, 4*(1), 6-13.

Takeuchi, H. (1998). *Beyond knowledge management: Lessons from Japan.* Retrieved July 10, 2002, from http://www.sveiby.com/articles/LessonsJapan.htm

Taylor, P. G., Pillay, H., & Clarke, J. A. (2003). Enriching the learning culture through peers and technology. In J. Searle, I. Yashin-Shaw, & R. Roebuck (Eds.), *Enriching learning cultures* (vol. 3, pp. 140-146). Brisbane: Australian Academic Press.

Taylor, P. G., Pillay, H., & Clarke, J. A. (2004a). Exploring student adaptation to new learning environments: Some unexpected outcomes. *International Journal of Learning Technology, 1*(1), 100-110.

Taylor, P. G., Pillay, H., & Clarke, J. A. (2004b). Investigating the consequences of sustained involvement in new learning environments. In J. Searle, C. McCavanagh, & R. Roebuck (Eds.), *Doing, thinking, activity, learning* (vol. 2, pp. 219-230). Brisbane: Australian Academic Press

Teh, G. P. L. (1999). Assessing student perceptions of Internet-based online learning environments. *International Journal of Instructional Media, 26*(4), 397-402.

Winn, W. (2002). Learning in artificial environments: Embodiment, embeddedness and dynamic adaption. *Technology, Instruction, Cognition and Learning, 1,* 87-114.

Section II

Chapter VI

Cultural Agents:
Who They Are and What
Role They Play

Salvatore Colazzo
University of Lecce, Italy

Abstract

Teaching function is a strategic factor in the improvement of teaching and learning. In online education teaching function involves cultural, pedagogical, and didactical mediation. Thus conceived, the business of teaching aims to improve the aptitudes, intelligence, and personal qualities of the students, by engaging with the competence already in their possession, raising to consciousness their implicit knowledge, and favoring group interaction. By dint of cooperation, the students acquire important opportunities to construct, understand, and share knowledge and information. The teaching function conceived as a mediating function leads us towards the assumption of the socio-constructivist paradigm, which may be considered the key development of post-modern pedagogy.

Introduction

Online education is now shaping up as a completely new domain of pedagogical knowledge. This sector appears to be characterized by a multitude of elements which make it unique, compared to both traditional teaching practices and previous types of distance learning. Online education seems to be able to maximize the advantages of traditional forms of communication (group interaction and two-way communicative exchange between teachers and learners) while overcoming its limitations (the need for all the participants to be physically present). At the same time it enjoys the advantages of previous forms of distance learning (exploitation of the materials at times and in ways chosen autonomously by the learner), without having to suffer the isolation which they involve.

Online education is held to be particularly effective in facilitating learning in virtue of three possibilities that it provides:

1. The involvement of a number of sensory channels (multi-media) which particularly enrich communication

2. The use of a number of communicative possibilities (in real time or deferred), which implement the relationship not only between the teacher and the individual learner, but all the players in the educational process concerned

3. The high level of interaction with the study materials, which can be produced by the learning community itself, in such a way that the learning environment is modeled by the actions of the individual learners, with important effects on motivation and the acquisition of competence, which is thus richer, deeper, and more stable

The possibilities provided by online education, rather than streamlining and simplifying (or even making obsolete) the work of the teacher, actually make it more complex (and certainly more interesting). In the presence of a wealth of instruments and technological potential, the choices made by the teacher are crucial for developing the systematic and combined use of the available media and providing diversified forms of learning support; as such, the teacher's choices constitute the real strategic factor determining the quality of the training on offer. When we speak of the teaching function, we refer to a series of features that characterize the provision of teaching and training services by an institution whose *mission* is education, accomplished via one or more people, with recourse to appropriate technologies (Damiano, 1976).[1] The advent of online education has led to a reappraisal of this teaching function, which has seen the rise to preeminence of an important feature, that of the *mediation of learning.*[2]

The Professional E-Learning Mediator

Who is the *e-learning mediator?* He or she is a figure who performs the task of educational and pedagogical mediation, within and by means of the electronic platform being used.

In order to better define mediation in pedagogy we shall refer to Vygotskij, who firstly provided a convincing formulation of this concept (Vygotskij, 1974; cf. also Di Mauro, 2004).

He stresses that human culture is constituted thanks to the transformation of nature, which human beings accomplish through the use of instruments, and he argues that human beings transform social relations with the *mediation* of instruments of thought. Just as we design and create instruments for interacting with (and transforming) nature, we create instruments of thought which enable us to manage social relations, to transform them, and to bring about change in ourselves. These instruments of thought are of a social nature, because we learn to create them and to manipulate them through the practice of social relations. We may be said to learn through *mediators* (who in the initial phase of life are above all our parents), who in various ways that are moreover implicit and informal, give us indications on how to structure instruments suitable for acting with others and on others.

In an educational context, planning an intervention whose purpose is mediation involves the definition of the objectives to be achieved on the basis of a careful analysis of the educational needs of the subject, the selection of the tasks, the expectation of the possible difficulties he or she can meet and the providing for alternative routes to achieve the same objectives.

The mediator must have a clear idea of the significance of the efforts required from the learners and be able to communicate this effectively (why are we learning what we set out to learn?); he or she must know how to analyze the task and its characteristics (he or she must have a clear idea of what to do); he or she must have a very detailed and precise idea of the learners and of their characteristics (mediators are people who know who they are working with); he or she must know how to promote the acquisition of the content that the students need to learn (he or she must therefore be aware of the methodological strategies to activate, which must also take account of any difficulties that that the students may have).

Therefore he or she must know how to work in accordance with the principles of objective-based pedagogy, that is, he or she must know the prerequisites required for the adequate accomplishment of the task, he or she must know how to present the content and understand the feedback from the student concerning the task while it being performed, and he or she must have a very precise idea of the level of complexity of the task, so as to be able to identify the difficulties that learners may be expected to have. The mediator-educator is a person who can identify the proximal zone of development (Vygotskij, 1974), taking account of the heterogeneity of the group, and who can therefore pedagogically manage this heterogeneity.

The mediator is a person who stands between the characteristics of the situation and context and the characteristics of the student, selecting the strategies for maximizing the relationship between the student and the context and using tools and technologies as appropriate.

In this regard, when faced with the failure of a test, the mediator asks him or herself why this has happened. He or she knows that it is only by answering this question correctly that he or she will be able to help the student to organize the skills that are indispensable to the correct performance of the task, or (more probably) to appropriately activate the student's knowledge so that it can be used in the execution of the task. The mediator is therefore someone who knows how to diagnose: he or she understands why a performance is not a good performance and helps the learner to understand the reasons why he or she has failed.

The mediator, furthermore, is aware of, and monitors as appropriate, the social and effective dimensions of learning: he or she knows well the role played by the socio-effective context in the mobilization of cognitive resources.

All the indications relative to the educational mechanism being used, the possibilities it provides, and its limitations may be considered mediatory functions (regardless of whether there will be assigned to the teacher, the tutor or any other specific professional category). E-learning platforms also include an induction/ orientation activity, which enables the learner to find out about the institution or organization promoting the educational initiative, to understand how he or she is expected to participate in the educational activities, who his or her interlocutors will be and what their roles are, what the aims and general objectives are, the chosen topics, and how knowledge is monitored.

In the same way, all the support concerning the self-esteem of the users, the handling of the frustrations consequent on the failure to perform a task, and the help that can be offered to the users so that they become aware of the their progress, constitutes a form of mediation. Concern for the development of meta-cognitive abilities, the work which can be done to facilitate cognitive transfer[3] is also mediation. The mediator may be said to be a person who helps improve the knowledge acquisition process.

Managing the Learning Group

This conception of the work of teaching and the role of the student is oriented towards a democratic and innovative framework of values. The group which learns and is educated in the virtual universe of cyberspace is a social system in miniature; it therefore functions on the basis of norms, has objectives and implies the presence of roles.

The methodologies inspired by cooperative learning draw their efficacy from:

1. Their ability to establish defined spaces and periods within which synergies can develop
2. The possibility of defining the roles of the participants and their position with respect to each other
3. The applicability of systematic observation and retrieval techniques
4. The possibility of guiding the group dynamics and of introducing deliberate changes

In addition, Lewin argues that the group is a system of integrated movements that may be ordered and measured. Those who belong to a cooperative learning group have a great advantage: they can acquire information on how a group functions, on how it evolves: it is a direct and valuable experience of sociality.

The teacher (mediator) is called upon to orient and guide the group: by his or her actions, he or she aims to act on the culture of the group. He or she is part of the group, and can perceive its dynamics; he or she is participating in a common experience which he or she interprets from a specific point of view. The personal traits that he or she must possess include the capacity to express "involvement" in the situations, "enthusiasm" for the exchanges and participation. He or she must create a democratic, cooperative, welcoming and tolerant climate, so that meaningful learning can take place. It is interesting to reconsider teaching-learning strategies that have been tried out in the traditional classroom, which seem to draw new strength from the ease of computer-mediated communication: we refer here above all to the strategies associated with collaborative and cooperative learning. These strategies may be usefully applied not only in the context of school, but also (perhaps even more so) in the fields of in-company training, adult education, and professional follow-up courses.

There is a convergence between the reorganization, now in progress of the system of production, with its emphasis on the restructuring of large organizations, making them more flexible and less bureaucratic in order to better respond to the needs of a mature market. The new approaches to training, which is beginning to be understood as a whole complex of actions designed to promote in learners a willingness to work as a group, thus learning mechanisms of mutual adaptation. Work groups today, especially in complex organizations where the prevailing tasks are not of a routine nature, tend to function in accordance with non-hierarchical, immediate, and informal mechanisms, along the lines of what once used to happen in artisans' workshops. They work on specific objectives, on the basis of models and templates[4]; the capacity of the individuals to learn from the situation they find themselves in enables them—in the presence of adequate organization—to bring about significant transformations in the firm, enabling it in turn to respond more flexibly to environmental stimuli.

Collaborative learning and cooperative learning are part of the psycho-pedagogical constructivist paradigm, which is considered the central paradigm of post-modern pedagogy (Dalle Fratte, 2003). If one wished to place collaborative learning and cooperative learning in a broader cultural frame of reference, it could be said that they are the expression of an ideology of "rationality without foundations." This ideology seems to be characterized by eclecticism (the possibility of combining ideas from different cultural contexts), pragmatism (pre-eminence of action), historicism-contextualism (truths are not stable, but change according to the socio-cultural context and the historical moment), and emphasis on the communicative dimension (meaning derives from communicative trans-actions).

Towards New Ethics of Social Relations

Further testimony to the transformation in progress in western society is provided by the numerous attempts that have made over the last two decades to substantially modify the welfare state. There is a shift towards an approach which sees the possibility of resolving social problems, exclusion and marginalization through the universal promotion of well-being and the quality of life. A new notion of citizenship is emerging, leading to a re-evaluation of the function of those institutions which provide services. These are now expected to open up spaces and opportunities by promoting and protecting above all the right to information on the services that the user is entitled to, and therefore by guaranteeing the right of access to the network of services, eliminating any obstacles present in situations where exercising this right might be more difficult. Moreover, they need to enhance the right to the personalization of services and the recognition of differences, via personalized intervention; to promote the right that each of us has to enjoy a satisfactory social life and be active members of society. We dealing therefore with an approach to social services that aims to enhance the resources and the skills of the individual: these must be recognized and developed, with the collaboration of the relational and social context, in order to bring about changes in the practices of the individual, with a view to enabling the development of autonomy while taking account of the problems.

It can thus be said that new ethics are maturing, and the emphasis on collaboration and social interaction in learning tasks can be considered an expression of this. We are dealing with ethics whose purpose is overall well-being, that is, a well-being that is the result of a number of factors: physical health, psychological health, quality of social relations, autonomy and self-determination of the individual, and spirituality. Cooperative learning and collaborative learning, therefore, must be understood as the maximum expression of individuality, which enters into relationships with others, finding the possibility of complete fulfillment. The idea of sociality that emerges is, in a manner of speaking, that of a sustainable sociality, characterized in terms of *ecological equilibrium* between the needs of the individual and the social context of reference.

Constructivist models generally assign a fundamental value to the power of language in structuring thought (thus following an important intuition of Vygotskij). Through verbal interaction, a more expert subject, making his or her actions explicit, helps the less expert to internalize the explanations to the point of integrating them into his or her cognitive structure. In fact, this work of making something verbally explicit is also useful to the more expert subject. He or she can also learn, in that any difficulties of comprehension experienced by the less expert subject can help the more expert subject to acquire greater awareness of his or her theory, which becomes better organized.

The more expert subject can moreover understand the mechanisms through which the process of comprehension in the other takes place. By means of language, therefore, it is possible to make explicit and exchange points of view and activate cooperation. In the learning environments which are inspired by this theoretical model, the process of acquisition of individual knowledge is seen as the result of the weaving together of a number of discourses that exist within the learning space, but above all outside it, in the space that constitutes the culture in which the object of learning is inscribed and the social context in which the subject who learns is located.

Collaborative and cooperative learning thus seek to educate a subject who is then able to contribute positively to the growth of knowledge thus conceived, in the ambit of communities that assign a significant value to communication. They do this by focusing attention on the interactions within the group, facilitating the collective commitment of students to complex tasks,[5] regarding the teacher as a facilitator of interactions within the group and as a source of expert knowledge, promoting skills that can bring about the sharing of information and knowledge. Collaborative and cooperative learning favor the organization of the players in didactic communication into a collaborative community, within which—through the interactions—the subjects can learn to know themselves and to express their potential.

The new media are particularly suitable to the promotion of collaborative and cooperative learning, in that they are able to create a conversational environment and provide a rational organization of the content of knowledge, which, when suitably archived, can subsequently be reused and modified, in relation to the specific problems to be resolved.

Supported by computers, the collaborative community makes it easier to develop meta-cognitive abilities, favors the solution of problems through comparison of different interpretations of the situation, and teaches people how to negotiate meanings and to appreciate the differences.

It does this insofar as it:

1. Makes it possible to develop problem-solving skills by helping learners to interiorize the implicit cognitive processes through interaction and communication

2. Obliges learners to make explicit and communicate their knowledge, ideas and opinions, making it possible to share different perspectives

3. Acts on motivation: belonging to a group is an emotive factor that favors learning processes

4. Brings out attitudes that can be of great use in the world of work, where the success of an action is often made possible by the existence of an adequate collaborative spirit among colleagues

The Mediating Function of the Teacher and Learning Through the Group

Communication and collaboration should not be confused. Communication is a pre-requisite for collaborative activities but the two concepts (and the two practices) are not entirely coterminous. When communicative technologies have been introduced into an educational institution then only the pre-conditions for their justified use have been created. Indeed, care needs to taken to give these technologies a new meaning; they must become *educative* technologies, inscribed in an educational project, and they need to be looked at in terms of clearly defined objectives. There is one technology, in the end, on which all the others depend and this technology is the brain of the teacher, which indeed needs to be well made, in the words of Edgar Morin (2000, 2002).

There are teachers who are excellent communicators and very effective at generating learning, but who may not be sufficiently able to inculcate in the students aptitude for building, through collaborative activity, their own knowledge. A specific approach is necessary to create the right environment for the sharing of information and the collaborative resolution of problems. Collaboration, if we look at the etymology of the term, means *working together*, in the belief that four eyes see more than two, that there is a particular satisfaction in doing something together. The result obtained through collaboration has a greater value which derives from the process that has brought it into being.

The teaching function is the factor that determines the success or failure of a learning community: its actions will either enable the group to develop cooperative attitudes or prompt the emergence of forms of competition that will cause the community to disintegrate.

The pioneering studies of Kurt Lewin have a strong contemporary relevance in that they help us understand the importance of leadership in determining the dynamics of the learning group. While guiding a small cooperative research community, Lewin came to the result, supported by significant experimental data, that both autocratic-*dirigiste* and permissive attitudes are deleterious for the functioning of the group (Lippit & White, 1960). The results obtained by the group are strongly conditioned by the overall attitude assumed by the teacher. If, in the ambit of the group, the teacher assumes an autocratic attitude, the students will be very argumentative, they behave as individuals that do not engage with each other, and have no interest in the objectives of the group or the activities of the other members.

The *laissez-faire* attitude, however, does not produce good results either: it generates frustration, due to the lack of fundamental rules which inspire the action. This frustration manifests itself in the mocking of the less competent or less popular members within the group.

From this experience, Lewin drew the idea that the difference in the behavior observed in a situation characterized by autocratic leadership with respect to that of a more democratic situation is not attributable to individual differences. The social climate can have a profound influence on the group. A group led by a democratic leader is active, cooperative and creative; if the leadership changes and becomes autocratic, the group rapidly becomes apathetic and without initiative (Marrow, 1977, pp. 145-8).

Collaborative learning is based on the assumption that learning is an intrinsically individual process, though it comes about in a social context. For example, Bruner stresses how the knowledge that is created in the mind of a person is formed thanks to conversations, comparisons and discussions, and is thus a practical, here-and-now activity: the subject who learns does not engage with the content of knowledge in a solipsistic way, but acquires his or her knowledge by taking advantage of all the possibilities and opportunities that the environment provides. And if the relational dimension is limited, one can be certain that the learning will be less profound and less significant than would be the case in a social context rich in communicative exchanges.

In addition, Vygotskij spoke of the "proximal zone of development," by which is meant those possibilities for development that the subject has (and which would otherwise remain unused) in virtue of the presence of others, be they peers or more expert adults (scaffolding).

From this intuition, the next step is to posit the notion of optimal teaching. The teaching is optimal when it is collocated in the proximal zone of the individual learner: the teacher selects and organizes the stimuli, which, in order to work properly, must correspond to the proximal zone of development of each learner. This is the proper function of the teacher mediator.

It is possible to take account of the social dimension of learning only by observing the operations that we put into effect when we really want to know something: we go through our notes in exercise books and writing pads, we take books off the shelves and we look through them quickly, letting ourselves be guided by previous jottings made when we read them and studied them originally, looking for the passage that could be relevant to us right now, we telephone a friend who might be able to give us an important reference, we consult the internet, we recover files from our computers that might contain knowledge which is important to us. The process of acquisition of knowledge in our society is complex and in some ways is culturally conditioned: we do not learn as our ancestors did. We know what we know in a different way to them, our way of learning is of a specificity that would be interesting to decipher.

If that is true, then learning, which in one sense is an individual phenomenon, is also intrinsically social: it is thanks to interactions with others that we are prompted to reorganize and modify the structure of our knowledge. It is safe to say therefore that while learning is an individual set of knowledge and skills, it is the system of social interactions however that we establish in the environment that helps to form it, to keep it efficient and to enrich it. The teacher is a person who, seeing himself or herself as the facilitator of learning, intervenes in the environment and on the environment in order to constantly maintain the educational potential.

Conclusion

The mediating dimension in teaching and tutoring creates the conditions for the student to be able to construct, discover, transform and extend his or her knowledge. It places materials at the disposal of the student so that he or she may exploit them; it helps the students become aware of what they already know. It considers learning not so much a memorization of data as a practical-operational experience, characterized that is by actions which, thanks to the mediation provided, is taken to the level of reflection. It assigns to instruction the task of emphasizing and developing the capacities and the inclinations of the students. The work of teaching aims to improve the aptitudes, intelligence and personalities of the students. It sees cooperation between students as an important opportunity to construct, understand and share knowledge and information.

Future Trends

In this chapter the issue of the need to develop teaching programs able to, with the support of the new technologies, the individual differences between the subjects who learn has remained in the background, barely developed as a theme in itself. Subsequent research will better tackle this issue.

Online education is based on the idea that the student, when entering the world of education or training, brings his or her own baggage of experiences that make him or her surely unique; this baggage furthermore prompts him or her to compare himself or herself with other subjects who bear the imprint of other experiences and therefore see the world and the objects with different eyes.

In the virtual space of the new communicative tools, it should be clear that every viewpoint has the right to express itself, to exist, and to be represented. However this viewpoint cannot presume to be as it was constitutive of the world, that is, to contain the whole truth of the world. It must be correlated with other, different perspectives. The world is what the encounter and the dialogue are able to construct together.

The virtual community, oriented by a new kind of teacher, can become the space that makes community experience possible through the exchange of experiences, bringing them together with the aim of creating an object which is the result of debate, of the negotiation of meaning and of mutual agreement.

The problem is to understand how diverse subjectivities, with highly dissimilar experiences, can effectively enjoy a community experience. And this is exactly where the role of pedagogy, of didactics and of technology comes in. By acting together, they must indicate the operational solutions to adopt. They must tackle the problem of how to enable every individual to recognize the other individuals, their identity, and their specific way of interpreting the world. On this basis it will then be possible to think together, evaluate together, plan and act together.

References

Bonazzi, G. (2002). *Storia del pensiero organizzativo*. Milano: Franco Angeli.

Dalle Fratte, G. (Ed.). (2003). *Postmodernità e problematiche pedagogiche. Vol 1: Modernità e postmodernità tra discontinuità, crisi e ipotesi di superamento*. Roma: Armando.

Damiano, E. (1976). *Funzione docente*. Brescia: La Scuola.

Di Mauro, M. (2004). *La pedagogia della mediazione e l'apprendimento mediato*. Retrieved December 7, 2004, from http://www.univirtual.it/real/download/REAL_LezioneDistanza16Febbraio2004.pdf

Lippit, R., & White, R. (1960). *Autocracy and democracy: An experimental inquiry*. New York: Harpen & Low.

Marrow, A. J. (1977). *Kurt Lewin fra teoria e pratica*. Firenze: La Nuova Italia.

Morin, E. (2000). *La testa ben fatta. Riforma dell'insegnamento e riforma del pensiero*. Milano: Raffaello Cortina.

Morin, E. (2002). *Educare gli educatori. Una riforma del pensiero per la democrazia cognitiva*. Interview of Antonella Martini. Roma: Edup.

Vygotskij, L. S. (1974). *Storia dello sviluppo delle funzioni psichiche superiori ed altri scritti*. Ancona: Giunti Barbera.

Endnotes

[1] Elio Damiano points out that the teaching function does not coincide with the "role of the teacher." The teaching function is provided by the institution, in the ways and under the terms that it considers most appropriate.

[2] Convinced of the importance of the mediating dimension in e-learning, we have designed and implemented a post-graduate specialization course for the training of professional "e-learning mediators" at the University of Lecce. The course, which benefited from funding provided by the European Social Fund, was designed by professors Nicola Paparella and Salvatore Colazzo, respectively director and coordinator of this initiative. Taught in the academic year 2003/2004, it saw the participation of 70 young graduates from various disciplines, thus forming a pilot experience among those pertaining to the training of professionals needed for e-learning.

3   *Transfer* is the influence that the learning of one activity exerts on the learning of another, facilitating it. It is therefore the capacity to perform a task or resolve a problem after having had experience with similar tasks or after having acquired adequate cognitive tools for predicting the outcomes of given behaviors.

4   To describe this modality of organization the term "ad hocracy" was coined. We find a definition of the term in Bonazzi: "Ad hocracy is characterized by a highly integrated nucleus of specialists of great sophistication, with informal behaviors, absence of hierarchy, lack of standardization, and a pronounced aptitude for the exploration of solutions along routes that are not pre-defined" (Bonazzi, 2002, p. 314).

5   By *complex task* we mean a task that has open solutions. It requires the use of multiple intellective abilities; it promotes processes of thought of a higher order; it stimulates the use of multiple sensory channels. A complex task is a problem in which the exact properties of the initial state, of the final state and of the obstacles are unknown and change dynamically during the process of resolution.

Chapter VII

A Model to Measure the Impact of Web-Based Technologies in Different Teaching Styles

Carmen de Pablos Heredero
Rey Juan Carlos University, Spain

Abstract

Information and communication technologies offer us new possibilities to improve the way we develop our work as educators and give our students new opportunities to relate with us and other stakeholders in the process of learning. In higher education we can differentiate three different teaching styles, the traditional one, with the need of the presence of the students and the teacher in a classical classroom, the distance teaching style that substitutes the personal interaction in the class between student and professor with a distance relation based in different materials, and the virtual style, in which a permanent relation between students and lectures is established via a network. Some past analysis have tried to measure the importance and variables that have an impact in the implementation of information and communication technologies and the final results achieved for each of the different styles. In this chapter, we try to study the variables that have a greater impact in the IT implementation and final success and try to integrate all them in a model. Future studies should try to contrast the presented model in the three main mentioned university styles.

Introduction

Since the '90s, there has been an increase in the number of universities implementing Web technologies to complete or improve the way they offer their services (Alavi & Leidner, 2001). Among the areas of interest in the studies that measure the impact of Internet in Educational Institutions, we can mention: virtual teams (Knoll & Jarvenpaa, 1995), the improvement of work group by using technological tools (Alavi 1994; Alavi et al., 1995), the virtual interaction amongst students and teachers produced by Internet (Leidner & Fuller, 1997) and the new contents for pedagogical material (Leidner & Jarvenpaa, 1993).

Khan (2001) developed a framework for e-learning containing some of the following dimensions: the institutional one, focused on aspects and issues affecting the organization such as the administrative affairs, academic affairs and student services; the pedagogical one, focused on learning and teaching styles in the virtual context; the technological dimension, focused in the technical required tools; the management dimension concerned with aspects such as maintenance and distribution of information (close to our rules and procedures); resource support related to all types of online support and ethical dimension focused on aspects such as social, cultural diversity, bias, geographical diversity, learner diversity, legal issues, etc. (these last aspects are quite close to our organizational inertia concept).

The literature centered in the analysis of the variables that can explain the behavior of educational Institutions that incorporate Internet as a work tool have shown some partial factors as the responsible ones. Although we have found references of notable interest, we have detected a very important lag when trying to find an explanatory model. For that reason, in this work we have tried to collect the main literature references and after that to create a model containing the main variables considered from an integral perspective. After that, we will contrast the model offered in future research.

The Model

In the last decade the sociological models have generated a great debate in the role that information and communication technologies play in organizations (Poole & de Sanctis, 1990, 1992; Walsham 1993; de Sanctis & Poole, 1994). The human behavior is of importance for these models, in particular, the use of these technologies. New approaches that give a special importance, not only to the information and communication technologies in the firm, but the use that firms give to these technologies and derived consequences (Weick, 1990; Roberts & Gravowski, 1995). In this orientation, Orliwoski (2000) proposes a practical understanding of the relationship amongst the people, the technology, and the social action.

By considering the different mentioned studies and others to mention afterwards, De Pablos, Romaniello, and Quintana (2005) integrated the different variables, partially considered in the literature in an only model. They are now trying to contrast the model in three different kinds of educational styles: traditional, virtual, and distance ones.

The following figure presents the model we propose for further contrasts. We have named our model "internalizing Web-based technologies in the university education model."

As shown in Figure 1, we have considered two different levels in the model. One first, behavior, referred to the internalization of Web technologies from the involved individuals (professors and students) and a second one, organizational climate, referred to the internalization of Web technologies in the involved organizations (universities in our case).

In our model we hypothesize that the way in which individuals and organizations internalize Web-based technologies has a positive impact in the individual's

Figure 1. A variation from the De Pablos and Romaniello (2004) model "internalizing Web-based technologies in the university education model"

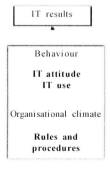

satisfaction degree (professors and students) and the organizational performance.

In relation to the behavior, we have considered two dimensions: the individual attitude people have towards the use of information technologies and the individual use they make of them.

The attitude, following the theory of the reasoned action (Fishbein & Ajzenis, 1975) reflects the degree of affection one feels about the information and communication technologies. In the use dimension, we have considered the resource based view. This theory promotes new technology as one more resource, a resource that does not necessarily bring a competitive advantage to the organization. Companies achieve desired results depending on the kind of information technology implementation they develop. Only those institutions that have been able to develop appropriate rules and procedures will benefit from its use.

In a second step, our chapter follows Block and Novell's (1999) orientation: the reach and extension of the incorporation of new technologies depends on a group of factors identified as "organizational climate." The organizational climate helps to promote some professor and students' behaviors towards new technologies with a clear impact in the final results and satisfaction they attempt to achieve.

We specially identify two variables that the literature considers very important ones: rules and procedures and the organizational inertia. Each university expresses via its rules and procedures the way they interiorize new technologies, how they are going to use them and the explicit and implicit objectives they pursue with them. The organizational inertia has to do with aspects in relation to culture, values and ways of group expression in the organization. The literature analyzed suggests that all these aspects could promote the use of these technologies in educational environments.

The last part of the model, IT results, refers to the impacts of the implementation of new technologies and the degree of satisfaction it promotes in students and professors. Clemons and Row's analysis (1991) consider performance and satisfaction as very important variables to analyze the impact of Web based technologies internalization.

Figure 2. Main facts in the model proposed (De Pablos, 2005)

POSITIVE IT BEHAVIOUR
+
ADEQUATE ORGANISATIONAL CLIMATE
=
IT POSITIVE RESULTS

The model tries to contrast as main hypotheses how a positive behavior of people towards information technologies joint to an adequate organizational climate leads to better satisfaction of the information technologies use in educational institutions.

The Attitudes

Argyle (1991) points out that one of the best ways of encouraging group cohesion is sheer physical proximity. Evolution seems to have provided us with social rewards for co-operating with others. However, the complex human interaction methods we use to establish trust, cohesion, and so on in groups, are largely innate and normally very subtle. They often include facial gestures, body language, and tone of voice. Even with efforts put into exercises to introduce and engage online participants, it is immensely more difficult to build up commitment, trust, and understanding in fully virtual groups (Castelfranchi & Tan, 2002).

The attitude reflects the degree of affect that one feels "to or against" any object or behavior (Fishbein & Ajzenis, 1975). A person's attitude in relation with the information technology makes a reference about the perception (positive or negative) a person feels about the information technology. Davis (1989) shows that the attitude of people to the use of the information technologies is directly related to the perception these persons have about the technologies. Orliwoski and Gash (1994) suggest that the use that people make of technologies is critic to understand their interaction. Yates and Orliwoski (1992, 1994) speak of genres of organizational communication. The purpose of communication in a genre is not an individual and private motive for communication but a built propose recognized by a community and used in some situations. Rhodes and Cox (1990), in an analysis they made on today's practices and policies concerning computer use in primary schools, study the effects of the student's attitudes through information technologies in the learning. Fullan (1993) stresses the importance of positively motivating the students in relation to the information technologies to reach a better empathy with them. Rusell et al. (1997) try to measure the anxiety that people develops towards the computers and the implications they have in the worker's professional career. From their analysis we can understand that higher degrees of anxiety lead to a decrease in the worker's final results. In the concrete case of the virtual education, Mikropoulos et al. (1998) analyze the attitudes of students towards the modality of virtual learning, by stressing the characteristics that make a student the appropriate customer for the use of Web technologies in this learning style. Collis et al. (1999) emphasize the importance of training to achieve a positive attitude in the education by using distance means. Shrum and Hong (2002) develop a more complete analysis by introducing the two implied parts: students and lecturers. In their analysis they stress how it is needed to know the characteristics of the students, users of Web technologies, so that the lectures can develop appropriate strategies for these characteristics. Njagi et al. (2003) propose a methodology that helps to develop attitudes in the students that enable them a more efficient use of the resources based in the network.

IT Use, Procedures, and Work Routines

Brown and Duguid (2002) argue that innovation is not just about technology; it is also about human beings and for technology to be implemented effectively it must be accommodated within the social context in which human beings operate.

In the study of the impacts of information technologies in our context, we do not defend technology as a specific asset (Peteraf, 1993), but as one more resource that properly internalized in the management information system can allow to achieve a group of efficiencies of different nature, it could be a decrease in the cost, an improvement in the quality of the offered services or an increase in the communication channels offered. In this sense, Web technologies are resources at the reach of any educational institution. However, not all the educational centers internalize the technology in a same way. In this sense to have the technology does not necessarily means that the results are going to be improved. Only those Institutions that use them, even in a secondary phase, have developed the adequate routines and procedures of use, and can then benefit from the advantages they offer.

Below this perspective and around the relation between information technologies and organizational results, Clemons and Row (1991) developed an analysis showing how the competitive imitation removes a great part of advantages coming from the technology itself. The authors conclude in their analysis that *"although it is possible to find examples of the use of information technologies in order to reach a sustainable competitive advantage; however, they are not as frequent as we think"* (1991, p. 278). Anyway, educational institutions are going to try to reach efficiencies in the IT use, and in this sense, they consider that a higher degree of use and the development of routines and procedures in the firm will help to reach IT's objectives.

Organizational Inertia

Educational technology and change are intricately linked. Just as the introduction of new technology has brought about changes in society and in the workplace, the introduction of computers at school is also laden with change implications, although this relationship has rarely been acknowledged by policymakers and techno researchers alike. Knuffer (1993) points out two important points about the relationship between computers, schools, and change. First, she argues that the successful implementation of computers in education requires an understanding of the process of educational change and that this understanding must precede the actual implementation of the innovation itself. Second, the teacher's role must be seen as central to any change due to the fact that successful education change depends on what stakeholders do and think.

Culture is the context that defines the organizational inertia. It is the context in which things happen in society, institutions and organizations. Culture is not easily defined because it is largely implicit. Schein (1992) notes are at a great extent intertwined with organizational norms and values which influence and shape how groups and individuals think and behave and through which systems of shared meanings evolve.

The literature on this issue has paid special attention to another factor that can influence in the way of internalizing Web technologies in educational institutions. It is maybe a more abstract consideration of the group as it appears in the organizations and that, in view of the analyzed studies, could promote or emphasize the use of these technologies in educational environments. It has more to do with aspects related to culture, values, and ways of group expression in the organization. Under these considerations we support what we name organizational inertia, and it includes these mentioned aspects.

IT Results

Where, with no doubt, we can find more contrasted references and the more representative studies, is in the field of user's satisfactions and results obtained after using a certain IT through the time. Satisfaction and results are considered, variables of the greatest importance when defining different styles of internalizing Web technologies in the educational field. Maybe the most outstanding analysis is developed by Ives and Olson (1983) who developed a complete method for allowing the measure of users' satisfaction in IT use. This approach has been mentioned in various analyses for the studying of the impact of information and communication technologies in firms of different nature. It seems to be a very useful tool for the organizations due to the difficulty in measuring such abstract term as satisfaction. Bailey and Pearson (1983) take part of the before mentioned analysis to develop a tool trying to measure and analyze computer user satisfaction. Compeau and Higgins (1995) develop a framework to measure what they call computer self-efficacy. Webster and Hackley (1997) and Duvall and Schwartz (2000) apply the Ives and Olson's model to measure the teaching effectiveness in technology mediated distance in the first case and to measure the relationship between academic performance and technology-adept adult students in the second case.

Due to the different aims and objectives that students and lectures have on IT for work motives, De Pablos, Romaniello, and Quintana (2005) have elaborated two different questionnaires to contrast the model we present in this chapter. The model attempts to analyze how different upper learning styles behave in the use of IT by considering two different actors: students and lectures. It integrates the various variables that the literature has collected as explaining ones: attitudes, use of IT, routines and procedures developed by the Institution, organizational inertia, satisfaction and results. Now we are in the process of offering the survey in academic forums so that people working in this field can give us an opinion about our model. It could be an opportunity for us to receive valuable feedback and improve it.

Conclusion and Future Trends

Information and communication technologies cannot be considered as a viable solution to university growth and profitability unless they can deliver educational benefits. Universities, for research and lecturing purposes, daily use information and communication technologies. There have been many studies done in the field of key factors surrounding the use of technology in education. However, these studies were more focused on one perspective (students or lectures), and analyze one only variable effect (Henly & Reid, 2001; Peterson, 2001). We assume that different kinds of universities do not use information and communication technologies with the same intensity. For some of them, the pure virtual ones, the use is more critical than for the rest. Apart from the main aim in the lecturing and researching objectives, in that case we can distinguish amongst the traditional, the distance, and the virtual styles. In this chapter we have tried to create a model in order to incorporate some other variables that can better explain the use that universities make of information and communication technologies. With that aim, we have integrated in a single model the variables partially studied in the literature up to the moment. Further research consists of contrasting the model in the different mentioned university teaching models.

References

Alavi, M. (1994). Computer-mediated collaborative learning: An empirical evaluation. *MIS Quarterly, 18*(2), 150-174.

Alavi, M., & Leidner, D. E. (2001). Research commentary: Technology-mediated learning—A call for greater depth and breadth of research. *Information Systems Research, 12*(1), 1-10.

Alavi, M., Wheeler, J., & Valacich, J. (1995). Using IT to reengineer business education: An exploratory investigation of collaborative tele-learning. *MIS Quarterly, 19*(3), 294-312.

Argyle, M. (1991). *Cooperation: The basis of sociability*. London: Routledge.

Bailey, J., & Pearson, S. (1983). Development of a tool for measuring and analyzing computer user satisfaction. *Management Science, 29*(5), 114-130.

Block, H., & Dobell, B. (1999). *The e-Bang Theory: Education industry overview*. San Francisco: Equity Research, Bank of America Securities, Montgomery Division.

Brown, J., & Duguid, P. (2002). *The social life of information*. Boston: Harvard Business School Publishing

Castelfranchi, C., & Tan, Y. H. (2002). The role of trust and deception in virtual societies. In C. Clegg, W. R. Hardy, & Nord (Eds.), *Handbook of organization studies* (pp. 409-423). Thousand Oaks, CA: Sage Publications.

Clemons, E., & Row, M. (1991). Sustaining IT advantage: The role of structural differences. *MIS Quarterly, 6*(4), 275-292.

Collis, B., Peters, O., & Pals, N. (2000). Influences on the educational use of WWW, email and videoconferencing. *Innovations in Education and Teaching International, 37*(2), 108-119.

Compeau, D., & Higgings, C. A. (1995). Computer self-efficacy: Development of a measure and initial test. *MIS Quarterly, 19*(2), 189-211.

Davis, F. (1989). Perceived usefulness, perceived ease of use, and end user acceptance of information technology. *MIS Quarterly, 5*(3), 219-339.

De Pablos, C., Romaniello, A., & Quintana, D. (2005, May). A model explaining the degree of success of web based technologies in the university education. In *Proceedings of the IRMA 2005 Conference*, San Diego, CA.

De Pablos, C., Romaniello, A., & Quintana, D. (2005, May). Un modelo explicativo de la aplicación de tecnologías web a deferentes entornos universitarios. In *I Congreso Internacional de Tecnología Educativa 2004, UNED*, Madrid, June.

De Sanctis, G. M., & Poole, M. S. (1994). Capturing the complexity in advanced technology use: Adaptive structuration theory. *Organization Science, 5*(2), 121-147.

Duvall, C., & Schwartz, R. (2000). Distance education: Relationship between academic performance and technology-adept adult students. *Education and Information Technologies, 5*(3), 177-187.

Fishbein, M., & Ajzenis, Y. (1975). *Belief, attitude, intentions, and behavior: An introduction to theory and research.* Boston: Addison-Wesley.

Henly, D. C., & Reid, A. (2001). Use of Web to provide learning support for a large metabolism and nutrition class. *Biochemistry and Molecular Biology Education, 29*(6), 229-233.

Ives, B., & Olson, M. (1983). The measurement of user information satisfaction. *Management of Computing, 26*(10), 55-94.

Khan, B. H. (2001). *A framework for e-learning.* Retrieved March 15, 2005, from http://www.elearning.com/elearning/article/articleDetail.jsp

Knoll, K., & Jarvenpaa, S. (1995). Learning to work in distributed global teams. In *Proceedings of the 28th Hawaii International Conference System Science,* Maui, HI (Vol. 4, pp. 92-101).

Knuffer, N. (1993). Teachers and educational computing. Changing roles and changing pedagogy. *Computers in Education: Social, Political and Historical Perspectives, 1*(1), 163-179.

Leidner, D., & Fuller, M. (1997). Improving student learning of conceptual information: GSS supported collaborative learning vs. individual constructive learning. *Decision Support Systems, 20*(2), 149-163.

Leidner, D., & Jarvenpaa, M. (1993). The information age confronts education: Case studies on electronic classrooms. *Information Systems Research, 4*(1), 24-54.

Mikropoulos, T, Chalkidis, A., Katsikis, A., & Emvalotis, A. (1998). Students' attitudes towards educational virtual environments. *Education and Information Technologies, 3,* 137-148.

Njagi, K., Smith, R., & Isbell, K. (2003). *Assesing students' attitudes towards Web-based learning resources.* Retrieved from http://naweb.unb.ca/procceding/2003/PosterNjagilsbell.htm

Orliwoski, W. (2000). Using technology and constituting structures: A practice lens for studying technology in organizations. *Organization Science, 11*(4), 404-428.

Orliwoski, W. J., & Gash, D. C. (1994). Technological frames: Making sense of information technology in organizations. *ACM Transactions on Information Systems, 12*(2), 174-207.

Peteraf, M. (1993). The cornerstones of competitive advantage: A resource-based view. *Strategic Management Journal, 4*(2), 179-191.

Peterson, P. W. (2001). The debate about online learning: Key issues for writing teachers, computers, and compositions. *Computers and Compositions, 18*(4), 359-370.

Poole, M. S., & De Sanctis, G. (1990). Understanding the use of group decisions support systems: The theory of adaptive structuration. In J. Fulk, & C. W. Steinfield (Eds.), *Organizations and communication technology* (pp. 173-193). Thousand Oaks, CA: Sage Publications.

Roberts, K. H., & Grabowski, M. (1995). Organizations, technology and structuring. *International Journal of Electronic Commerce, 6*(3), 55-70.

Rusell, G., & Bradley, G. (1997). Teachers' computer anxiety: Implications for professional development. *Education and Information Technologies, 2*, 17-30.

Schein, E. H. (1992). *Organizational culture and leadership.* San Francisco: Jossey-Bass.

Shrum, L., & Hong, S. (2002). The role of trust and deception in virtual societies. In C. Hardy Clegg, & W. R. P. Nord (Eds.), *Handbook of organization studies* (pp. 409-423). California: Sage.

Walsham, G. (1993). *Interpreting information systems in organisations.* New York: Wiley.

Weick, K. (1990). Technology as equivoque. In P. S. Goodman, L. S. Sproull, et al. (Eds.), *Technology and organizations* (pp. 1-44). San Francisco: Jossey-Bass.

Webster, J., & Hackley, P. (1987). Teaching effectiveness in technology-mediated distance learning. *Academy of Management Journal, 40*(6), 1282-1309.

Yates, J., & Orliwoski, W. J. (1992). Genre of organizational communication: A structurational approach to studying communication and media. *The Academy of Management Review, 17*(2), 299-326.

Yates, J., & Orliwoski, W. J. (1994). Genre repertoire: Examining the structuring of communicative practices in organizations. *Administrative Science Quarterly, 39*(4), 541-574.

Chapter VIII

Teachers, Tutors, and Mentors:
New Roles or Professionals?

Paolo Ardizzone
Catholic University of Milan, Italy

Pier Cesare Rivoltella
Catholic University of Milan, Italy

Abstract*

The goal of this chapter is to describe the main transformations of our Information Society and to show how these kinds of transformations are changing teaching roles in schools and universities. Particularly, the focus is on teachers and tutors in on line education: the first ones are gradually passing from the "sage on the stage" to the "guide on the side" (of the learner) and understanding that their job is no longer individual, because their activities are much more staff activities; the second ones are really important because the learner, in an online environment, needs more than in presence to be helped from the cognitive and emotive point of view. The chapter provides a description of the main activities of these professionals: organization, knowledge and experience sharing, and evaluation. In conclusion, we try to indicate some problems whose importance decision makers should consider.

The Challenge of Complexity:
From Teacher to Staff

The Information Society, according to the point of view of philosophers and sociologists (Baudrillard, 1976; Castells, 2001; Feenberg, 1999), is characterized by a new centrality of symbolic goods: these kinds of immaterial goods (images, knowledge, cultural products) find their value in what they represent, and not in what they are.

The effect, in the last few years, is the birth and development of a new class of workers that the French sociologist Erik Neveu (2001) names "workers of the symbolic," actualizing what Peter Drucker (1965) has already defined as "knowledge workers": their specialization isn't the production of anything, but the building and circulation of meanings.

Communication professionals (journalists, PR, television workers), tourist and culture operators, and people working in the digital economy also belong in this category.

They have three main characteristics:

1.   They are "low definition professionals" because they are space- and time-independent: they can work in their house, out of regular work time.

2.   They are hybrid figures, because they need a strong integration of disparate competencies (informatics, marketing, communication, course design, etc.).

3.   They work with great flexibility, according to the needs of the companies, consumers, and projects on which they are working.

This worker profile is also the same for that particular category of knowledge workers who work in e-learning and in the application of ICTs in education. In fact, in this case, the core component (technology, materials) is not enough to explain and describe the teaching and learning process; value is found into what people are able to do *with* technology.

Starting from the job descriptions of the staff of Texas University[1] (and synthesizing its very analytical plan), it is possible to describe these workers by referencing to two types of variables: according to the role/function they play, we can distinguish management figures, administration figures, and intermediation figures; according to the educative actions they do, we can talk about professionals involved in organization, interaction and evaluation/assessment.

The interaction between these two sets of variables is summarized in Figure 1.

Figure 1. E-learning professionals

	Organization	Interaction	Evaluation/assessment
Management	Project leader Project manager	E-tutor	Technical analyst Change manager Quality manager
Administration	Web master Instructional designer Web programmer Web editor		
Intermediation	Surfer Database manager		

When we teach with technologies, in a school or university, we must play all these roles and do all these actions: we must search for didactical materials (surfer) and organize them into a repository (database manager); we must create our online courses (Web master) taking care of their didactical structure (instructional designer); we must manage this course (project manager), interacting with students with synchronous and asynchronous tools (e-tutor), assessing students' performances and evaluating the educational process quality (technical analyst, quality manager). These multiple roles are too much for one person and herein we find the challenges of applying ICTs to education.

First of all, there is *a knowledge challenge*, because the teacher working with technologies needs to know more, not only about his discipline, but also about informatics suites, design and editing principles, and projecting techniques. Particularly, he needs to transform his tacit didactical competences into explicit ones (Nonaka & Takeuchi, 1995): when teachers work in a technological environment, experience is not enough; it is necessary that this experience becomes reflexive (Schön, 1983) and this fact implies the formalization of the steps and strategies in which teaching is organized. This process is difficult for professionals who have habitual experiences but are not able to be reflexive about what they have experienced: teaching is an *habitu*—according to the Aristotelian definition of *habitus,* as the capacity of doing anything and learning it by doing it more and more.

Secondly, the challenge of ICT for education is also an *organization challenge*. Working with technologies in the classroom, in a school or university, implies a new way for teachers to organize their job. Often a teaching activity is a sort of cognitive *bricolage*: it means that experience leads teachers to take micro decisions at the last minute rather than planning their activities in the classroom. This kind of improvisation is absolutely impossible when teaching involves technology. Teachers, in this case, need to preview and outline all the individual steps of their activity: they need to prepare materials, plan how and when to use them, put them into the learning environment, make sure the environment has upgraded information and materials, and interact with students using online tools communication. This is more a problem of teaching engineering than of teaching performance.

Finally, we also have an *identity challenge*. Our didactical tradition is made up of great teachers. These teachers, usually (in Italian and European experience), stand alone (the sage on the stage) and conceptualize teaching as an activity of cultural diffusion: the consequence is the adoption of a transmissive communication scheme, where the teacher speaks and the students take notes. Clearly, here we do not mean that this model needs to be erased. It has its own value because it is a chance for students to learn using the teacher model (this is the meaning of socialization). What we mean is that, working with technologies, the teacher is not yet able to perform in the same way and is forced to change roles in two main ways (both of which redefine their identity):

1. The *lateralization of presence*, which means that teachers lose their centrality in the classroom and are invited to re-conceptualize it using new forms. Here, the main goal is not information transfer, but cognitive cooperation and scaffolding, tutoring, mentoring (the sage by the side).

2. The *distribution of self*, which means that perhaps the teacher is not able to be a tutor, a mentor, an instructional designer, etc. at the same time. The teaching function needs to be re-imagined in a different way from the past: the change is from one person that performs a system of functions to a system of roles that perform a complex function into. In short: *from the teacher to the staff.*

Teachers, Tutors, Mentors

In a distributed social situation such as we have described, every actor has a different role and is called upon to perform several actions. This principle is also valid for didactical situations, like e-learning. The presence of e-learning itself helps to show that educational behavior is a complex function. If this complexity and plurality of roles was in part hidden in traditional teaching, it becomes more explicit in teaching environments characterized by the presence of ICT. In fact, technologies create shared and permanent spaces, where teachers and students leave their footprints, connecting them reciprocally. Therefore, it is no longer possible for the teacher or the student to avoid using the forms of textual and audiovisual writing that software and learning management systems place at their disposal.

These tools are destined to grow in the future, spreading throughout didactics, and it will be more and more difficult to get away from them. In other words,

Figure 2. Teacher's and tutor's activity

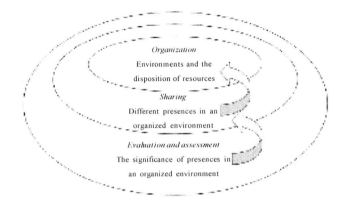

when ICT is present in didactics as a common use cultural object, there will be a social request pressing on the educational institutions and that future doesn't seem so far.

In this frame, we will now see the functions of teacher, tutor and mentor. We can try to describe the principal actions of these figures through the categories of the organization, sharing and evaluation-assessment, which are, in our proposal, the three macro-actions of the didactical field (Rivoltella 2003, p. 63-99). They refer to: (see Figure 2) (a) environments and the disposition of resources (*organization*), (b) different presences in an organized environment (*sharing*), (c) the significance of presences in an organized environment (*evaluation-assessment*).

Organization

Fundamentally, the figures of organization are involved in projecting and coordinating activities. Projecting teachers act at two levels: the strategic level and the distributive level. In the first case, they articulate the learning plan in modules and working steps (from problem-posing to problem-solving to the conclusion of the learning experience). The content selection and the educational design may be decided individually or with other members of the staff, or even with the students: it depends on the personal competencies of the individuals and on the didactical model adopted. At this level ICT are present like fields containing different forms of knowledge representation (regarding texts, documents, and the project itself). Also, the teacher must look at the opportunities offered by technologies, possibly including online activities in the general plan.

At the distributive level of projecting, the teacher works to structure personalized learning opportunities and to exploit individual and group resources. The coordination activity required by the teacher involves several levels: the level of the didactical formats (lesson, exercises, simulation, discussion, role playing, ...), the level of the setting (face-to-face, teleconferencing, online), the level of learning (formal and informal), the level of the different technologies, etc. This means a continuous blending activity, that is realized not only by integrating presence and distance (see, for instance, Singh, 2003), but also other levels. After all, it is a typically didactical competence, perhaps "the" didactical competence: the competence of choosing the right solution out of several situations, in a general framework of different and integrated solutions.

From the point of view of organization, the *tutor*'s and *mentor*'s role is very significant.[2] They facilitate the student's guidance: in a high-technology environment the student is shaped like a campus user. It means, we could say, that education no longer goes to the student, but it is the student who has to go towards education.

Teachers need a guide to help them organize their work and choose the activity to be successful, such as facilitating the approach to ICT and socialization.

E-learning, in fact, often presents a variety of opportunities that are the student's task to take. This happens when the didactical process is building-oriented, but the complexity of the field is sometimes evident in auto-instructional situations as well.

We said that the teacher has to control the function of integration among different educational components. Now we can add that who guarantees it on the operative plan are the tutors (at system level) and the mentors (at the discipline level). People contribute from their own perspective, to develop the integration among learning forms, phases of the process, participants, available resources, and among these levels themselves.

Sharing

At this level, the *teacher* must speak not only with students, but also with the other members of the staff, such as other teachers. In this direction, in some experiences this knowledge- and competence-sharing activity includes dedicated online communities (of teachers, of staff, of the course, etc.).

Teacher practices the sharing function with the students especially in interaction activities. This happens in the lesson, when teachers show their professional way of posing a problem or of investigating a knowledge field. Online interaction (chat, forum, teleconferencing, community, etc.) completes this process providing important application and re-elaboration opportunities. Sharing activities may also be auto-reflective and lead to negotiation forums about the educational course itself. The group (staff + students) may also re-design the project or advance not initially foreseen proposals, if necessary. This is possible when students participate in areas dedicated to interaction, especially by using blended activities in checking and following up. In fact, the timing of these exchanges may generate the growth of a public opinion: it is the teacher's duty to give it the right space so that it can become significant.

In the *tutor* perspective, sharing assumes the nature of scaffolding. It is an emotional kind of scaffolding, oriented to stimulate the motivation and participation of the various forms of activities. And it is also an organizational kind of scaffolding, as was already said. Sharing means scaffolding in the *mentor*'s perspective, as well, but in a more disciplined point of view. In fact, in this case it is a question, above all, of cognitive scaffolding, oriented to help students make their needs explicit regarding comprehension, in a sort of cultural mediation between teacher and student. Tutors and mentors must coordinate their work to help students reach and share a realistic vision of their educational course. This function is particularly important when the activity plan foresees the long-time phases of online job; in this case the student risks forgetting the aims defined at the beginning of the activity itself.

Finally, it is important to remember that the distinctions between tutor and mentor and between their profiles are not univocal. Their meaning depends largely on the roles and functions that the educational system in which they are involved assign to them.

Evaluation

Evaluation is the third aspect we have to consider. Briefly, we can say that this function, in e-learning environments, is distributed among the staff members. On one side of evaluation (concerning structural aspects such as needs analysis, monitoring, and customer satisfaction) the staff has to analyze the setting (the students' localization and profile, the learning management system configuration, the didactical architecture, etc.), the lay-out (the organization and quality of materials, editing, course navigability, interface friendliness, etc.), and interaction (quality and quantity of messages, their typology, contents and tones, etc.). Tools for evaluation are on-site observation, screen analysis (for instance interaction), and tracking elaboration.

On the other side, assessment regards learning goals: knowledge, competences, and meta-qualities. Generally it concerns the balance of competences (*ex ante*), formative assessment (*in itinere*) and terminal assessment (*ex post*).

These activities are generally done through *in itinere* and final tests and surveys, papers, questionnaires, reports, and so on.

One teacher cannot manage a so complex an activity. Tutors and mentors are dedicated figures that, respectively, are interested in evaluation and assessment. Although these functions are often overlapped, the required competences become more and more sophisticated. For instance, we can think about what it means to organize periodical reporting about the state of a course, or to describe the online behaviors in a class combining observation and e-data and meta-data.

A Case History in the School: E-Tutors' Functions in Italian Teachers' Training

The e-tutors are surely among the most important figures in e-learning. Their actions control the possibility of managing, monitoring, moderating and evaluating on line learning activities. There is much debate between scholars in education about their role and competencies. The problem is the double possibility of conceiving the e-tutor as a role or as a function and, on the other hand, as an expert of a discipline or as a moderator with competences in psychology and education. Here we have three different profiles:

1. The case of a tutor (role + discipline) who takes care of the student's training about the discipline he is studying. This tutor (we can refer to as an e-mentor) is a dedicated person that helps the teacher in managing online activities of the course: they manage course contents and FAQs about them, they help teachers interact with students in the virtual classroom (problem solving, supplementary explications, etc.), and finally they take care of monitoring learning, assessing it with tests and discussions.

2. A second profile is that of a tutor (role + moderation) whose goal is animating and moderating interactions between students in the virtual classroom. In this case we can really talk about an e-tutor, that is a dedicated person who: facilitates the access and motivation of the learning environment and learning activities, promotes the socialization of the students in it, allows information to be exchanged among them, assists students in knowledge-building, and supports them in developing a learning community (Salmon, 2000; 2002).

3. In the third case we do not have a specific profile, but only functions that must be played by teachers themselves.

Figure 3. E-tutor models

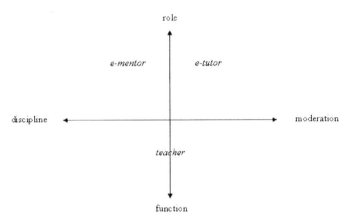

It's clear from Figure 3 that the e-tutor identity is increasingly thought of as a role instead of a function. To imagine an e-tutor as a role means to think that he must be a new profile that does not belong to traditional education systems; on the other hand, if tutoring is a function we must imagine that this function belongs to traditional figures. In the first case we need tutors cooperating with teachers, in the second case we need to teach the teachers how they can be tutors as well. Our point of view is that, in an e-learning environment, the complexity of activities is so high that it will be impossible for one teacher to control everything without help. So the e-tutor must be imagined as a new and very important role and education systems must be able to create conditions for their institutional accreditation.

Since 2001, Italy has had an interesting experience that is leading to the recognition of the e-tutor as a role. The Ministry of Education charged INDIRE (The National Institute for Documentation of Teaching and Educational Research) in 2000 to put mind to an e-learning plan for in-service teachers' training. After a preliminary study, INDIRE chose to implement a blended learning system that provides e-contents in an online learning environment[3] (*PuntoEdu*). It also facilitates interaction among teachers, and supports learning processes with in-presence activities. The large number of participants[4] was fragmented in classrooms of 25/30 teachers, each of which was moderated, in presence and online, by a tutor. The tutor is not a disciplinary expert, however. Teachers' training, in fact, is about informatics and foreign language (English) and most of the tutors are neither computer scientists nor linguistics. They have didactical and psychological competences.

PuntoEdu's tutor formation has been developed by my research group at the Catholic University of Milan. The project was defined using remarks we collected during the three previous years when we monitored INDIRE's experience in order to perform a quality evaluation. The training target was made by pioneer teachers in ICT whose goal was to implement a technological training for teachers that were only beginners in ICT. We have isolated four training areas. The first one is the communication area in a virtual classroom. Teachers' competencies here are to be able to create and manage scripts with which to regulate the communication of virtual groups; that is, providing a netiquette, moderating communication, and creating and managing a virtual community. The second area provides e-tutors with skills in the analysis and evaluation of didactic products. In their class activities, teachers often produce some objects with students, such as hypertexts, Web-pages, multimedia materials. It is very important for an e-tutor to be able to evaluate them, not only from the technological point of view, but also from the educational one. The training provides criteria with which they can evaluate and the tools for doing so (tables, check lists, etc.). In the third area, teachers can learn about techniques and methodologies for evaluating online learning processes. Particularly they collaboratively produce indicators and tables with which to analyze online communication. Finally, in the fourth area, an e-tutor must learn how to project and manage the entire formative process; that is, to understand how to analyze the needs of formation, to create and manage groups, to manage e-portfolios, etc. This syllabus of competencies generates some questions. How can we check which of them are fundamental and which not? What is the role of the e-tutor? What are their characteristics? And who will certificate this formation? It may be that in Italy the answer comes from ANITEL, the Italian Association of E-Learning Tutors, an association in which most of the Italian teachers who are experts in technologies are enrolled. One of their goals is the recognition by the Ministry of education of the role of the e-tutor and their specifications.

A Case History into the University: The Teacher in a Context of Blended Learning

In the past few years the Catholic University of Milan, in Italy, created some First Graduate Degrees in blended learning. This innovative experience uses a didactical model based on three ways of communication: in presence, through videoconferencing, and online. A peculiar characteristic of this educational proposal is the presence of a central campus (in Brescia) and of three other campuses, distributed among Italy: Sarzana (Liguria), Cemmo di Capodiponte (Lombardia) and Comiso (Sicilia). A research group of the same University studied the evolution of teachers in this context, through semi-structured interviews of the teachers of the degree in "Tourist Activities." The results of the research highlight three fundamental points.

The first point regards the impact of ICT on teachers' procedures. Generally speaking, there is a double movement, that we can call "destabilization" and "stabilization." The destabilizing characteristic of ICT is due to the fact that they break the balance of the teacher's routine. Every teacher interviewed felt this turbulence: the dilatation of time and space, the modular re-projecting of their courses, the necessity of working in a group, the importance of interaction with students, etc. Thus, the teacher must rediscover the lost equilibrium. But another process, more subconscious, follows the arrival of ICT: it consists of the re-comprehension of the educational situations that are stimulated by the presence of ICT. And so the research of a new balance also becomes there discovery of solutions not yet emerged: they may already be present, but not yet explicit. For instance, the availability of interaction zones helped some teachers discover the way to rationalize a didactics based on communication. So, this second aspect is the stabilizing characteristic of technology towards teaching.

The second emerging observation regards the effort of rationalizing of educational praxis. Many teachers underline that: the course plan need to be detailed, and possibly broken down, and published from the beginning; documents and texts need to be produced, possibly before the lesson; sections of the learning management system need to be selected and checked everyday; and conversation zones need to be opened and periodically monitored. The organization and the planning become professional style: a style that—as some interviewed assert—is based on meta-quality not regarding only this kind of experience, but experience exportable in other contests.

This meta-quality seems to be, among other things, a sense of complexity, a meta-cognition, a sensibility toward differentiated users, and an informal communication.

Finally, a common emphasis coming from the interviewed teachers was the satisfaction in institutional forms of support. This was accompanied by a clear disposition to participate in distributed activities of continuing education. Here, the problem is the absence of a formal academic appreciation of these kinds of didactics. Perhaps one of the most crucial problems, from the teachers' point of view, is about the future of possibilities like these.

Conclusion

Looking at what we briefly said about the relationship between teaching and ICT, we can talk about two main processes. On one hand, the teacher is no longer alone in the integrated (presence + online) classroom: they need to be helped by new figures with specific competencies. The e-tutor is perhaps the most important of them. We can imagine them as cognitive and emotional scaffolders whose goal is to facilitate learning both from the point of view of knowledge and of psycho-social. On the other hand, we can say that ICT promotes an "expanded view of teachers" (Davis, 2001. p. 37). This means two things: first, it means that in the Information Age teachers are no longer the only experts in this role, but also all those community workers (such as librarians, educators, an so on) with which pupils are in daily contact; second, it also means that the teacher's spectrum of competencies is wider today than just 10 years ago. Among these competencies ICT occupies a very important position with its three broad dimensions:

1.   ICT aspects of core skills
2.   ICT as a theme of knowledge
3.   ICT as a means of enriching learning

To understand this complexity we must take into account three big topics:

1.   **An organizational question:** For the institutions (schools, universities) the recognition of other figures different from teachers. Here the problem is economic (it means to pay other professionals in a time when the problem of the big organizations is to reduce their employees) and structural (how can we integrate and coordinate these new figures?).

2.   **A cultural question:** To understand that education today is a process wider than just schooling. In each social context schools must promote forms of collaboration with other education agencies; ICT can be the focus of this collaboration.

3.   **A formative question:** This is the most important one. The necessity here is to provide good training for all these professionals, both teachers and tutors. The aim of this training must be not only to provide teachers and tutors with technical skills, but to move them from a traditional curricular vision towards critical media literacy. ICT is part of our culture, and if it is both an information and a visual culture, our teaching aim must be to

improve our pupils' capacity to think critically and to become citizens of the culture itself.

References

Ardizzone, P., & Rivoltella, P. C. (2003). *Didattiche per l'e-learning, Metodi e strumenti per l'innovazione dell'insegnamento universitario.* Roma: Carocci.

Baudrillard, J. (1976). *L'echange simbolique et la mort.* Paris: Gallimard.

Castells, M. (2001). *Internet galaxy.* Oxford, MA: Oxford University Press.

Davis, N. (2001). The virtual communities of teachers. In M. Leask (Ed.), *Issues in teaching using ICT* (pp. 31-48). London: New York: Routledge.

Drucker, P. (1965). *Landmarks of tomorrow: A report on the new "Postmodern" world.* San Francisco: Harper & Row.

Feenberg, A. (1999). *Questioning technology.* London: Routledge.

Neveu, E. (2001). *Une societé de communication?* Paris: Montchrestien.

Nonaka, I., & Takeuchi, H. (1995). *The knowledge-creating company: How Japanese companies create the dynamics of innovation.* Oxford, MA: Oxford University Press.

Salmon, G. (2000). *E-moderating: The key to teaching and learning online.* London: Kogan Page.

Salmon, G. (2002). *Etivities: The key to active online learning.* London: Kogan Page.

Schön, D. A. (1983). *The reflective practitioner: How professionals think in action.* New York: Basic Books.

Singh, H. (2003). Building effective blended learning programs. *Educational Technology, 6*(43), 51-54. Retrieved March 15, 2005, from: http://www.bookstoread.com/framework/blended-learning.pdf

Endnotes

*   Paolo Ardizzone wrote § 2 and 4. Pier Cesare Rivoltella wrote § 1, 3 and 5.

1   Online, URL: http://www.elearningguild.com/

2   A definition of tutor and mentor can be found in point 3 of this text.

3   Online, URL: http://puntoedu.indire.it

4   Training in 2002 referred to 46,000 incoming teachers; in 2003 and 2004, to an ever increasing number of teachers experimenting with the new regulations of School Reformation (from 3,500 in 2003 to 61,000 in 2004).

Section III

Chapter IX

Assessing Satisfaction and Academic Locus of Control of Dropout Students in Online Learning Courses

Yair Levy
Nova Southeastern University, USA

Abstract

Numerous studies have been conducted related to dropouts from on-campus and distance education courses. However, no clear definition of dropout from academic courses was provided. Additionally, literature suggest that students attending e-learning courses dropout at substantially higher rates than their counterparts in on-campus courses. However, little attention has been given in literature for key constructs related to this difference. This chapter explores two main constructs (students' satisfaction and academic locus of control) with online learning. Results show that students' satisfaction with e-learning is a key indicator in students' decision to dropout from online learning courses. Additionally, completer students reported to have significantly higher satisfaction with online learning than students who dropped out from the same courses. Moreover, results suggest that the academic locus of control appears to have no significant impact on students' decision to drop from online learning courses.

Introduction and Background

The growing use of Internet as a mainstream vehicle for online courses enables some educational institutions to go "campusless" (Thor & Scarafiotti, 2004). The staggering increase of e-learning courses in the past decade by traditional universities has also raised concerns about the dropout rates associated with such courses (Munro, 1987; Dirkx & Jha, 1994; Parker, 1999, 2003; Ariwa, 2002; Xenos, Pierrakeas, & Pintelas, 2002; Sikora & Carrol, 2002). Literature suggests that students attending e-learning courses dropout at a substantially higher rate than their counterparts in on-campus courses (Parker, 1999). Dropout rates from online learning courses were documented around 25% to 40% as compared to 10% to 20% in on-campus courses (Dirkx & Jha, 1994; Carter, 1996; Parker, 1999, 2003; McLaren, 2004). More dramatic results were reported for online training centers where more than 50% of learners dropped out compared to only 10% in standard on-site training (Zielinski, 2000). Moreover, even before the Internet became a major educational delivery vehicle, estimates of dropouts from distance and correspondence education range from 25% to 60% (Kember, 1989a, 1989b; Wilkinson & Sherman, 1989; Dirkx & Jha 1994). Nevertheless, little attention has been given in literature to the key factors associated with such substantial differences in dropout rate in the context of online learning (Parker, 1999). Fjortoft (1995) suggested that further research needs to expand beyond the current models of dropout and look at other factors and their interrelations as the nature of distance education is ever changing.

Several hypothetical explanations have been raised to indicate why the dropout rate in e-learning courses is higher. There is a clear consensus in literature that dropping out, especially in distance education, is a perplexing phenomenon. Kember (1989a, 1989b) developed a model based on Tinto's (1975) model of dropout from correspondence distance education courses. His model includes components such as demographics characteristics, students' motivation, academic abilities, and students' social factors. Fjortoft (1995) criticized Kember's (1989b, p. 199) model for failing to "take into consideration the job-related motivation of adults."

Several other scholars suggested that demographics characteristics have a minimal effect on dropouts from distance education courses (Williamson & Creamer, 1988; Volkwein & Lorang, 1995). While others suggested that demographics characteristics do have significant effect on dropouts from distance education courses (Dille & Mezack, 1991; Xenos, Pierrakeas, & Pintelas, 2002; McLaren, 2004). Dille and Mezack (1991) conducted a study comparing completer and dropout students attending television broadcasting (telelearning) courses. They concluded that completer students in telelearning courses are older, have higher grade point average, and have more college credits than dropout students (Dille & Mezack, 1991). Moreover, they suggested that locus of control is an important factor when investigating dropouts from distance education courses. Xenos, Pierrakeas, and Pintelas, (2002) conducted field interviews with dropout students in distance education courses. They claimed that dropout students were older and were employed more hours per week than completer students. Moreover, their results indicate that gender and students' family status were not found to play a key role as a predictor of dropout from distance education courses. McLaren (2004, p. 2) claimed that there is a conflict in reports of findings associated with demographics characteristics. She suggested future studies should measure demographics characteristics as it remains fruitful to continue exploring the effects of demographics characteristics on dropout and completion in online courses. Therefore, this study will measure and explore the impact of demographics characteristics on dropouts in online learning courses.

The locus of control was reported as a key factor in "understanding the nature of the learning process in various kinds of learning situations" (Whittington, 1995). Rotter (1966, 1989) introduced the instrument to measure the locus of control (LOC) individuals may perceive regarding outcomes of certain behavioral actions with two polar outcomes. The first is labeled as the *external control* that indicates ones' perceptions of outcomes that are due to chance, lack, fate, or actions of others; thus the notation *external*. Whereas the second is labeled as the *internal control*, this indicates ones' perceptions of outcomes that are mainly due to their own actions; thus the notation *internal*.

Considerable research has been done using LOC in diverse settings such as children education, management, intellectual achievement responsibility, marital satisfaction, parenting, general health, mental health, drinking, weight loss, and sexual issues (Lefcourt, 1991). Although Rotter's (1966) instrument was developed to measure general LOC, he noted that it "is of major significance in understanding the nature of learning processes in different kinds of learning situations" (p. 1). Trice (1985) noted that although Rotter's (1966) instrument has been used over several decades in various settings, it was not fully tailored for educational settings. Consequently, Trice (1985) proposed an abbreviated instrument based on his work to specifically measure Academic Locus of Control (ALOC). Using this ALOC instrument, students were to report on their perceptions of locus of control in regards to their academic achievements. Richardson (1995) conducted a study on over a thousand university students in the Caribbean using ALOC. His results indicate that there is no significant difference on ALOC between gender distributions, however there was a significant difference on ALOC across different academic majors and age categories. Additionally, older students (over 30) scored more internally on

ALOC than younger students. Dollinger (2000) conducted a study looking at the effect of ALOC on students' grades in college courses. His results suggest that students that scored more internally on ALOC received significantly higher grades than students that scored more external on the ALOC measure.

Parker (1999) conducted a study on various variables as predictors of students' dropout from distance education courses. The focus of her study was in LOC and some demographics characteristics such as gender, age, and the number of hours employed as the main predictors for dropout or completion in distance learning courses. Parker (1999) concluded that LOC was the main variable in predicting dropout with an overall accuracy of 80%. She suggests that further research is needed to confirm such findings in online courses. Consequently, this study will investigate the impact of locus of control on dropout in the context of online learning courses.

A second key factor proposed in literature deals with students' satisfaction with online learning. Several studies reported students' satisfaction as a major factor that is related to students' decision to dropout from distance education courses (Chyung, Winiecki, & Fenner, 1998). Chyung, Winiecki, and Fenner (1998) reported that "42% of the students who dropped out expressed dissatisfaction with the learning environment as the reason [for dropping]" (p. 7). Fredericksen, Pickett, Shea, Pelz, and Swan (2000) noted that students who reported the highest levels of satisfaction also reported significantly higher levels of learning than students who rated their satisfaction level as lower. Levy and Murphy (2002) noted that administrators, practitioners, and researchers should have a great interest in understanding the key factors that affect student perception of online learning effectiveness. Levy (2003) conducted a study with over 200 students attending e-learning courses on the relationship of students' satisfaction and online learning effectiveness. He reported that students' satisfaction with online learning is a significant factor in measuring the effectiveness of online learning (Levy, 2003). Additionally, Sachs and Hale (2003) noted that universities and colleges that offer e-learning courses should put major emphasis in students' satisfaction in measuring the success of such programs and students' potential to successfully complete the program.

Shea, Pickett, and Pelz (2003) reported on the relationship of pedagogy, design, and faculty development issues to students' satisfaction in e-learning courses. Their results indicate that students' satisfaction level in online learning courses is highly correlated with various issues such as instructional design and organization of the courses, instructors' discourse facilitation, and instructors' direct interaction. They concluded by noting that the key factors that contribute to students' satisfaction can help uncover the drivers for effective online learning environments. Nonetheless, this study proposes taking this notion further by looking at the impact of students' satisfaction on dropout from online learning courses. Moreover, other scholars suggest that students' satisfaction with online learning is an important factor in measuring the success or effectiveness of such a medium (Hiltz & Johonson 1990; Alavi, Wheeler, & Valacich, 1995; Swan, Shea, Fredericksen, Pickett, and Pelz, 2000; Bures, Abrami, & Amundsen, 2000; Piccoli, Ahmad, and Ives, 2001). Consequently, this study also proposes to measure students' satisfaction with online learning in order to find its impact on dropouts from online learning courses. The central aim of this study is to investigate the differences of these two main factors (academic locus of control and students' satisfaction with online learning) among dropout and completer students in online learning courses. In the context of this study, completer students are defined as students that successfully completed an online learning course.

Several studies have been conducted related to dropouts from academic courses, both on-campus and distance, however, no clear definition of dropout from online learning courses is provided. Thus, in the context of online learning courses, this chapter will define dropout students (or non-completers) as students that voluntarily withdraw from online learning courses while acquiring financial penalties. As such, students who opt to drop a course during the "add/drop period" are not considered by the definition as dropout students since they are fully refunded for their tuition or have no financial penalties for dropping out during that period. Moreover, students that drop a course during this early period have no indication on their transcript for it.

Students that drop a course after the early period of the term (known as "late drop") are not refunded for their tuition and are not able to switch to another course. In this case, the dropped course remains on the students' transcript with a note that the course was dropped late without a reported grade. Dropped courses remain on students' transcript until graduation.

Hypotheses and Methodology

The remaining paragraphs of this chapter are organized as follows: the subsequent section will present the hypotheses guiding this research study and some rationale for each hypothesis. Next, the methodology guiding this research is reviewed including the instrument and validity issues. Data collection, analysis and results of the study are presented subsequently. The last section concludes this research study with discussion of findings, contributions of the study, limitations, and suggestions for future research trends.

Hypotheses

From the relevant literature above it is evident that locus of control, or more specifically academic locus of control (ALOC), may be a potential factor related to students' dropout from college courses (Whittington, 1995; Parker, 1999). This study attempts to validate such theoretical impact using two groups of students: one that successfully completed online learning courses (completers) and another that dropped from online learning courses (non-completers). Thus, this study proposes the first hypothesis as follows:

H1: The Academic Locus of Control (ALOC) score of dropout students will be more external than that of completer students in online learning courses.

Several studies suggested that students' satisfaction with online learning is another major factor in the success or effectiveness of such medium, thus also determining students' completion of online learning courses (Hiltz & Johonson 1990; Alavi et al., 1995; Webster & Hackley, 1997; Chyung et al., 1998; Swan et al., 2000; Bures et al., 2000; Piccoli et al., 2001). Consequently, this study proposes the second hypothesis as follows:

H2: The level of satisfaction of dropout students will be lower than that of completer students in online learning courses.

Other studies suggested that aside from the students' perceived measures, such as locus of control and satisfaction, demographic variables should have been given attention in future studies of dropouts from distance learning and online learning courses (Dille & Mezack, 1991; McLaren, 2004). Thus, this study proposes the following set of hypotheses related to demographics factors:

H3a: The gender distribution of dropout students will be different than that of completer students in online learning courses.

H3b: The college status of dropout students will be different than that of completer students in online learning courses.

H3c: The age distribution of dropout students will be different than that of completer students in online learning courses.

H3d: The residency status of dropout students will be different than that of completer students in online learning courses.

H3e: The academic major distribution of dropout students will be different than that of completer students in online learning courses.

Figure 1. Proposed research model and hypotheses

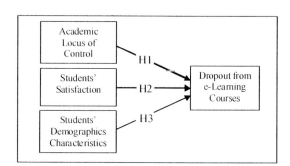

H3f: The graduating term of dropout students will be different than that of completer students in online learning courses.

H3g: The GPA score of dropout students will be different than that of completer students in online learning courses.

H3h: The weekly working hours of dropout students will be different than that of completer students in online learning courses.

Figure 1 presents an overview of the major constructs along with the research hypotheses addressed by this study.

Methodology and Instruments

There were two instruments used in this study along with a general students' demographics information sheet. The first one includes a 12-item instrument based on Trice's (1985) Academic Locus of Control instrument. Studies have also shown that Likert-type measures of locus of control are as valid as the original forced-choice proposed by Rotter (Harris & Salomone, 1981). Thus, students were asked to rate each item on a five-score Likert-type scale ranging from "Strongly Disagree" to "Strongly Agree." The total score can be generated by summing up all the internally answered scores. Total score can range from minimum of 12 (external ALOC) to a maximum of 72 (internal ALOC).

The second instrument is a 7-item survey based on Bures et al.'s (2000) instrument and it measures students' satisfaction with online learning. This instrument also provides students with a 5-score Likert-type scale ranging from "Strongly Disagree" to "Strongly Agree." Some of the questions are intentionally set in a negative form. Therefore, prior to generating the total score, a simple transformation to a positive form was required. Following the transformation, a total score can be generated by summing up the scores. Students' satisfaction total score can range from a minimum of 7 (very low satisfaction level) to a maximum of 35 (very high satisfaction level). Examples for questions asked as part of the user satisfaction survey included *"learning to use WebCT was easy"* and *"I learned a great deal because of the use of WebCT."*

Data Collection and Results

Data Collection

It was suggested in prior literature that the use of online surveys can greatly improve the reliability of the data as it eliminates the human data entry step that includes some natural human errors (Fowler, 1993, p. 63). Consequently, the surveys and the demographics sheet were delivered via the Web to dropout and completer students attended (or drop) online learning courses. The Web-based survey system was set to collect responses via the Internet and Web browser, where students submitted a Web form to a server that collected the data and submitted it to a centralized database. To eliminate duplications and insure the integrity of the data, the surveys were administered on a server that captured the Internet Protocol (IP) number when submitting the data. Both the date/time of submission and the IP numbers were use to spot any duplication in data submitted. Data submission was anonymous with no link between a submission and an individual student.

The study was conducted during spring of 2003. The study includes 18 under-graduate and graduate online learning courses at a major state university in the southeastern U.S. The courses were all from the college of business administration and included a variety of subjects such as MIS, general management, accounting, finance, and marketing.

Initially, there were 453 students registered to the 18 online learning courses. At the end of the term, a student assistant was asked to review the class-rolls of the online learning courses and generate two e-mail lists: one of completer students and another of dropout students. This resulted in a sample of 372 completers and 81 dropout students, resulting in about 18% overall dropout rate, which is slightly higher than the average 12% dropout reported in on-campus courses. An e-mail request to take part in this study was sent to the two groups. Twenty-five dropout and 108 completer students completed the survey representing about 31% response rate of the dropout group and about 29% response rate of the completer students with a total of 133 submissions or about 30% overall response rate. Respondents had similar demographics characteristics as the whole sample. No duplications were found in the data collected.

Analysis and Results

Group comparison using one-way ANOVA and non-parametric tests (Mann-Whitney) for satisfaction, as well as for ALOC were conducted. Results from both analyses are presented in Table 1. Results show that students' ALOC was found non-significantly different between the two groups: completer and dropout students from online learning courses. This indicates that the first hypothesis (H1) was rejected due to the fact that the level of ALOC appears not to be significantly different between completer and dropout students in online courses. Additionally, results show that students' satisfaction was found significantly different (at $p<.01$) between the two groups indicating that the second hypothesis (H2) is supported as the level of students' satisfaction with online learning for dropout students is significantly lower than that of completer students.

The same analysis was repeated also on several demographics characteristics between the two groups of students. Results are presented in Table 2. The demographics characteristics include: gender (H3a), college status (H3b), age group (H3c), residency status (H3d), academic major (H3e), graduating term (H3f), GPA (H3g), and weekly working hours (H3h). Results of both analyses support only two out of the eight demographics hypotheses (H3b and H3f). The first supported hypothesis is college status (H3b), which indicates that the college status of dropout students was found to be significantly lower (at $p<.05$) than that of completer students. Thus, results of this study indicate that largely,

Table 1. Students' satisfaction and ALOC group comparison

	Non-Completers (Dropout) (n=25)		Completers (n=108)		Oneway ANOVA		Noparametric (Mann Whitney Test)	
	M	S.D.	M	S.D.	F	P	Z	Sig. (2-t)
ALOC	46.36	6.94	46.08	7.27	0.030	0.863	-0.084	0.933
Satisfaction	23.76	6.99	27.52	4.49	*11.28* **	*0.001*	*-2.35* *	*0.019*

* - p< 0.05
** - p< 0.01

Table 2. Group comparison—Demographics variables

Variable	Non-completers (n=25)		Completers (n=108)		Oneway ANOVA		Noparametric (Mann-Whitney Test)	
	M	S.D.	M	S.D.	F	P	Z	Sig. (2-t)
Gender	16F, 9M		60F, 48M		0.58	0.446	-0.77	0.444
College Status	3.68	0.85	4.09	0.88	*4.504* *	*0.036*	*-2.273* *	*0.023*
Age Group	3.32	1.41	3.17	1.26	0.286	0.594	-0.489	0.625
Residancy Status	1.40	1.00	1.70	1.23	1.315	0.254	-1.263	0.207
Major	4.60	3.23	5.31	2.47	1.504	0.222	-0.919	0.358
Graduateing Term	4.16	1.03	3.52	1.09	*7.184* **	*0.008*	*-2.826* **	*0.005*
GPA	3.12	0.56	3.23	0.56	0.759	0.385	-0.829	0.407
Work (hrs/wk)	3.04	1.88	3.06	1.66	0.002	0.967	-0.033	0.974

* - p< 0.05
** - p< 0.01

Figure 2. College status distribution for dropouts vs. completer students in online learning courses

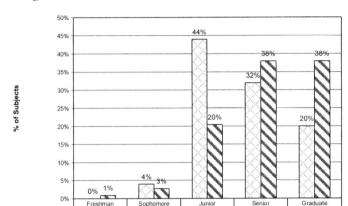

dropout students from online learning courses are in a lower college status than completer students. Figure 2 presents the college status distribution across dropout and completer students in online learning courses.

The second supported demographic characteristic hypothesis is graduating term (H3f), which indicates that the graduating term of dropout students was found to be significantly higher (at $p<.01$) than that of completer students. Therefore, results of this study indicate that dropped students appear to graduate in a later term than completer students in online learning courses. This is consistent with the previous supported hypothesis (H3b) about students attending online learning courses that are in higher college status are less likely to drop as they may need to graduate in that term or next one. Figure 3 presents the graduating term distribution across dropout students and completer students in online learning courses.

Six more demographic characteristic hypotheses were not supported by this study. They indicated that there is no difference between dropout and completer students in online learning courses for gender (H3a), age group (H3c), residency status (H3d), academic major (H3e), GPA (H3g), and weekly work hours (H3h). These results are consistent with prior research (Xenos et al., 2002).

Table 3 presents the Pearson correlations for all variables including the "group" variable. The group variable is the binary indicator to note the status of the student with regards to the online learning course at the end of the term, where zero represents a dropout and one represents completion of the course. Results indicate that students' satisfaction and graduating term are correlated significantly (at $p<.01$ level) with the group indicator. This is consistent with the

Figure 3. Graduating term distribution for dropouts vs. completer students in online learning courses

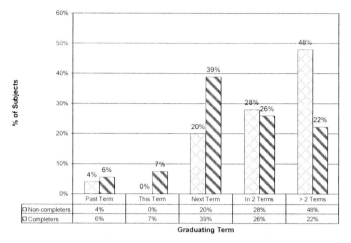

	Past Term	This Term	Next Term	In 2 Terms	> 2 Terms
□ Non-completers	4%	0%	20%	28%	48%
□ Completers	6%	7%	39%	26%	22%

Graduating Term

Table 3. Pearson correlations for all variables in the study

(n=133)	Group (Drop & Comp)	Satisfaction	ALOC	Gender	College Status	Age Group	Residancy Status	Major	Graduateing Term	GPA	Work
Group (Dr & Comp)	1.000										
Satisfaction	0.282 **	1.000									
ALOC	-0.015	0.101	1.000								
Gender	-0.067	-0.089	0.040	1.000							
College Status	0.182 *	0.317 **	-0.289 **	-0.260 **	1.000						
Age Group	-0.047	0.092	-0.078	-0.164	0.369 **	1.000					
Residancy Status	0.100	0.049	-0.111	-0.015	0.105	-0.078	1.000				
Major	0.107	0.285 **	-0.093	-0.311 **	0.242 **	0.108	-0.033	1.000			
Graduateing Term	-0.228 **	-0.059	0.150	0.158	-0.381 **	-0.153	-0.029	-0.210 *	1.000		
GPA	0.048	0.056	-0.049	-0.149	0.181 *	0.160	0.131	0.152	-0.023	1.000	
Work (hrs/wk)	0.004	0.144	-0.004	-0.378 **	0.231 **	0.228 **	-0.073	0.187 *	-0.136	0.103	1.000

** - Correlation is significant at the 0.01 level (2-tailed).
* - Correlation is significant at the 0.05 level (2-tailed).

previous results showing that these are the two main indicators of dropout from online learning courses. Moreover, college status was found to be correlated significantly (at $p<.05$ level) with the group indicator, thereby supporting prior results. This is further supported by the significant correlation (at $p<.01$ level) between college status and graduating term.

Straub (1989) suggests that the reliability of an instrument is generally measured by Cronbach's α High Cronbach's α ($>.75$) is usually a sign that survey items are reliable (Straub, 1989, p.150). Cronbach's reliability measure was tested for each of the instruments indicating high reliability ranging from .74 to .86. Results for both students' satisfaction and students' ALOC instruments are presented in Table 4.

Table 4. Cronbach's α for ALOC and students' satisfaction instruments

	Non-Completers (n=25)	Completers (n=108)
ALOC (12-item)	0.80	0.86
Satisfaction (7-item)	0.83	0.74

Conclusion

Discussion of Findings

This study looked at literature of dropout from higher education courses, dropout from distance education courses, locus of control, academic locus of control, and students' satisfaction as the theoretical background fostering this study. Better understanding of the key attributes that contribute to dropout from online learning courses can help instructional designers and faculty to improve online courses. Additionally, better understanding of such key attributes can help decrease dropouts, which in turns is hoped to increases reduce students' frustration.

This study suggests that students' satisfaction from online learning is a key attribute in students' decisions to complete or dropout from online learning courses. This is consistent with prior literature. However, in contrast to prior literature that primarily concentrated on correspondence courses and earlier types of distance learning, academic locus of control was not found as a key predictor of dropouts from online learning course.

Moreover, most of the demographics characteristics (gender, age group, residency status, academic major, GPA, and weekly working hours) were not found to be significantly different between completer and dropout students. This is also consistent with prior literature. However, college status and graduating term were found to be significantly different between completer and dropout students. These results indicate that students are likely to drop online learning courses if they have a lower college status and are in an earlier term of their academic studies. This may well be due to the students' lack of time to invest in successfully completing such courses. Therefore, students that dropout from online learning course may register again and will successfully complete the course in a later term. It may well be that their decision to drop is a calculated one to ensure a higher grade in the course, or just to attempt to register for the same course with another professor in the following term that may ensure a higher perceived level of satisfaction, which in turn may yield a higher grade.

The results also may suggest that students with lower motivation, probably as a result from low user satisfaction, are tends to drop at a significantly higher rate than those who have higher motivation to finish the course. It also may be that some students just tend to drop from online courses due to frustration with the system rather than learning related issues. Clearly this should be also investigated in future studies.

Limitations and Future Trends

There are two main limitations observed in this study. The first one is the low sample size for the dropped students (n=25). As a result, it may be that the measure of significance was impacted. Future studies are encouraged to look at larger sample size; specifically when the interest in online learning courses is growing, it will be more productive to find the results of similar study on a substantially higher group of online students. The second limitation observed deals with the large spectrum of majors for the participants under this study. Participants of this study include students from various majors such as MIS, general management, accounting, finance, and marketing. Consequently, the measure of academic locus of control may have been somewhat impacted as it was documented that students from different majors may have different levels of locus of control which may also be associated with the students' personality, and thus the selection of their academic major. Future studies are encouraged to look at the factors within one or two closely related subjects for add reliability.

Future research should continue the school of thoughts proposed by this study. Additionally, it is needed to uncover all of the factors that impact dropout from online learning courses. Such studies should attempt to focus on target students that dropout and complete online learning courses, rather than other types of distance education. Moreover, additional studies should use a less diverse population of courses and students' majors than the current study, in order to provide a better understanding of the key factors that drive students to dropout from online learning courses.

It will also be extremely fruitful if future studies can look at similar factors (academic locus of control and user satisfaction from online learning) in other educational level such as high school and post-graduate students to uncover the similarities or differences among the various academic levels. Moreover, it will also be fruitful for future studies to look how cultural differences may impact the dropout level in the various academic levels (high school, undergraduate, and graduate/post-graduate) in online learning courses. Measuring cultural related issues along with the measures used in this study (academic locus of control and user satisfaction from online learning) will also help researchers get a better picture of the key factors that may ultimately inhibit dropout from online learning courses.

References

Alavi, M., Wheeler, B., & Valacich, J. (1995). Using IT to reengineer business education: An exploratory investigation of collaborative telelearning. *MIS Quarterly, 19*(3) 293-311.

Ariwa, E. (2002). Evaluation of the information, communication and technology capabilities, and online learning. *USDLA Journal, 16*(11), 59-63.

Bloom, B. J. (1956). *Taxonomy of educational objectives, Handbook I: Cognitive domain.*

Bures, E. M., Abrami, P. C., & Amundsen, C. (2000). Student motivation to learn via computer conferencing. *Research in Higher Education, 41*(5), 593-621.

Chyung, Y., Winiecki, D. J., & Fenner, J. A. (1998). A case study: Increase enrollment by reducing dropout rates in adult distance education. In *Proceedings of the Annual Conference on Distance Teaching & Learning,* Madison, WI.

Carter, V. (1996). Do media influence learning? Revisiting the debate in the context of distance education. *Open Learning, 11*(1), 31-40.

Dille, B., & Mezack, M. (1991). Identifying predictors of high risk among community college telecourse students. *The American Journal of Distance Education, 5*(1), 24-35.

Dirkx, J. M., & Jha, L. R. (1994). Completion and attrition in adult basic education: A test of two pragmatic prediction models. *Adult Education Quarterly, 45*(1), 269-285.

Dollinger, S. J. (2000). Locus of control and incidental learning: An application to college student success. *College Student Journal, 34*(4), 537-540.

Fjortoft, N. P. (1995). *Predicting persistence in distance learning programs.* Paper presented at the Mid-Western Educational Research Meeting, Chicago, IL.

Fowler, F. J. (1993). *Survey research methods.* Newbury Park, CA: Sage Publications.

Fredericksen, E., Pickett, A., Shea, P., Pelz, W., & Swan, K. (2000). Student satisfaction and perceived learning with online courses: Principles and examples from the SUNY learning network. *Journal of Asynchronous Learning Networks, 4*(2), 7-41.

Harris, R. M., & Salomone, P. R. (1981). Toward an abbreviated internal-external locus of control scale. *Measurement and Evaluation in Guidance, 13*(4), 229-234.

Hilz, R. S., & Johnson, D. W. (1990). User satisfaction with computer-mediated communication systems. *Management Science, 36*(6), 739-765.

Kember, D. (1989a). A longitudinal-process model of dropout from distance education. *Journal of Higher Education, 60*(3), 278-301.

Kember, D. (1989b) An illustration, with case studies, of a linear process model of drop-out from distance education. *Distance Education, 10*(2), 196-211.

Lefcourt, H. M. (1991). Locus of control. In J. P. Robinson, P. R. Shaver, & L. S. Wrightsman (Eds.), *Measures of personality and social psychological attitudes* (pp. 413-499). San Diego, CA: Academic Press, Inc.

Levy, Y. (2003). A study of learners' perceived value and satisfaction for implied effectiveness of online learning systems. *Dissertation Abstracts International, 65*(03), 1014A. (UMI No. AAT 3126765). Retrieved October 13, 2004, from Digital Dissertations Database.

Levy, Y., & Murphy, K. E. (2002). Toward a value framework for online learning systems. In *Proceeding for the 35th Hawaii International Conference on System Sciences (HICSS-35)*, Big Island, HI.

McLaren, C. H. (2004). A comparison of student persistence and performance in online and classroom business statistics experiences. *Decision Sciences Journal of Innovative Education, 2*(1), 1-10.

Munro, J. (1987). *The discourse of dropout in distance education: A theoretical analysis*. Paper presented at the Annual Conference of the Canadian Association for the Study of Adult Education.

Parker, A. (1999). A study of variables that predict dropout from distance education. *International Journal of Educational Technology, 1*(2), 1-12.

Parker, A. (2003). Identifying predictors of academic persistence in distance education. *USDLA Journal, 17*(1), 55-62.

Piccoli, G., Ahmad, R., & Ives, B. (2001). Web-based virtual learning environments: A research framework and a preliminary assessment of effectiveness in basic IT skills training. *MIS Quarterly, 25*(4), 401-426.

Richardson, A. G. (1995). Academic locus of control of university students: A Caribbean case study. *Perceptual and Motor Skills, 81*(3), 1388-1390.

Rotter, J. (1966). Generalized expectations for internal versus external control of reinforcement. *Psychological Monographs, 80*(1), 1-28.

Rotter, J. (1989). Internal vs. external control of reinforcement. *American Psychologist, 45*(4), 489-493.

Sachs, D., & Hale, N. (2003). Pace university's focus on student satisfaction with student services in online education. *Journal of Asynchronous Learning Networks, 7*(2), 36-42.

Shea, P. J., Pickett, A. M., & Pelz, W. E. (2003). A follow-up investigation of "teaching presence" in the SUNY learning network. *Journal of Asynchronous Learning Networks, 7*(2), 61-80.

Sikora, A., & Carrol, D. (2002). *A profile of participation in distance education: 1999-2000* (Research Report). National Center for Education Statistics. Retrieved from http://www.nces.ed.gov/pubs2003/2003154.pdf

Straub, D. (1989). Validating instruments in MIS research. *MIS Quarterly, 13*(2), 147-170.

Swan, K., Shea, P., Fredericksen, E. E., Pickett, A. M., & Pelz, W. E. (2000). Course design factors influencing the success of online learning. In *Proceedings of WebNet 2000 World Conference on the WWW and Internet,* San Antonio, TX.

Thor, L. M., & Scarafiotti, C. (2004). Mainstreaming distance learning into the community college. *Journal of Asynchronous Learning Networks, 8*(1), 16-25.

Tinto, V. (1975). Dropout from higher education: A theoretical synthesis of recent research. *Review of Educational Research, 45*(1), 89-125.

Trice, A. D. (1985). An academic locus of control scale for college students. *Perceptual & Motor Skills, 61*(3), 1043-1046.

Volkwein, J. F., & Lorang, W. G. (1995). *Characteristics of extenders: Full-time students who take light credit loads and graduate in more than four years.* A research paper presented in the Association for Institutional Research (AIR) Annual Forum, Boston.

Webster, J., & Hackley, P. (1997). Teaching effectiveness in technology-mediated distance learning. *Academy of Management Journal, 40*(6), 1282-1309.

Whittington, L. A. (1995). *Factors impacting on the success of distance education students of the university of the West Indies: A review of the literature.* East Lansing, MI: National Center for Research on Teacher Learning. (ERIC Document Reproduction Service No. ED453740)

Williamson, D. R., & Creamer, D. G. (1988). Student attrition in 2- and 4-year colleges: Application of a theoretical model. *Journal of College Student Development, 29*(3), 210-217.

Xenos, M., Pierrakeas, C., & Pintelas, P. (2002). A survey on student dropout rates and dropout causes concerning the students in the course of informatics of the Hellenic Open University. *Computers & Education, 39*(4), 361-377.

Zielinski, D. (2000). The lie of online learning. *Training, 37*(2), 38-40.

Chapter X

Learning Styles and Adaptive ICT-Based Learning Environment

Zlatko J. Kovačić
The Open Polytechnic of New Zealand, New Zealand

Abstract

This chapter has two aims. First, to provide an overview of learning styles research and secondly, to provide an overview of research in adaptive hypermedia learning environment systems, those where different learning styles are considered and used to create a personalized learning environment. For most distance education institutions individualization of the learning environment for each student is not an option because economies of scale are the determining factor of cost reduction. However, the latest advances in database management, artificial intelligent systems and intelligent agents provide a technological infrastructure for individualizing the learning path for every learner at a lower cost. This chapter focuses on learning styles and how we can integrate and use them as a source of adaptation in an adaptive hypermedia learning environment systems.

Introduction

Teachers and researchers have long recognized the differences between learners and the impact these differences can have on learning. Concern for these differences has been the focus for academics and practitioners for decades and led to research on learning styles, i.e., "the composite of characteristic cognitive, affective, and physiological factors that serve as relatively stable indicators of how a learner perceives, interacts with, and responds to the learning environment" (Keefe, 1979). Research efforts in the theory and application of learning styles have proliferated a wide spectrum of models and instruments. Coffield, Moseley, Hall, and Ecclestone (2004a), who provided the latest and the most comprehensive overview of the learning style theories and instruments, have identified and critically discussed 13 major models of learning styles among the 71 models reported in literature.

Important messages emerge from the learning style research both for educators and course designers. Teachers should identify the learning styles of their students, encourage them to reflect on their own learning styles, and provide a teaching approach and support that will cater for individual learning styles. Course designers should create a learning environment that would address differences between learners. Though the idea of individualization is not new to education many of the larger distance education institutions offer little individualization for the students because economies of scale are the determining factor of cost reduction.

In the last few decades, with the emergence of information and communication technologies (hereafter labeled ICT) and their use in education research, we have witnessed new revival of interest in the individualization of learning and learning style research. There is a strong belief that ICT will provide the necessary foundation to individualize instruction, even in further education with large class sizes and a modular curriculum. At the same time emerging ICT raises expectations, as was pointed out by Kolb, the teacher's role will change from "dispenser of information, to coach or manager of the learning process" (1984, p. 202).

In the distance education we may achieve true individualization of the learning process by using emerging technologies such as intelligent agents and artificial intelligence systems which could store relevant data into a database and generate ad hoc completely customized course material, (i.e., an individualized learning path) for every single learner, according to their individual needs and preferences. An intelligent system which uses information about learners' preferences to dynamically organize course material is labeled an adaptive learning environment. If this learning environment involves the use of hypertext and multimedia (and most recently is Web-based) then we are describing an adaptive hypermedia learning environment (hereafter labeled AHLE). Peter Brusilovsky (1996, 2001) provided an overview of adaptive hypermedia systems from the early 1990s until now. He shows that the research on adaptive hypermedia systems in the last decade produced framework, techniques, prototyping models and authoring tools to create courses deliverable in the AHLE.

There are many different criteria for the adaptation of the learning environment to suit individual learner's needs and preferences. In this chapter we are focusing on the use and integration of learning styles as the only criteria for adaptation of the learning environment.

This chapter has four objectives: (a) to summarize and present learning style models in a systematic manner using proposed learning styles meta-models, (b) to review systematic efforts to establish and implement adaptive hypermedia systems in education, particularly those based on using learning styles as an adaptation criteria, (c) to discuss the problems and limitations of the current approach in using learning styles in adaptive hypermedia systems, and (d) to discuss the implication of the adaptive hypermedia systems based on learning styles on pedagogy, course design, and developers of an adaptive hypermedia system.

Overview of Learning Style Models and Instruments

There is a proliferation of definitions, concepts, models, and instruments related to individual learner's preference which makes it very difficult to summarize and classify learning styles models. What makes such an effort even more difficult is that there is no clear separation between the various models, as De Bello (1990, p. 217) suggests, "there are many areas of overlap among the models."

The taxonomy of learning styles models proposed by Lynn Curry (1983) uses an onion metaphor consisting of three layers. The core, the innermost layer of Curry's "Onion Model" deals with the most stable component of style, (i.e., cognitive personality style). Models from this layer focus on impact of personality on the ability to acquire and integrate information. Models from the middle layer are labeled as "information processing models" which concentrate on the ways learners obtain, sort, store, and utilize information. The models from this layer are more stable than the models from the outer layer ("instructional preference models") but are still modifiable by learning strategies. Finally, environmental, emotional, sociological, physiological, and psychological features of both learners and teachers are included in the models from the outer layer—

"instructional preference models." Claxton and Murrell (1987) added a fourth layer, social integration, which they placed between Curry's outer two layers. Models from this layer focus on how a learner interacts with other learners during the learning process. Finally, Given (1996) included physical elements (such as visual, auditory, tactile and kinesthetic) between social interactions and environmental/instructional layers to make the metaphorical model more complete.

In this chapter we have adopted the classification proposed by Coffield, Moseley, Hall, and Ecclestone (2004a). Presenting the learning style models in a continuum, they have allocated each model to one of the "families of learning styles." This continuum is based on the extent to which the authors of learning styles models and instruments appear to believe that learning styles are fixed. They have identified the following five families of learning styles:

- Constitutionally-based learning styles and preferences
- Cognitive structure
- Stable personality type
- "Flexibly stable" learning preferences
- Learning approaches and strategies

The first family encompasses those models which consider influence of genetics on fixed inherited traits and the interaction of personality and cognition as the dominant factors. Moving along the continuum, we locate learning style models which are based on the idea of dynamic interaction between personality and experience. On the opposite side of the continuum is a family of learning styles models where the authors paid particular attention to personal factors, curriculum design, institutional and course culture and their impact on learning.

Using learning style as a source of adaptation of the learning environment raises the question of which learning style model to select and build in the AHLE system. Sampson and Karagiannidis (2002) proposed a certain number of conditions that each candidate, for use in AHLE systems among learning styles models, should be tested against. They suggested a check on the theoretical and empirical justification of the model, the suitability of the learning style model in the specific learning context; whether the model or its constructs are measurable or not; the time effectiveness in applying a particular model; does the model provide sufficient instruction about what should be adapted for each learner category and finally the cost of using a particular learning style instrument.

In this chapter we focus on those learning styles models which could be used or are already built in the AHLE systems (both prototyping and conceptual AHLE systems are considered). Most of these learning styles models belong to the middle layer of the Curry's model or to the stable personality type or "flexibly stable" learning preferences family in case of Coffield, Moseley, Hall, and Ecclestone classification. The reason for this is that the models which belong to this layer or family are more stable than the others, and do not interact directly with the environment, though they are modifiable by learning strategies (Atkins, Moore, Sharpe, & Hobbs, 2001).

We begin with the first family of learning styles (i.e., constitutionally based). The most prominent representative of this family of learning styles is the Dunn and Dunn model (Dunn, 2003) based on five dimensions that mark various preferences: environmental, emotional, sociological, psychological, and psychological. However, from the perspective of using learning styles models in the AHLE systems Del Corso et al. (2001) did not recommend the Dunn and Dunn model, because this model is focusing on less relevant aspects of learning such as the senses and environmental factors.

Next, we consider learning style models which belong to the cognitive structure family. Coffield, Moseley, Hall, and Ecclestone (2004a) provided a detailed analysis of the Riding's model of cognitive styles (Riding & Cheema, 1991) as the representative for this family. However, in the research literature about AHLE systems, Witkin's model (Witkin, Moore, Goodenough, & Cox, 1977) or better known as the Field Dependent/Field Independent model, was more frequently used than any other from this family of learning styles. Witkin's model divides learners into two groups: Field Dependent learners (externally motivated, like collaborative work and are people-oriented) and Field Independent learners (intrinsically motivated, prefer to work alone and take an impersonal approach to learning). Degrees of field dependence or field independence could be defined as a continuum with field independent at one end and field dependent at the other end. In the middle of the continuum is the group termed as field mixed who do not have clear orientation like the group of field dependent or field independent. This has a practical implication for use of Witkin's model in the AHLE system. According to Sampson and Karagiannidis (2002) criteria in case of field-mixed learners we may say that the model did not provide sufficient instruction on what should be adapted for this particular learner category.

The stable personality type family of learning styles models was rarely used in AHLE systems. The most popular learning style model which belongs to this family is the Myers-Briggs model. This model is based on psychologist Carl Jung's theory of psychological types and uses four bipolar dimensions to characterize people according to 16 personality types. Each of these types has a primary orientation toward the world, one which affects their ability to learn and to work. Del Corso et al. (2001) recommended not considering implementation of the Myers-Briggs model in the AHLE systems. According to them, this model goes beyond cognitive controls and behavior related to learning, focusing on the whole personality rather than information perceiving and processing dimensions which is the main focus of the Kolb's and Honey and Mumford's model.

The flexibly stable learning preferences family comprises, among other models, Kolb's experiential learning cycles model (1984), Honey and Mumford (1992), McCarthy (1990), and Felder-Silverman model (1988). Honey and Mumford's and McCarty's model were inspired by the Kolb's model and share basically the same pedagogical approach to learning. This family of learning styles was most frequently implemented as one of adaptation criteria in the AHLE systems. The Kolb model uses the learner's experience as a starting point in the learning process. Learners are perceived as passing through four stages of learning. Initially they are experimenting with the topic accumulating enough concrete experience to be able to reflect in the second stage on the observation gathered in the concrete experimenting stage. As a result of reflective activities, learners derive abstract concepts and make generalizations in the third abstract conceptualization stage. Finally, new concepts are subject to testing to see if they provide a solid explanation in new situations. In other words, learners begin a new learning cycle, gathering new evidence, and concrete experience. Though learners are moving through each stage, they tend to use a specific learning mode. Therefore we can describe them as a learner with a preference for a particular mode. By looking at the quadrants, Kolb identified four types of learners: Diverger (creative, generates alternatives), Assimilator (defines problems, creates theoretical models), Converger (practical applications, makes decisions), and Accomodator (takes risks, gets things done).

Initially the Felder-Silverman model was developed as a five-dimensional model, with the following dimensions: Perception, Input, Processing, Understanding, and Organization. Later the organization dimension was omitted because Felder (1993) believes that the best approach to teaching undergraduates is always inductive and therefore his learning styles instrument does not differentiate between inductive and deductive learners. Both the Kolb's and Felder-Silverman's models are based on the same educational philosophy of John Dewey, which emphasizes the nature of experience as of fundamental importance in education.

There appears to be a close relationship between the Felder-Silverman and the Kolb model. They share the same two dimensions: processing (the preferred way learners are processing information, with two poles: actively/reflectively) and perception (the preferred way learners are perceiving information, with two poles: sensing/intuitive). However, the Felder-Silverman model also partly belongs to the second and third families of learning styles, (i.e., cognitive structure and stable personality type, because it adds two new dimensions, which address the learners' approaches to adapting and assimilating information.) These two dimensions are: input (the preferred way learners are inputting information, with two poles: visually/verbally) and understanding (the preferred way learners are adapting information, with two poles: sequentially/globally).

The last family of learning styles we are considering is labeled "learning approaches and strategies." The well-known model in this family is the Grasha and Reichmann model (Hruska-Riechmann & Grasha, 1982). They developed a set of student learner types that indicate the likely attitudes, habits, and strategies students will take toward their work. Grasha (1996) indicates ways in which teachers can adjust their teaching styles to create better connections with various types of students. This model has three personality dimensions: (1) competitive—collaborative, (2) avoidant—participant, and (3) dependent—independent.

We would expect that when the learning environment and teaching methods are modified to cater for various learning styles, that the student outcome, (i.e., academic performance) would improve. Therefore, as an illustration of the applied learning styles research that might be relevant for AHLE systems, the relationship between learning styles and academic performance is discussed. There are many factors which influence academic performance in addition to learning styles, such as gender, age, and work experience (Dille & Mezack, 1991). While it is preferable that a student uses and develops an array of learning styles to deal with course content and the real world, most of the applied work in this area focus only on a student's currently preferred learning style. Though there have been numerous studies on the relationship between preferred learning styles and academic performance (Zywno & Waalen, 2002), the evidence remains contradictory. For example for first-year programming courses, Thomas, Ratcliffe, Woodbury, and Jarman (2002) suggest that there is a relationship between student learning style and academic performance, while Byrne and Lyons (2001) suggest that no such relationship exists. Weak evidence of a relationship and impact on academic performance has been found for the way students on an IT course are inputting and understanding the information by using the Felder-Silverman model (Kovačić & Green, 2004).

Implications of Learning Styles Research For Pedagogy

Each of the learning styles models has its own specific implications for pedagogy. In this section we are addressing two general issues related to pedagogical implications which are relevant for all presented models: meta-cognition and "matching hypothesis." We conclude this section with critiques of the learning style models and instruments.

Even if the idea of learning styles is not fully accepted we believe there might be a benefit from discussing the concept. Coffield, Moseley, Hall, and Ecclestone (2004a, p. 120) stated that "A knowledge of learning styles can be used to increase the self-awareness of students and tutors about their strengths and weaknesses as learners." This self-awareness of learners and teachers is known in literature as the meta-cognition. By increasing meta-cognitive abilities learner can take full ownership of his or her learning. When we are able to understand how we learn, how deeply we learn and our reasons for learning then we can, in some situations, manipulate the learning strategy to best suit our learning styles. At the same time learners with developed meta-cognitive abilities can be expected to be more adaptive to changes in the learning environment.

"Matching hypothesis" describes the situation in education when there is congruence between teaching styles and learning styles. Whichever model of the learning styles one prefers or implements the expectation is that there is a mismatch between learning and teaching style preferences. To minimize conflict between teacher's and student's style, some researchers in the area of learning styles recommend teaching and learning styles be matched (e.g., Charkins, O'Toole, & Wetzel, 1985; Griggs & Dunn, 1984; Smith & Renzulli, 1984). On the other side we can argue equally well that mismatches are sometime desirable and that learners should be exposed to multiple alternative teaching-learning strategies for their own benefits. Exposure to different teaching styles or deliberate mismatching is what Grasha (1996) recommends. He argued that people need to be "stretched" to learn, and such a situation he describes as a "creative mismatch" between teaching and learning style. Therefore, the issue remains whether to teach to learners' strengths or to challenge them and expand their styles?

A mismatch can lead to poor teaching outcomes, low retention of students on courses (Felder & Silverman, 1988), and to poor academic performance (Ford & Chen, 2001). Though Felder (1993) advocates teaching strategies that incorporate all of the learning style preferences, there is still discussion on whether mismatches of teaching and learning styles should be sought or avoided and whether there is a benefit from eliminating mismatches or not. Coffield, Moseley, Hall, and Ecclestone (2004a, p. 123) for example, claim they "failed to find...hard empirical evidence that matching the styles of learner and tutor improves the attainment of the learner significantly."

The learning styles model continues to be the subject of debate and critique. Curry (1990) identified three problems with making the learning style model the basis of educational practice. Firstly, different learning style models and instruments use different style categorization to define the learning style continuum. Even the fundamental elements such as definition of learning style are not unanimously accepted and almost every author has his or her own definition. Though there is an overlap among concepts and models it is not an easy task to classify these models or to compare them. Secondly, evidence of the reliability and validity of learning style instruments is weak. Coffield, Moseley, Hall, and Ecclestone (2004b, p. 55) go even further by saying "that some of the best known and widely used instruments have such serious weaknesses (e.g., low reliability, poor validity and negligible impact on pedagogy) that we recommend that their use in research and in practice should be discontinued." Thirdly, the pedagogical implications and changes in educational practices that complement particular learning styles are in some cases hard to identify or it is not clear whether the increase in performance should be attributed to other factors rather than to the implementation of a learning style model. More comprehensive critical reflection on the theory and practice of learning style is given in Coffield, Moseley, Hall, and Ecclestone (2004a, 2004b).

Adaptive Hypermedia Learning Environment

The birth and the rapid growth of the Internet have transformed education and the way we learn. The dominant paradigm in today's education uses a traditional hypermedia based learning environment which assumes that "one size fits all." However, since the early 1980s, with advances in artificial intelligence research, there has been a significant development of systems to provide an individualized and intelligent response to users interacting with computers. These artificial intelligence systems were based on strategies to "learn" users' interactions with the learning environment and respond accordingly. Brusilovsky (2000, 2001) described two phases in the historical development of adaptive systems. Before 1996 adaptive systems were based on pre-Web hypertext and hypermedia. The most dominant systems at that time were intelligent tutoring systems, which were from a pedagogical perspective, teacher-centered systems with the main focus in problem-solving support. After 1996 research interest moved toward Web-based adaptive hypermedia, along with a shift in pedagogy toward a student-centered learning, based on constructivist approach. In regard to the application of adaptive hypermedia in education Brusilovsky (2004b) identified three generations of AHLE systems. The research focus of the latest generation of AHLE systems is the integration of adaptive hypermedia technologies into the regular educational process, answering the challenge posed by dominant learning management systems such as Blackboard and WebCT.

AHLE systems usually provide two forms of adaptation: adaptability and adaptivity. Both terms describe personalization on the Internet. However, they are two quite different concepts dependent upon whether the learner or the system is in control of the adaptation. Kay (2001) discussed different levels of adaptation which should be considered when designing an AHLE system: (a) *adaptability*—the system is adaptable when the learner modifies the visual appearance of the learning environment; and (b) *adaptivity*—the system is adaptive when it monitors a learner's behavior and updates a learner model. Then the presentation is updated according to the learner model, which in turn is updated during browsing process.

Summarizing the various conceptual and prototyping models of the AHLE systems we came up with a generic model which encompasses most of the existing AHLE systems. The conceptual model of an AHLE system is presented in Figure 1 and consists of four sub-models:

1. **Learner model:** Stores information about each learner (user profile) including a learning style profile in the database. Magoulas, Papanikolaou, and Grigoriadou (2003) provided a detailed structure of the learner model (goals, knowledge, learning styles, preferences, background, and hyper-space experience). A learner's understanding about the domain in this model is typically represented as an overlay model of the domain model. This means that for every "concept" in the domain model there is a corresponding "concept" in the learner model that represents how the learner relates to that concept (De Bra, Aroyo, & Chepegin, 2004). Alternative models describing the learner's knowledge level of domain are listed in Danchak (2004).

2. **Domain model:** Contains information content of the course, which includes also the relationship between course components (Kelly & Tangney, 2004; Wu, 2002).

3. **Pedagogical model:** Defines the roles of each person, such as instructor and learner, and stores details about pedagogical approach used. This model has not been included or discussed in most of the AHLE systems. Shute and Towle (2003) argued that existing AHLE systems concentrate more on the adaptation of the format of the content rather than on adaptive instruction. In other words, the pedagogical component of AHLE system is quite often neglected.

4. **Adaptation model:** Consists of a description of how to update the learner model by monitoring a learner's behavior and also how to generate the adaptation.

There are some variations of the presented conceptual model. Paramythis and Loidl (2004) for example, added the Group Model to the AHLE model. It captures the characteristics of groups of learners, which is important when collaborative instructional design is used.

Figure 1. Conceptual model of an adaptive hypermedia learning environment system

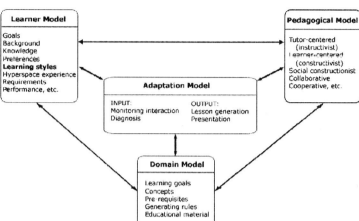

In order to select the appropriate technology of adaptation we need to answer the following questions: what features of the learners or their environment are used as the source of adaptation and which features of the AHLE system can be different for different learners. Most of the AHLE systems use the learner's previous knowledge of domain as a source of adaptation. Recently, learning style information has been used as a source of adaptation in AHLE systems (see Table 1). The answer to the second question brings technologies of adaptation into focus. Brusilovsky (1999, 2001) identified the following adaptive and intelligent technologies for Web-based education:

1. **Curriculum sequencing (or instructional planning) technology:** Adapting the sequence of the content to the learners' learning preferences (Brusilovsky & Vassileva, 2003).

2. **Problem solving support technologies:** The intelligent analysis of learner solutions, example-based problem solving, and interactive problem solving support.

3. **Adaptive navigation support:** Direct guidance, adaptive annotation, adaptive sorting, and adaptive link hiding and disabling. Helps the learner orientation and navigation in hyperspace by changing the appearance of visible links (Brusilovsky, 2004a; Brusilovsky, Chavan, & Farzan, 2004).

4. **Adaptive presentation:** Adapts the content to learners' learning preferences.

5. **Learner model matching technologies:** Adaptive collaboration support and intelligent class monitoring—uses the system's knowledge about

Table 1. Adaptive hypermedia learning environment systems that use learning styles as a source of adaptation

AHLE system (working/ conceptual model); author(s)	Learning style model and author(s)	Initial identification & dynamic adaptation	Adaptation technology	Teaching/learning approaches
3DE; Del Corso et al. (2001)	Honey & Mumford (1992)	Questionnaire. Learners' profiles are described on all four basic dimensions.	AP	Content is stored as a set of micro modules, specifically designed for each learning style. Teacher supervises course creation.
ACE; Specth & Opperman (1998)	Model not specified. Learner's media preferences	Learner directly modifies learner model.	ANS (adaptive annotation and incremental linking), CS	Teaching strategy is modifiable by the system.
AES-CS; Triantafillou, Demetriadis & Pomportsis (2002)	Witkin et al. (1997)	Questionnaire. Learner directly modifies learner model.	ANS (link annotation)	Learners can switch between different instructional strategies.
AHA!, Stash, Cristea, & De Bra (2004) Stash & De Bra (2004)	Any could be used. Honey & Mumford (1992) Witkin et al. (1997)	Learners initially specify their learning style. System adapts learner model.	CS, AP, ANS (adaptive annotation)	Learners can switch between different instructional strategies and change attributes of the concepts in their learner model.
Arthur; Gilbert & Han (1999, 2002)	Any could be used. Witkin et al. (1997)	Alternative styles of instruction differ in the type of media they use.	CS	Mastery learning – dynamically adapts the instructional style according to learner's performance.
CS383; Carver, Howard, & Lavelle (1996, 1999)	Felder & Silverman (1988)	Questionnaire	AP	Media elements are sorted, ranked and presented according to learners' learning style
Danchak (2004)	4MAT; McCarthy (1990)	Questionnaire. Naïve Bayes Classifiers and Case-based Reasoning.	AP	Reflective teaching method of instruction
ILASH; Bajraktarevic, Hall, & Fullick (2003a, 2003b)	Felder & Silverman (1988)	Questionnaire	ANS (adaptive annotation and hiding of links), AP	Adapt the method of navigation with special emphasis on the approaches of global and sequential learners.
INSPIRE; Papanikolaou, Grogoriadou, Kornilakis, & Magoulas (2002, 2003)	Honey & Mumford (1992)	Questionnaire. Direct manipulation of learner model.	ANS (adaptive annotation and hiding of links), AP, CS	Adapt method and order of presentation of multiple types of educational resources.
iWeaver; Wolf (2002, 2003)	Dunn & Dunn; Dunn (2003)	Questionnaire. System allows for fluctuations in learning styles.		Learners can switch and combine media representations and system adapts dynamically.
MANIC; Stern & Woolf (2000)	Model not specified; Text vs. graphic	System adapts learner model. Naïve Bayes Classifiers	AP	Presentation of content objects using *stretchtext* which allows certain parts of a page to be opened or closed.
Peña, Narzo, & de la Rosa (2002)	Felder & Silverman (1988)	Questionnaire. Case-Based Reasoning	ANS (adaptive annotation and hiding of links), AP	
TANGOW; Paredas & Rodriguez (2002a, 2002b, 2004)	Felder & Silverman (1988)	Questionnaire. Learner directly modifies learner model.	AP, CS	Learning style was used to adapt the exposition-example sequencing (sensing/intuitive learners).

Acronyms used in the "Adaptation technology" column: ANS: Adaptive Navigation Support, AP: Adaptive Presentation, CS: Curriculum Sequencing different learners to form a cohesive group for different kinds of collaboration, or to identify a mismatch between learners.

The most frequently used adaptation techniques in the AHLE systems are: adaptive presentation, curriculum sequencing and adaptive navigation support (see Table 1, column "Adaptation technology"). On first use of an AHLE system which uses learning style preferences as a source of adaptation, the learner has to complete a learning style questionnaire; the result from this questionnaire initializes the learner model and classifies the learner into a particular learning style group. Most of the AHLE systems assess the learning styles through psychometric questionnaires (Stash, Cristea, & De Bra, 2004). The disadvantage of this approach is that the learners are classified into stereotypical groups and assumptions about their learning styles were not updated during the subsequent interactions with the system in most of the early AHLE systems. However, in the latest AHLE systems, during the use of the system, the learner model is dynamically updated in terms of preferred learning components and changes in learning preferences. In other words, these systems assume that learning preferences are not fixed, and that a learner's learning style may change from one occasion to another. These systems do not require an initial diagnosis of a learner's learning preferences but simply pick them up from browsing behavior of the learner. Danchak (2004) suggests using two alternative techniques for dynamic adaptation of learning preferences, namely the Naïve Bayes Classifiers and the Case-Based Reasoning (see Castillo, Gama, & Breda, 2003; Funk & Conlan, 2003; Zukerman & Albrecht, 2001). These techniques could be used to dynamically update learning preferences in the learner model. Furthermore, an ideal AHLE system should provide learners with full control over the learner model, allowing them to change their learning preferences in spite of initial classification in a particular learning style group.

Although systematic efforts have been made to evaluate adaptive systems (Weibelzahl, 2003; Weibelzahl & Weber, 2001) only a few empirical studies, mostly small scale studies conducted in experimental conditions, have been conducted that seek to prove the effectiveness of the adopted approaches based on learning styles (Papanikolaou & Grigoriadou, 2004).

Conclusion

Awareness about learning styles is very important both to academic staff and learners. Learners will gain an understanding of why academic staff is using different teaching approaches on the course and how they can benefit from them. Academic staff will recognize the diversity of learning styles among learners and adjust their teaching style to take account of this. The discussion in this chapter also sends a clear message to instructional designers to create a learning environment that will support the construction of knowledge in learners.

Coffield, Moseley, Hall, and Ecclestone (2004b) answering the question in the title of their study "Should we be using learning styles?" claim that there are no clear implications of learning styles research for pedagogy. They state that, for example, there is no consensus on whether the style of teaching should be consonant with the style of learning or not. However, one of the benefits that an AHLE system with learning styles could have over a non-adaptable learning environment is that it could help students to develop meta-cognition skills. An AHLE system provides learners with alternative paths through the course material based on different learning styles. Learners could reflect on the way they are learning and then decide to use an alternative path through the course, i.e., a different learning approach to the course material. In other words, AHLE systems could stimulate learners to think more about the way they are learning and what the best learning strategy for them is. Of course an AHLE system to some extent should also expose learners to teaching styles and instructional material which is different from their preferences to increase their readiness for the real world (Felder, 1993, 1996; Montgomery & Groat, 1998).

Learning styles which belong to the stable personality type and "flexibly stable" learning preferences families in Coffield, Moseley, Hall, and Ecclestone's (2004a) classification of learning style models, are used in AHLE systems as a source of adaptation more often than others. These models are the Felder and Silverman, Honey and Mumford, McCarthy, Dunn and Dunn, and Witkin models and provide sufficient information for AHLE systems designers to incorporate them in the system. They also fulfill most of the conditions stated by Sampson and Karagiannidis (2002) for any learning style model, which is a candidate for use in an AHLE system as a source of adaptation. Of course this does not mean that the other learning style models should not be tried in an AHLE system. This may be a possible topic for further research in this area.

Most of the AHLE systems which incorporate learning preferences as a source of adaptation use the following adaptation technologies: adaptive presentation, curriculum sequencing and adaptive navigation support to adapt learning environment to individual learning preferences. However, because of the increasing role of collaborative learning in distance education, adaptive collaborative support technologies together with learning style information should be considered for the construction of groups and implementation in an AHLE system in future development.

Future Trends

One of the reasons why AHLE systems are not widely used as an alternative for course management systems such as WebCT and Blackboard, lies in fact that most of them are not content-free, (i.e., they are developed for a particular domain and/or particular learning style model). In other words, domain and learning style are embedded in the code of the AHLE system. This is the area where Brusilovsky (2001, 2003b) expects future progress and the development of new architectures and authoring tools for AHLEs. He predicts that "we may expect better markup-based and form-based tools. I also expect the appearance of a new kind of 'really graphic' user interface design tools" (2003b). At the moment the only available content-free authoring tool is De Bra's AHA.

The use of learning style as a source of adaptation in a new generation of AHLE systems raises the following question: How do we address the meta models of learning styles in adaptive hypermedia? (Brusilovsky, 2003a). In other words the question is whether the AHLE system is capable of addressing not only one selected learning style, but whole families of learning styles. Berlanga and Garcia (2004a, 2004b) proposed a flexible design of an AHLE system with learning preferences as a source of adaptation where learning styles approach and adaptation rules are not prescribed. They argued that different learning style approaches should be used for different knowledge and types of learners. The idea is not to set down any particular learning style, but a flexible structure where the different learning style approaches can be easily described and used to characterize the learning style of learners and activities.

Future AHLE system should provide learners with full access to the learner model. Learners should be able to choose a particular path through the course material, even if it is not the same path recommended by the system and based on their learning styles. As was recommended before, learners should be exposed to different approaches to learning to improve their meta-cognition skills and to gain an understanding of how other people in their collaborative team learn. Future AHLE systems should have built-in options similar to the computer chess game, where a player might select an opponent with certain characteristics, for example, a defensive or offensive player.

Learning style processing may require fuzzy logic in the diagnosis (Triantafillou, Pomportsis, & Georgiadou, 2002), allowing for the fact that not all users are located at the poles of each dimension of the learning style model (for example, global and sequential poles in the case of Felder and Silverman model), but they combine the characteristics of both global and sequential dimensions. However, as they argued, it is questionable if all different shades of learning styles can be handled by an adaptive hypermedia system, or if the system should be simpler for the user's benefit. It is a matter of future research to find a trade-off between the degree of adaptation and the level of complexity of an AHLE system.

There are also other issues related to learning styles in AHLE systems that need to be addressed in the future, such as delivering an adaptive course for mobile devices (Brusilovsky & Rizzo, 2002c, 2004; Kinshuk & Lin, 2004) and creating a framework or at least adaptive navigation support, which would integrate closed corpus course material (a standard AHLE system with well-structured homogeneous course material) with open corpus Web material, i.e., all the other relevant resources on the Internet (Brusilovsky & Rizzo, 2002a, 2002b).

References

Atkins, H., Moore, D., Sharpe, S., & Hobbs, D. (2001). Learning style theory and computer mediated communication. In *Proceedings of ED-MEDIA 2001*, Tampere, Finland.

Bajraktarevic, N., Hall, W., & Fullick, P. (2003a). ILASH: Incorporating learning strategies in hypermedia. In *AH2003: Workshop on Adaptive Hypermedia and Adaptive Web-Based Systems*.

Bajraktarevic, N., Hall, W., & Fullick, P. (2003b). Incorporating learning styles in hypermedia environment: Empirical evaluation. In *AH2003: Workshop on Adaptive Hypermedia and Adaptive Web-Based Systems*.

Berlanga, A., & García, F. J. (2004a). A proposal to define adaptive learning designs. In *Proceedings of the 2nd International Workshop on Applications of Semantic Web Technologies for E-Learning, SW-EL'04*, Auckland, New Zealand.

Berlanga, A., & García, F. J. (2004b). An adaptive meta-model for eLearning. In *Proceedings of the 5th International Conference Human-Computer Interaction*, Lleida, Spain.

Brusilovsky, P. (1996). Methods and techniques of adaptive hypermedia. *User Modeling and User-Adapted Interaction, 6*(2-3), 87-129.

Brusilovsky, P. (1999). Adaptive and intelligent technologies for Web-based education. *Künstliche Intelligenz, 13*(4), 19-25.

Brusilovsky, P. (2000). Adaptive hypermedia: From intelligent tutoring systems to Web-based education. In G. Gauthier, C. Frasson, & K. VanLehn (Eds.), *Intelligent tutoring systems: Lecture notes in computer science, 1839* (pp. 1-7). Berlin: Springer Verlag.

Brusilovsky, P. (2001). Adaptive hypermedia. *User Modeling and User Adapted Interaction, 11*(1/2), 87-110.

Brusilovsky, P. (2003a). Adaptive navigation support in educational hypermedia: The role of student knowledge level and the case for meta-adaptation. *British Journal of Educational Technology, 34*(4), 487-497.

Brusilovsky, P. (2003b). Developing adaptive educational hypermedia systems: From design models to authoring tools. In T. Murray, S. Blessing, & S. Ainsworth (Eds.), *Authoring tools for advanced technology learning environment* (pp. 377-409). Dordrecht, Netherlands: Kluwer Academic Publishers.

Brusilovsky, P. (2004a). Adaptive navigation support: From adaptive hypermedia to the adaptive Web and beyond. *Psychology, 2*(1), 7-23.

Brusilovsky, P. (2004b). Adaptive educational hypermedia: From generation to generation. In *Proceedings of 4th Hellenic Conference on Information and Communication Technologies in Education,* Athens, Greece (pp. 19-33).

Brusilovsky, P., Chavan, G., & Farzan, R. (2004). Social adaptive navigation support for open corpus electronic textbooks. In P. De Bra (Ed.), *Proceedings of 3rd International Conference on Adaptive Hypermedia and Adaptive Web-Based Systems (AH2004),* Eindhoven, The Netherlands.

Brusilovsky, P., & Rizzo, R. (2002a). Map-based horizontal navigation in educational hypertext. *Journal of Digital Information, 3*(1). Retrieved January 7, 2005, from http://jodi.tamu.edu/Articles/v03/i01/Brusilovsky/

Brusilovsky, P., & Rizzo, R. (2002b). Using maps and landmarks for navigation between closed and open corpus hyperspace in Web-based education. *The New Review of Hypermedia and Multimedia, 8,* 59-82.

Brusilovsky, P., & Rizzo, R. (2002c). Map-based access to multiple educational online resources from mobile wireless devices. In F. Paterno (Ed.), *Mobile human-computer interaction: Lecture notes in computer science, 2411* (pp. 404-408). Berlin: Springer-Verlag.

Brusilovsky, P., & Rizzo, R. (2004). Accessing Web educational resources from mobile wireless devices: The knowledge sea approach. In F. Crestiani, M. Dunlop, & S. Mizzaro (Eds.), *Mobile and ubiquitous information access. Lecture Notes in Computer Science, 2954* (pp. 54-66). Berlin: Springer Verlag.

Brusilovsky, P., & Vassileva, J. (2003). Course sequencing techniques for large-scale Web-based education. *International Journal of Continuing Engineering Education and Lifelong Learning, 13*(1-2), 75-94.

Byrne, P., & Lyons, G. (2001). The effect of student attributes on success in programming. In *Proceedings of the 6th Annual Conference on Innovation and Technology in Computer Science Education,* Canterbury, UK (pp. 49-52).

Carver, C. A., Richard, A. H., & Edward, L. (1996). Enhancing student learning by incorporating learning styles into adaptive hypermedia. In *Proceedings of ED-MEDIA 96, Association for the Advancement of Computing in Education*, Charlottesville, VA (pp. 118-123).

Carver, C. A., Richard, A. H., & Edward, L. (1999). Enhancing student learning through mypermedia courseware and incorporation of student learning styles. *IEEE Transactions on Education, 42*(1), 33-38.

Castillo, G., Gama, J., & Breda, A. M. (2003). Adaptive Bayes for a student modeling prediction task based on learning styles. In P. Brusilovsky, A. Corbett, & F. de Rosis (Eds.), *User Modeling 2003, 9th International Conference, Lecture Notes in Artificial Intelligence, 2702* (pp. 328-332). Berlin: Springer Verlag.

Charkins, R. J., O'Toole, D. M., & Wetzel, J. N. (1985). Linking teacher and student learning styles with student achievement and attitudes. *Journal of Economic Education, 16*(2), 111-120.

Claxton, C. S., & Murrell, P. H. (1987). *Learning styles: Implication for improving educational practices* (ASHE-ERIC Higher Education Report No. 4). Association for the Study of Higher Education. Washington, DC.

Coffield, F., Moseley, D., Hall, E., & Ecclestone, K. (2004a). *Learning styles and pedagogy in post-16 learning: A systematic and critical review*. London: Learning and Skills Research Centre/University of Newcastle upon Tyne.

Coffield, F., Moseley, D., Hall, E., & Ecclestone, K. (2004b). *Should we be using learning styles? What research has to say to practice*. London: Learning and Skills Research Centre/University of Newcastle upon Tyne.

Curry, L. (1983). *An organisation of learning style theory and constructs*. Paper presented at the Annual Meeting of the American Educational Research Association, Montreal, Quebec, Canada. (ERIC Document Reproduction Service No. ED235185)

Curry, L. (1990). A critique of the research on learning styles. *Educational Leadership, 48*(2), 50-55.

Danchak, M. M. (2004). Using adaptive hypermedia to match Web presentation to learning styles. In *Elements of quality online education: Into the mainstream* (93-108). Sloan Consortium.

De Bello, T. C. (1990). Comparison of eleven major learning styles models: Variables, appropriate populations, validity of instrumentation, and the research behind them. *Journal of Reading, Writing, and Learning Disabilities, 6*, 203-222.

De Bra, P., Aroyo, L., & Chepegin, V. (2004). The next big thing: Adaptive Web-based systems. *Journal of Digital Information, 5*(1). Retrieved January 7, 2005, from http://jodi.tamu.edu/Articles/v05/i01/DeBra/

Del Corso, D. D., Ovcin, E., Morrone, G., Gianesini, D., Salojarvi, S., & Kvist, T. (2001). 3DE: An environment for the development of learner-centered custom educational packages. In *Proceedings of 31ˢᵗ ASEE/IEEE Frontiers in Education Conference.*

Dille, B., & Mezack, M. (1991). Identifying predictors of high risk among community college telecourse students. *The American Journal of Distance Education, 5*(1), 24-35.

Dunn, R. (2003). The Dunn and Dunn learning style model and its theoretical cornerstone. In R. Dunn, & S. Griggs (Eds), *Synthesis of the Dunn and Dunn learning styles models research: Who, what, when, where, and so what* (pp. 1-6). New York: St John's University.

Felder, R. M. (1993). Reaching the second tier: Learning and teaching styles in college science education. *Journal of College Science Teaching, 78*(7), 674-681.

Felder, R. M. (1996). Matters of style. *ASEE Prism, 6*(4), 18-23.

Felder, R. M., & Silverman, L. K. (1988). Learning and teaching styles in engineering education. *Engineering Education, 78*(7), 674-681.

Ford, N., & Chen, S.Y. (2001). Matching/mismatching revisited: An empirical study of learning and teaching styles. *British Journal of Educational Technology, 32*(1), 5-22.

Funk, P., & Conlan, O. (2003). Using case-based reasoning to support authors of adaptive hypermedia systems. In *AH2003: Workshop on Adaptive Hypermedia and Adaptive Web-Based Systems.*

Gilbert, J. E., & Han, C. Y. (1999). Arthur: Adapting instruction to accommodate learning styles. In *Proceedings of WebNet '99 World Conference of the WWW and Internet* (pp. 433-438).

Gilbert, J. E., & Han, C. Y. (2002). Arthur: A personalized instructional system. *Journal of Computing in Higher Education, 14*(1), 113-129.

Given, B. K. (1996). Learning styles: A synthesized model. *Journal of Accelerated Learning and Teaching, 2*(1&2), 11-43.

Grasha, A. F. (1996). *Teaching with style: A practical guide to enhancing leaning by understanding teaching and learning styles.* Pittsburgh, PA: Alliance Publishers.

Griggs, S. A., & Dunn. R. S. (1984). Selected case studies of the learning style preferences of gifted students. *Gifted Child Quarterly, 28*(3), 115-119.

Honey, P., & Mumford, A. (1992). *The manual of learning styles*. Maidenhead, UK: Peter Honey Publications.

Hruska-Riechmann, S., & Grasha, A. F. (1982). The Grasha-Riechmann student learning style scales: Research findings and applications. In J. Keefe (Ed.), *Student learning styles and brain behaviour*. Reston, VA: NASSP.

Kay, J. (2001). Learner control. *User Modeling and User-Adapted Interaction, 11*(1-2), 111-127.

Keefe, J. W. (1979). Learning styles: An overview. In *NASSP's student learning styles: Diagnosing and prescribing programs* (pp. 1-17). Reston, VA: National Association of Secondary School Principals.

Kelly, D., & Tangney, B. (2004). Evaluating presentation strategy and choice in an adaptive multiple intelligence based tutoring system. In G. D. Magoulas, & S. Y. Chen (Eds.), *Individual Differences in Adaptive Hypermedia. Proceedings of the Adaptive Hypermedia 2004 Workshop*, London (pp. 21-30).

Kinshuk, & Lin, T. (2004). Application of learning styles adaptivity in mobile learning environments. In *Proceedings of the 3rd Pan Commonwealth Forum on Open Learning*, Dunedin, New Zealand.

Kolb, D. (1984). *Experiential learning: Experience as the source of learning and development*. Englewood Cliffs, NJ: Prentice-Hall.

Kommers, P., & Mizzoguchi, R. (2000). Intelligent systems/tools in training and lifelong learning. *Journal of Interactive Learning Research, 11*(3/4), 259-264.

Kovačić, Z., & Green, J. (2004). Are all learners created equal? A quantitative analysis of academic performance in a distance tertiary institution. *Journal of Issues in Informing Science and Information Technology, 1*, 965-976.

Magoulas, G., Papanikolaou, K., & Grigoriadou, M. (2003). Adaptive Web-based learning: Accommodating individual differences through system's adaptation. *British Journal of Educational Technology, 34*(4), 1-19.

McCarthy, B. (1990). Using the 4MAT system to bring learning styles to schools. *Educational Leadership, 48*(2), 31-37.

Montgomery, S. M., & Groat, L. N. (1998). Student learning styles and their implications for teaching. *CRLT Occasional Papers, No. 10*. The University of Michigan, The Center for Research on Learning and Teaching.

Papanikolaou, K. A., & Grigoriadou, M. (2004). Accommodating learning style characteristics in adaptive educational hypermedia systems. In G. D. Magoulas, & S. Y. Chen (Eds.), *Individual Differences in Adaptive Hypermedia. Proceedings of the Adaptive Hypermedia 2004 Workshop*, London (pp. 1-10).

Papanikolaou, K. A., Grigoriadou, M., Kornilakis, H., & Magoulas, G. D. (2003). Personalizing the interaction in a Web-based educational hypermedia system: The case of INSPIRE. *User-Modeling and User-Adapted Interaction, 13*(3), 213-267.

Paramythis, A., & Loidl, S. R. (2004). Adaptive learning environments and eLearning standards. *Electronic Journal on e-Learning, 2*(1), 181-194.

Peña, C., Narzo, J., & de la Rosa, J. (2002). Intelligent agents in a teaching and learning environment on the Web. In *Proceedings of the IEEE International Conference on Advanced Learning Technologies (ICALT 2002)*, Kazan, Russia.

Riding, R., & Cheema, I. (1991). Cognitive styles: An overview and integration. *Educational Psychology, 11*(3-4), 193-216.

Sampson, D., & Karagiannidis, C. (2002). Accommodating learning styles in adaptation logics for personalised learning systems. In *Proceedings of the World Conference on Educational Multimedia, Hypermedia and Tele-communications (ED-MEDIA 02)*, Denver, CO.

Shute, V., & Towle, B. (2003). Adaptive eLearning. *Educational Psychologist, 38*(2), 105-114.

Smith, L., & Renzulli, J. (1984). Learning style preference: A practical approach for classroom teachers. *Theory into Practice, 23*(1), 45-50.

Specth, M., & Oppermann, R. (1998). ACE: Adaptive courseware environment. *The New Review of Hypermedia and Multimedia, 4*, 141-161.

Stash, N., Cristea, A., & De Bra, P. (2004). Authoring of learning styles in adaptive hypermedia: Problems and solutions. In *Proceedings of the WWW 2004 Conference*, New York (pp. 114-123).

Stash, N., & De Bra, P. (2004). Incorporating cognitive styles in AHA! (The adaptive hypermedia architecture). In *Proceedings of the IASTED International Conference Web-Based Education*, Innsbruck, Austria (pp. 378-383).

Stern, M. K., & Woolf, B. P. (2000). Adaptive content in an online lecture system. In P. Brusilovsky, O. Stock, & C. Strapparava. (Eds.), *Adaptive hypermedia and adaptive Web-based systems: Lecture notes in computer science, 1892* (pp. 227-238). Berlin: Springer-Verlag.

Thomas, L., Ratcliffe, M., Woodbury, J., & Jarman, E. (2002). Learning styles and performance in the introductory programming sequence. *SIGCSE Bulletin, 34*(1), 33-37.

Triantafillou, E., Demetriadis, S., & Pomportsis, A. (2002). Adaptive hypermedia and cognitive styles: Can performance be influenced? In *Proceedings of the 9th Panhellenic Conference in Informatics*, Thessaloniki, Greece (pp. 510-518).

Triantafillou, E., Pomportsis, A., & Georgiadou, E. (2002). AES-CS: Adaptive educational system based on cognitive styles. In *Workshop on Adaptive Systems for Web-based Education*, Málaga, Spain.

Weibelzahl, S. (2003). *Evaluation of adaptive systems*. Doctoral dissertation, University of Trier, Germany.

Weibelzahl, S., & Weber, G. (2001). A database of empirical evaluations of adaptive systems. In R. Klinkenberg, S. Rüping, A. Fick, N. Henze, C. Herzog, R. Molitor, & O. Schröder (Eds.), *Proceedings of Workshop Lernen - Lehren - Wissen - Adaptivität (LLWA 01)*, University of Dortmund (Research Report in Computer Science Nr. 763; pp. 302-306).

Witkin, H. A., Moore, C. A., Goodenough, D. R., & Cox, P. (1977). Field-dependent and field-independent cognitive styles and their educational implications. *Review of Educational Research, 47*(1), 1-64.

Wolf, C. (2002). iWeaver: Towards an interactive Web-based adaptive learning environment to address individual learning styles. In *Proceedings of Interactive Computer Aided Learning Workshop*, Villach, Austria.

Wolf, C. (2003). iWeaver: Towards 'learning style'-based e-Learning in computer science education. In *5th Australasian Computing Education Conference (ACE 2003)*, Adelaide, South Australia, Australia.

Wu, H. (2002). *A reference architecture for adaptive hypermedia applications*. SIKS Dissertation Series No. 2002-13. Eindhoven: Technische Universiteit Eindhoven.

Zukerman, I., & Albrecht D. W. (2001). Predictive statistical models for user modeling. *User Modeling and User-Adapted Interaction, 11*(1-2), 5-18.

Zywno, M. S., & Waalen, J. K. (2002). The effect of individual learning styles on student outcomes in technology-enabled education. *Global Journal of Engineering Education, 6*(1), 35-44.

Chapter XI

From the Monitoring of the Teaching-Learning Process to Didactics' Transparency

Antonio Cartelli
University of Cassino, Italy

Abstract

The chapter starts with a short introduction on students' assessment and school evaluation and the great changes investing them in last decades. Soon after the same topics are deeply analyzed with respect to results coming from educational research and to the introduction and use of ICT; as a consequence the limits of the partial application of ICT and information management to separated educational fields emerge. From the above remarks arises the author hypothesis of a paradigmatic change in education management and the consequent need for a deeper use of ICT and information systems in the management of educational data; contextually it is explained how the above change can lead to didactics' transparency in teaching-learning processes.

Introduction

The main concern of this chapter is the analysis of assessment and evaluation strategies and processes in education, the changes in their meaning and function cropping up with the time, and the problems that educational research recently evidenced in this field, mostly due to ICT.

The changes inducted in school systems during last century and especially mass education, firstly introduced the need for students' analytical assessment; there were, in fact, well established educational models students had to conform to. The measure of the student's identification with a given behavioral/"well performing" ideal model was expressed by the scores that teachers periodically and finally (at the end of predetermined school periods like semesters or the whole school year) assigned to their students.

Until the first half of the 20th century students' assessment was mostly made of teachers' judgments, which were absolute and independent from the evaluation of teaching and any other didactical aspect. In the second half of the century, the need for an objective assessment, free from teacher's environmental/personal conditioning, clearly emerged; curricular programming, under the perspective of the formalization of teaching-learning process and the influence of the cognitive educational paradigm, guided teaching planning and evolution and led to a separation between the student's assessment and the teaching process evaluation. The introduction of cognitive, sense-motor, and affective taxonomies (Mialaret, 1999) made the above division easier, both for the clear definition of the steps teaching process had to be based on (analysis of prerequisites, planning and carrying out of teaching action, assessment, feedback), and for the introduction of the cyclicity in that process, by means of the feedback from students' assessment and teaching evaluation (which had to produce new elements for further teaching actions) (Nicholls & Nicholls, 1983). As a consequence, very analytical instruments for students' knowledge and skills assessment were developed and teaching evaluation tools, in terms of correspondence between teachers' planned work and what they really did in the classroom, became more and more common.

During last two or three decades, at least in Europe, where many countries experimented school reforms, the introduction of organizations' theory in education led to the evaluation of single institutions and whole school systems. The above change was mostly based on the administrative decentralization and on the assignment to schools of administrative and didactical autonomy (Indire, 2005). Main ideas supporting administrative decentralization can be summarized in the following statements:

1. Decentralization produces better efficacy in problem solving, both in the finding of students' needs and in the management of resources.

2. Citizens and administration can easier cooperate due to their closeness.

3. School system organization can more easily adapt to local and regional peculiarities.

The administrative decentralization brought with itself the interest for more formal and systemic school evaluation strategies and gave rise to nation wide evaluation, inspection, and superintendence systems.

In the meanwhile, different elements intervened in modifying the meaning and the influence of assessment and evaluation procedures in education and some among them are reported below:

1. The discovery of wrong ideas and mental schemes in students' and, more generally, in people's minds, and the experience of their resistance to various teaching strategies.

2. The displacement of the general attention, mostly due to the coming of knowledge society, from the highly specialized knowledge acquisition to the development and improvement of personal operations and resources (e.g., self-guidance, self-investigation, etc.).

3. The results of psycho-pedagogical research on social-constructivism and knowledge construction and evolution in communities.

4. The growth of ICT use in education and the introduction of e-learning strategies in traditional education, which produced new interest for subject analysis in their interaction with new media.

ICT, Students' Assessment, and Teaching-Learning Monitoring

The introduction of the ICT in education intervened on students' assessment procedures and instruments at least in two ways:

1. The finding of adequate assessment/evaluation tools for the different distance education and e-learning contexts.

2. The need for new teaching management procedures and strategies within those contexts.

An explanation which is common to both above statements can be found in the four different kinds of platforms one can meet on the Net:

1.   **Content Management System (CMS):** Mostly devoted to the download of didactical materials (texts, images, movies, etc.).
2.   **Learning Management System (LMS):** Where great attention is devoted to Learning Objects management.
3.   **Computer Based Collaborative Learning Systems (CSCLS):** Which main aim is the construction of communities of learning and the displacement of subjects' actions from teaching-learning contents to developing interactions among community's members.
4.   **Knowledge Management Systems (KMS):** Instruments for the capture, the management, and the sharing of CoPs' (Communities of Practice) knowledge.

In all cases, the lack of physical interaction and the consequent need for different investigation instruments analyzing students behaviors, the students' drop-out in distance education or e-learning courses and the levels of students' performances, led to the introduction of monitoring functions for the teaching-learning process in platforms and systems for distance learning and/or e-learning.

Recent research experiences show how difficult the planning and carrying out of monitoring strategies helping students to overcome the difficulties they meet or in creating alternative assessment instruments can be. In what follows, two special cases are analyzed in a greater detail: the former one concerns the use of a special e-learning platform for helping students in overcoming their computing literacy misconception; the latter one reports the results of a study on the use of e-portfolios.

Students' Wrong Ideas and the Monitoring of Teaching-Learning

It is well known that people often manifest wrong ideas which can be interpreted in at least two different ways (Driver & Erickson, 1983): (a) mental schemes, if only the coherence of people's ideas in the interpretation of phenomena is considered (with no reference to scientific paradigms), or (b) preconceptions or misconceptions (when people's ideas are compared and evaluated with respect to the right scientific paradigms).

Many studies (Cartelli, 2002) carried out all over the world with differently aged people (from students to workers, professionals and teachers) show that:

1.   Almost all disciplinary fields report the presence of wrong ideas.

2.   A lot of strategies and instruments have been proposed until now to help students in overcoming the problems they meet in their study, based or not on IT and ICT strategies, adopting or not constructivist strategies (supported or not by ICT), and a good percentage of success has been measured in those experiences. Nonetheless they were rarely compared with traditional teaching experiences and were never used systematically or adopted on a large scale in education.

3.   Wrong ideas can persist in students' minds also after the above instruments and strategies have been used and the best practices have been adopted.

The work the author made in selecting wrong ideas in CS basic courses, computer programming, and computing literacy courses, the different experiences he planned and carried out with differently aged and skilled students, and the materials he produced and collected during his teaching, led him to hypothesize that a special e-learning platform continuously monitoring the didactic process could make the supervision of wrong ideas evolution easier and help students in the meaningful learning of CS topics (while giving to professors a powerful instrument for the management of their teaching).

The information system the author planned and carried out (Cartelli, 2003) was very similar for its features to an e-learning platform and especially: (1) it had a well structured knowledge-tree of the topics to be taught/learned, (2) special auto-evaluation tests, integrated within the pages of the course (they were planned on the basis of the detected wrong ideas) were available for students, (3) various communication areas implementing virtual environments for teachers/professors, tutors and students could be accessed from the actors of the didactic process, (4) a careful management of students' assessment tests was made available, and (5) two functions for the analysis of students' access to course materials and the use they made of the communication services could be used (the number of students' hits on the pages of the site and the temporal sequence of the pages they browsed could be obtained).

The management of all information in the site was guaranteed from five types of protected accesses: the system administrator, professors, tutors, students, and, at last, didactic researchers and scholars (who could only retrieve the information on the students' access at the course materials).

The system was experimented with two different sets of university students in two different academic years and had positive results as regards the number of students passing ending examinations, there was in fact only a 20% students' loss and more than 65% of them had positive scores.

A careful analysis of the data stored in the database showed on the contrary some limits for the system and the main aim it pursued: (1) at the end of the course, many students still evidenced the presence of misconceptions (more than 43% of the whole population), (2) the amount of data generated by the second set of students (more than 300 subjects) made it very difficult if not impossible to monitor the didactic process by means of the two functions. The main reason for the second difficulty has to be found in the lack of statistical operations in the functions analyzing students' behaviors; they reported in fact absolute values and didn't make any percentage with respect to the whole population.

Students' Assessment and Portfolios

The changes induced by knowledge society on everyday life put the problem of a more efficient evaluation/assessment of the knowledge and skill people have and/or develop while attending courses. Portfolios of competences have been among the best non formal instruments answering to the above needs; they were firstly developed in professional contexts (doctors and engineers adopted them as soon as they appeared), then they spread among teachers and students to alternatively assess their success in educational activities.

Over the last years there has been also a significant increase in the use of online portfolios in primary, secondary, tertiary, advanced, and professional education, to combine the benefits of traditional portfolio-based assessment with the paper saving and other benefits of online environments (Cartelli, 2005a). Love and Cooper (2004) while investigating the key factors necessary to design information systems for online portfolio-based assessment in education identify four weaknesses: (1) design brief omitting most of the key educational and administrative issues, and focusing mostly on identifying technical means, (2) "online portfolios" made only of a single essay, a project report, or a term paper presented as a Web-based electronic facsimile of a conventional document, (3) designs for online portfolio assessment systems based on an over-narrow view of value distribution that does not take all stakeholders into account, and (4) designing of online portfolio assessment systems not well integrated with overall course design processes.

In other words the authors found that online portfolio systems fell significantly short of their potential, and, in many cases, were inferior to conventional portfolio assessment and other more traditional assessment approaches. They suggested an alternative approach to designing online portfolio assessment systems which primary focus was the creation and distribution of benefits and value to all stakeholders. The main points of this alternative approach are:

1.   The identification of the nature and characteristics of the educational and institutional contexts for which the online portfolio assessment systems is designed (and evaluated).

2.   The identification of potential benefits and increase in value for all stakeholders.

3.   The development of heuristics for prioritizing value distributions.

4.   The development of an online system through the use of best practices in course design, the fulfillment of the requirements of the course criteria, the integration of the designing of the online portfolio system with the broader course design processes, and the focus on process automation to create and distribute increased value to all stakeholders.

ICT and Evaluation of Educational Systems

As already stated in the introduction, organizations' theory strongly contributed in the carrying out of the school system decentralization and introduced many innovation elements in the management of school processes. The concept of system evaluation is one of the most relevant innovations in the process described above. It has to be identified with the governance of situations/ organizations (i.e., the improvement of the system/process behavior for the hitting of predefined targets, continuously modified by a feedback process).

Different models for the evaluation of educational systems/institutions have been developed and all of them assign a great role to self-evaluation. Among the most interesting ones we have the following examples:

1.   One model is based on a central staff, planning and carrying out instruments and procedures for school self-analysis, and on the synergy between inner and outer evaluation of school data. The main target of this model is the global organizational diagnosis of the school with respect to the goals of its educational project.

2.   The second model is based on the outer evaluation of the school by means of simple and syncretic indices, to be used for diachronic and synchronic school/system evaluation. For its use to be effective a data base for school/ system memory has to be adopted; the creation/comparison of historical series of data is then made possible.

3.   The third model is based on the peer review strategy; for its use an external pool of observers and a shared checklist must be adopted. In such a way outer and inner subjects can focus on the evaluation of checklist items (they must be known to all the subjects before the starting of the evaluation process).

4.   The fourth model monitors both organizational and pedagogical-curricular features of the institution by means of an inner group of analysis and an outer set of instruments (checklist and questionnaires developed by an external agency).

Many pedagogists, at different times, recently suggested further elements for the school self-analysis:

1.   B. Vertecchi (1993) proposed the use of special indices numerically representing most important features of education, among which must be remembered: the development of students' curricula and the quality of learning.

2.   L. Guasti (2000) suggested the introduction of the evaluation of learning results, among which teachers (who must conform to behavioral general criteria) and teaching results.

3.   G. Domenici (2000) proposed the adoption of modular didactics as a strategy for the continuous monitoring of teaching-learning processes.

On a more general basis, many indices were developed for a better definition of evaluation/self-evaluation processes. Among them, the ones for the measure of performance, user satisfaction, additional value, frequency, and school success must be remembered (OCSE-CERI, 1996).

In regards to the use of ICT in school/system evaluation, most of the interventions have been devoted to the creation of Web sites for publicizing studies and results of researches nation widely, notwithstanding E. Liikanen's suggestions on e-government (2003). He suggested, in fact, a deeper use of ICT for the development of real e-democracy.

In the University, at least in Italy, the concomitance of various factors, not only due to the introduction of e-learning in advanced education, led to a more systematic use of ICT and especially of the Web. In what follows, the experience the author made in the Faculty of Humanities of his university is reported.

Italian University Reform and the Experience of the Faculty of Humanities at the University of Cassino

In 1999, Italian University had been reformed to overcome the difficulties and delays marking this specific segment of advanced education.

Main features of the university renovation were:

1. The creation of two separated study periods: a former triennium letting students graduate and a latter and subsequent biennium leading students to a special degree.

2. The introduction of the educational credit as a special unit for the measure of teaching-learning activities (each university credit is equivalent to 25 hours of student's work, including lecture, study, exercise, laboratory, etc.).

3. The introduction of absolute criteria for the analysis and evaluation of research and teaching and the correlation of the systemic evaluation of every academic institution and its economical resources.

Even if the above changes only partially describe the innovation involving the university, they are at the basis of an exponential growth of information production within academic institutions. Furthermore, the need for the efficient control, approval, storing and spreading of information, and the need for the increase in the speed of their circulation, forced universities to find newer and more appropriate instruments. For the above reasons the Web will become the cheaper, faster, and more efficient way for the spreading of information among students, teachers and all people working in the academy; furthermore, most parts of traditional university Web sites soon transformed in real portals.

In the faculty of Humanities at the University of Cassino, as soon as the law introduced the new regulations, the council decided to adopt them and converted former courses in the new ones; at that date there was no clear perspective of the commitment for all professors. Main steps of the reform application were (Cartelli, 2004):

1. In the academic year 2000/2001, the new organization of teaching started and the two regulations superposed each other.

2. In the academic year 2001/2002, new professionals (one didactics' manager for each course in the faculty) were engaged to help the transition from the old course organization to the new one.

3. In the academic year 2002/2003, on the basis of the author experiences on ICT and its introduction in education, the council approved the creation of "Faculty center for online teaching," with the main aim of helping teachers in introducing ICT in traditional teaching.

4. In 2004 the need for faster and more efficient information spreading within the faculty led to the attribution of new tasks to the faculty center which name become "Faculty center for ICT and online teaching." A task force, made by didactics' managers and the author, was involved in a restyling of the Web site and in the training of the same managers to let them autonomously update all Web pages containing information concerning courses' regulations, disciplines, teachers, lessons, classrooms, examinations and students' careers.

The above effort produced a generalized increase in students' satisfaction for more efficient communication services and less time consuming at offices' windows. The analysis of attained results, in term of students of educational courses who exactly graduated in three years, does not show equally positive results. They are reported in Table 1.

The following remarks must be noted:

1. The introduction of new regulations produced a little increase in the number of students exactly graduating at the end of their courses (in previous regulations, no more than 30-35% of the students generally graduated exactly at the end of their courses).

2. A discrepancy between local and national data must be noted and the national percentage of students exactly graduating at the end of their triennial course is set at 65% of the whole population.

3. It is too early to state if the systematic use of the Web for the increase of communication efficacy produced positive effects on students' performances (and their graduation in rightly three years) and further research is needed.

Table 1. Trend of graduating students in a.a. 2002/2003 and 2003/2004

Matriculation academic year	No. of students graduating in 3 years	% with respect to all matriculated students
2000/2001	89	40%
2001/2002	92	43%

Towards Didactics' Transparency

The experiences reported in the above sections show little positive effects for the introduction of ICT in education, both for the students' assessment and system evaluation.

Those difficulties have in the author's opinion the following reasons:

1. The sectoriality and bias of ICT use (i.e., ICT appears in special and particular educational areas like content/learning management, recovery actions, assessment/evaluation, etc.), but doesn't intervene in a radical change of teaching-learning processes.

2. The subsidiarity of ICT in educational process management, (i.e., ICT use in education is mostly limited to speedier information management more than in its re-organization). The limit of this perspective is mostly due to different theories recently intervening in the planning and carrying out of teaching; they produced a great deal of new information to be managed and shared among various actors, so requiring the help of ICT to avoid systems' collapse (e.g., what happened in Italian University with the application of Organization Theories to course management); but it has to be noted that all happened without the involvement of ICT in processes management.

The above remarks are at the basis of the author's hypothesis of the need for a paradigmatic change in education, (i.e., the planning and accomplishment of information systems making transparent teaching-learning processes and more generally didactics).

With "transparence of didactics" it has to be intended the chance, for all actors involved in the educational process, to access the information concerning themselves, the function they are entrusted of and the connections with other actors and functions of the whole system. More analytically some of the features for the system at the basis of the paradigmatic change can be:

1. Manage students' environmental data (everything influencing students' informal education, e.g., newspaper and magazine reading, TV seeing, extra-school activities, computer use, access to the Internet, etc.).

2. Manage student's participation in school activities and presence at school (i.e., student's absence, later entrance, and/or earlier exit from the school).

3. Manage students' learning styles.

4. Manage students' personalized study programs.

5. Manage students' formal assessment (as derived from structured and non structured tests at school).

6. Manage students' informal assessment (by means of portfolios of assessment and guidance).

7. Manage teachers' planning and carrying out of all school work.

8. Manage Learning Objects (depending on the school level).

9. Build and represent class data by extracting and transforming teachers and students specific data.

10. Manage school data both formally, by means of the description of available structures, educational offer, activities, etc., and statistically, by means of average data computed from students, teachers and classes general data.

11. Let students access their personal data and control them with respect to class and school data (in the respect of privacy and secrecy of personal data).

12. Let families access and manage students data and compare them with other data (in the respect of privacy and secrecy of personal data).

13. Let teachers analyze students' class work and assessment, produce historical series of personal data and statistical data of the whole class, compare those data with the school ones.

14. Let headmasters analyze students, classes and school evolution, in their entirety.

15. Let educational (human science) researchers access students, classes, and school data with a special attention to individual and population behaviors.

16. Let public officers analyze social data both at student class and school level for the planning of recovering intervention.

Figure 1 synthesizes what has been reported until now while giving a snapshot of the system structure and data flow.

The Implementation of the Information System

If the idea of an information system managing educational processes can appear easy and simple to transform into something real; on the contrary, difficulties of various kind must be noted: Why people must adopt such a system? Why people must change well settled procedures and protocols? etc.

The answers to the above questions generally imply two kinds of decisional processes: (a) top-down, where government autonomously decide the adoption

Figure 1. Information system draft and data flow

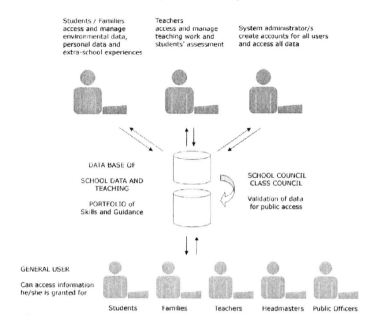

of instruments and strategies, (b) bottom-up, where people agree on the positive effects induced from new instruments and strategies and adopt them while conforming to traditional practices and respecting law prescriptions. The author could only choose the second one and was helped in the implementation of a prototype for the above system from the concomitance of various factors: first of all, Italian School reform, which introduced many elements of innovation in the school with the consequent increment in the information to be managed, the availability of hardware and software making the system easy to carry out and a teachers' sample for the testing of the prototype and its evaluation and amelioration. All above factors are discussed in a greater detail in the sections below.

The Italian School Reform

The reform of Italian school system started with law n. 53, published in 2003. It introduced only two school cycles in the Italian school system: the first one (including both Primary and Junior High Schools—eight years long) and the second one (where only vocational schools—four years long, and Liceos—five years long, can be found). That law found its first application in 2004 with the decree n. 59, concerning the first school cycle, and stated that the new school system had to start with the school year 2004/2005 (involving the first year of the primary school and the first year of the Junior High School).

Main features of the reform are:

1. It is based on the "Educational, cultural, and vocational profile" of the student, (i.e., the set of things he or she must know: discipline and inter-discipline knowledge) and be able to do (operating and vocational skills) at the end of his or her first school cycle, to be the man or woman and the citizen commonly meant in the society (the features of the profile are clearly defined and listed in the enclosure d of decree n. 59).

2. Schools must personalize students' curricula (called study programs), coherently with their educational profiles, by organizing and coordinating teaching work as it emerges from national suggestions, by the acceptance of cultural and educational proposals coming from families and by integrating school activities with the ones made available from local institutions (a part of school time must be devoted to these activities).

3. Teachers are charged of the organization of educational and teaching activities. Among them, a teacher having special training (called tutor-master) must carry out the following tasks: (a) be responsible for the continuous contact with families and environment, (b) have guidance functions for the choice of the activities to be included in the students' personalized study program, (c) coordinate educational and didactical activities, (d) mind the connections with students' families, and (e) mind the documentation of the student's instruction route, with the help of all other teachers.

4. Students' careers are documented in the "portfolio of individual skills." It collects notes coming from teachers, parents, and (eventually) the same student, which are selected among: (a) works describing the best skills of the student (made individually or in a group), (b) significant school tests, (c) remarks on student's learning coming from teachers and families, (d) remarks on special works, (e) examination papers the student, the family, or the school propose for the inclusion in the portfolio (reporting meaningful examples of the student's skill and wish), and (f) synthetics remarks coming from systematic observations, teachers-family meetings, speech with the student and questionnaires, or surveys concerning the student's bents and interests. The portfolio is made of two parts: the former one is devoted to the student's evaluation and assessment, the latter one is devoted to guidance; a portfolio must be compiled and brought up to date from the tutor-master teacher.

As already happened in the past, pros and cons marked the debate on the school reform and teachers and their organizations publicly declared their opposition to the law and its application.

Notwithstanding the opposition of teachers, educators, and some political parties, the government continued in the application of the law and published many other ordinances to make it effective.

It has to be noted that very little work has been done until now from the Ministry of education to spread information on the reform among teachers and to maintain up to date school professionals, so that there is a great amount of teachers asking for a deepen and more concrete information on it.

The Structure of the Information System

Structure and functions of the information system to be used for making the didactics transparent lay on the following elements: (a) hardware and software to be used, (b) the database structure, (c) the different access levels for the users allowed of data management, and (d) the query system. In what follows, each element is described in a greater detail:

1. Today's PCs can have all the features letting them manage the amount of data administered from the information system described above, when they are used as Internet servers, hosting Web and DBMS services; Open Source software like Apache Web server, PostgreSQL relational data base management system (RDBMS), and PHP language can be installed on Internet servers for the creation of dynamic Web sites interfacing with databases and storing all information they receive from the Web forms on the clients.

2. The list of the operations to be managed with the information system is such to imply a great number of tables in its structure. In the prototype version of the system, the author developed the following tables, which looked more relevant: (1) *student*, containing students' main data; (2) *family*, hosting the data of students' families and environmental parameters (it must be updated once a year); (3) *school*, identifying the school and its features (i.e., the formative offering plan or the set of all planned school activities, its main structures, etc.); (4) *teacher*, describing teachers' main features (their ID and password too) and the classes they are assigned to; (5) *stuscho*, linking every student to his or her class and to the corresponding teachers, it also identifies the tutor-master teacher for each student; (6) *stupres*, collecting students' presence at school, their later entry or earlier exit from the school; (7) *learnun*, describing learning units as suggested

from the Ministry of Education, with a special attention to taxonomies; (8) *persunit*, collecting for each student learning units belonging to his or her personal study program (it is not necessarily unique and all students in a class can have the same "study program"); (9) *assess*, containing the students' assessments as they emerge from the documents used to measure the acquisition of cognitive, sense-motor, and affective objectives in the learning units contained in personal study programs (a seven values scale, from null to optimum, for each item in the taxonomy is used); (10) *extra*, is the table for the description of special or extra-school experiences students and/or their families will like to include in the portfolio; it is made of four sections: the first one identifies and describes the experience, the second one evidences its main target and the student's self assessment of the experience, the third one contains remarks and comments of other students involved in that experience (if there are), the fourth one reports the judgment of the manager(s) of the organization accepting the student for the experience (if there are); and (11) *commun*, letting users communicate by special forums and electronic blackboards.

3.   Users accessing the database have different rights and powers: (1) the user with least rights on the data is the one who can only query the system to obtain general information on schools involved in the project and on the evolution of their educational activities (a general user can only access the school POF—*Piano dell'offerta formativa* = Formative Offering Plan and its evolution), (2) at an upper level are the students and their families, who can access special Web areas (by means of their ID and password) with a menu of the allowed operations, (i.e., they can input and modify their general data and all information concerning special or extra-school experiences to be included in the portfolio), can look at the evolution of teaching work, at the carrying out of the student's personal study program, at the student's presence at school and at the student's assessment, (3) just in the same way teachers can manage all data concerning teaching planning and evolution (with the assignment of learning units and personal study programs to the students), students' assessment (it has to be noted that these data become integral part of the portfolio and can be accessed from students and families only after validation from the tutor-master teacher; (i.e., after the definitive approval by the class council), (4) tutor-master, among all teachers, has a special role because validates students' assessment and all data to be included in the portfolio (after the class council), (5) further allowed access to special representation of system data are made for headmaster, researchers and public officers, and (6) at the top of the access pyramid is the system administrator who can do all the operations allowed to teachers and tutor-masters and can access the verified data to modify or to delete them.

4. As already remarked, not all information in the database can be accessed from everyone, (i.e., personal information can be seen only from people who are authorized to access them). Personal data like students' social status and environmental variables, students' study programs, evaluations, and assessments can be accessed only on a statistical basis from educational researchers. General school information, like the formative offering plan (FOP) and its specification in the different classes of the school are available to everyone.

The Teachers' Sample

The structure of the information system and its conformance to the needs of everyday teaching work have been discussed with some teachers recently involved in a guidance project (Cartelli, 2005b) so that a general agreement on its features and way of use has been stated. A prototype for the system was developed and ready for use on January 2005, but it was impossible to test it because its introduction in the school work would have caused a great amount of work to teachers, who already managed their school data with traditional instruments.

During the academic year 2004/2005, the author proposed an after degree course concerning the school reform to the council of the Faculty of Humanities, the procedures to be carried out for its application and the use of the information system. Changes in university regulations concerning the after degree courses delayed the course starting so that its opening session could be made only at the end of April 2005.

Notwithstanding those difficulties, 56 teachers enrolled for the course and are attending lectures (the course is blended and uses an e-learning CMS and CSCLS platform). During the course stage sessions, which will be held in the schools the teachers are employed in, the information system described above will be used for the management of teaching-learning activities.

Conclusion and Future Trends

It is too early to say if the author hypotheses on the paradigmatic change concerning didactics' transparency will hit the target or will fail, but some conclusion can be drawn on the general ideas inspiring the whole project.

A special role has been played in this context from informing science, the discipline that "provides its clientele information in a form, format and schedule

Figure 2. Informing science and educational sciences

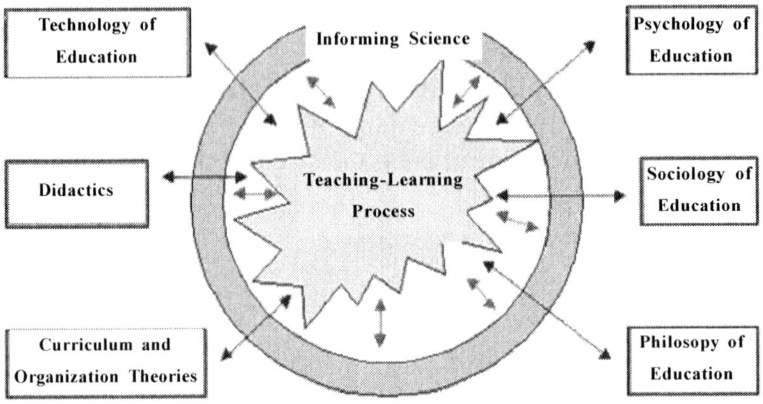

that maximizes its effectiveness" (Cohen, 1999). The clients are now of two kinds: on one hand there are the students, their families, the teachers and the institutions, (i.e., the actors of every educational process; on another hand there are scholars and researchers of the disciplines usually involved in the analysis of the teaching-learning process): Technologies of education, Didactics, Curriculum and Organization Theories, Psychology, Sociology and Philosophy. All clients together can work to help students in reaching better results and obtaining new elements for describing knowledge construction and development in mankind.

As already stated from the author (Cartelli, 2003), the use of information systems for didactics' transparency will lead to a special role for informing science with respect to other human sciences (it is shortly summarized in Figure 2).

Further research will show if ICT use will induce a diagnostic use for information systems in education (until now it has been mostly neglected), or not. In the author opinion the first option will lead all actors involved in educational processes to help students in overcoming their difficulties.

References

Cartelli, A. (2002). Web technologies and sciences epistemologies. In E. Cohen, & E. Boyd (Eds.), *Proceedings of IS + IT Education 2002 International Conference* (pp. 225-238). Retrieved June 10, 2005, from http://

proceedings.informingscience.org/IS2002Proceedings/papers/
Carte203Webte.pdf

Cartelli, A. (2003). Misinforming, misunderstanding, misconceptions: What
informing science can do. In E. Cohen, & E. Boyds (Eds.), *Proceedings
of IS + IT Education 2003 International Conference* (pp. 1259-1273).
Santa Rosa, CA: Informing Science Institute.

Cartelli, A. (2004). *Pedagogia, Didattica e nuove tecnologie.* Cassino, Italy:
U. Sambucci.

Cartelli, A. (2005a). Between tradition and innovation in ICT and teaching. In
C. Howard, P. L. Rogers, J. V. Boettcher, G. A. Berg, L. Justice, & K.
Schenk (Eds.), *Encyclopedia of distance learning* (pp. 159-165). Hershey,
PA: Idea Group Reference.

Cartelli, A. (2005b). Towards an information system making transparent teaching processes and applying informing science to education. *Issues in
Informing Science and Information Technology, 2*(1), 369-381.

Cohen, E. (1999). Reconceptualizing information systems as a field of the
transdiscipline informing science: From ugly duckling to swan. *Journal of
Computing and Information Technology, 7*(3), 213-219. Retrieved December 20, 2004, from http://informingscience.org/WhatIS.htm

Domenici, G. (2000). *Progettare e governare l'autonomia scolastica.* Naples:
Tecnodid.

Driver, R., & Erickson, G. (1983). Theories in action: Some theoretical and
empirical issues in the study of students' conceptual frameworks in
science. *Studies in Science Education, 10*(1), 37-60.

Guasti, L. (2000). *Valutazione degli apprendimenti e didattica.* Milan: Franco
Angeli.

Indire. (2005). *Il decentramento dell'istruzione nei paesi dell'UE.* Retrieved
May 02, 2005, from http://ospitiweb.indire.it/adi/Decentramento/
ueistr_decentro.htm

Liikanen, E. (2003). L'e-Government e l'Unione Europea. *UpGrade, 4*(2), 1-6
(CEPIS online magazine). Retrieved May 02, 2005, from http://
apache.tecnoteca.it/upgradepdf/it-up4-2Liikanen.pdf

Love, T., & Cooper, T. (2004). Designing online information systems for
portfolio-based assessment: Design criteria and heuristics. *Journal of
Information Technology Education, 3*(1), 65-81.

Mialaret, G. (1999). *Il Sapere Pedagogico* (It. trans. by V. A. Baldassarre).
Lecce: Pensa Multimedia.

Nicholls, A., & Nicholls, H. (1983). *Guida pratica all'elaborazione di un
curricolo.* Milan: Feltrinelli.

OCSE-CERI. (1996). *Uno sguardo sull'educazione. Gli indicatori internazionali dell'istruzione*. Rome: Armando.

Vertecchi, B. (1993). *Decisione didattica e valutazione*. Florence: La Nuova Italia.

Section IV

Chapter XII

Teaching Team Competencies

Tony Jewels
Queensland University of Technology, Australia

Rozz Albon
Curtin University of Technology, Malaysia

Abstract

Within institutes of higher education, the incorporation of various types of group work into pedagogies is already widespread, yet many examples fail to embrace a rationale for, or the potential benefits of, multiple contributor environments essential in a knowledge intensive society. We propose that for optimum IT workplace effectiveness, in which principles of knowledge management need to be applied, it is necessary to take into account the competencies of the teams in which individuals work and to explicitly teach team competency skills.

Introduction

Though the importance placed on knowledge is increasingly being recognised, applications of knowledge management principles are still inconsistent, the topic and even its definitions still being widely interpreted (Von Krogh, Ichijo, & Nonaka, 2000). The complexity of problems in our knowledge society requires that problem solving activities be shared across disciplinary, cognitive, geographic, and cultural boundaries (Leonard-Barton, 1995), with Jewels and Underwood, (2004, p. 1) synthesising these and providing a definition of knowledge management as *the collection and processing of disparate knowledge in order to affect mutual performance.*

It is expected that when IT graduates enter the professional workplace their ability to work as a team member will contribute to the team's immediate levels of productivity. Though various types of group work have already been incorporated into higher education pedagogies, many examples fail to embrace the potential benefits' of multiple contributor outputs in knowledge intensive environments. While perhaps being ideal candidates to capitalise on the benefits of knowledge sharing behaviours, higher education has generally not realised its potential. There has, according to Senge (1992), never been a greater need for mastering team learning in organizations.

> *Team learning is vital because teams, not individuals, are the fundamental learning unit in modern organisations* (p. 10) and

> *Until we have some theory of what happens when teams learn (as opposed to individuals in teams learning).... Until there are reliable methods for building teams that can learn together, its occurrence will remain a product of happenstance.* (p. 238)

The intent of this chapter is to provide a rationale for the teaching of team competencies by IT educators and to propose several innovative and successful learning opportunities in which team competencies have been developed.

Knowledge Within Teams

Forty years ago, Drucker (1964) defined knowledge workers as those people with a high degree of formal education and who apply knowledge to work, rather than manual skill or brawn. There is now an increasing awareness that the knowledge that had always been residing tacitly with workers, can be made explicit by capturing and codifying it for the purposes of re-use, transfer, and the creation of new knowledge (Nonaka, 1991).

However, Taylor's scientific management principles (Taylor, 1967) support the notion that it was only management who understand both the processes that workers undertake and the links between all the various processes in the production chain. The workers themselves needed to be instructed on how to perform these tasks more efficiently and were not encouraged to develop more efficient ways of performing their tasks (Grant, 1997). In this type of cultural environment, management hardly felt a need to capture and codify the knowledge of the workers as it was believed that the workers themselves contributed little to the knowledge processes embedded in their work, exemplified by the quotation:

> *I can say without the slightest hesitation that the science of handling pig-iron is so great that the man who is fit to handle pig-iron and is sufficiently phlegmatic and stupid enough to choose this for his occupation is rarely able to comprehend the science of handling pig-iron.* (Dubofsky, 1975 quoting Taylor in Grant, 1997)

There is now, however, according to Grant, an implicit acceptance by management that workers are able to provide worthwhile knowledge regarding their activities. Though much of the current literature discusses the role and importance of the type of work that knowledge workers perform, there is still relatively little literature that contradicts the fundamental scientific management approaches of Taylor that places little value on the knowledge contributions of workers. Unfortunately, these approaches are outdated, having been developed for an industrial era, yet are still being incorporated in pedagogies within our current knowledge society. Team competencies underpin the effectiveness of knowledge workers, thereby creating an imperative for higher education institutions to incorporate them into IT teaching practices. Newer and more innovative approaches are required to enable IT graduates to be effective knowledge workers and producers.

Pedagogy

It would appear that collaborative learning as a group approach as distinct from cooperative learning continues to monopolise the intention of teaching students to learn to work with others, a goal synonymous with team learning. The emergence of newer online learning approaches, such as "intergroup collaboration," still emphasise knowledge access as distinct from knowledge sharing

(Palloff & Pratt, 1999), dependant on the co-production of knowledge, which itself is dependant on particular contexts or environments in which learning is socially situated (Brown, Collins, & Duguid, 1989), (i.e., learning cannot be separated from the situations in which it is to be used). Abstractions, or in many cases, theories, if not grounded in multiple contexts will not transfer well, with Brown et al. (1989) emphasising that, "it is not learning the abstraction, but learning the appropriate circumstances in which to ground the abstraction that is difficult" (p. 19).

Teaching team competencies should extend beyond, for example, merely requesting groups of students to produce a report in which individuals can adopt a jig-saw approach (Biggs, 2003), where each individual places their piece in the final task or puzzle.

The traditional and popular belief is that it is the individuals within organizations, and not the organizations themselves, that learn (Simon, 1976; Weick, 1978). Yet there is now a proliferation of the use of "teams and communities" in the literature according to Ferrán-Urdaneta (1999), with Senge (1992) describing the types of teams that we are discussing: "…where new and expansive patterns of thinking are nurtured, where collective aspiration is set free, and where people are continually learning how to learn together" (p. 3).

Management approaches developed for an industrial era are still being applied in a new environment widely referred to as an "information or knowledge era." Described by Toffler and Toffler (1995) as "third wave" and by Drucker (1993) as "post capitalist society," this era demands new and innovative teaching practices that truly reflect multi-contributor environments in professional practice.

It would appear that in order to promote team competencies, IT educators not only need to incorporate the core tenets of sharing knowledge, but also need to understand the fundamental differences between teams and groups. Group work undoubtedly has a place in learning as one strategy which develops particular skills such as communication and providing avenues to practice small and discrete skills. In contrast, learning using teams is a significant approach to knowledge sharing which harnesses the synergy of collective knowledge.

To advance the teaching of team competencies and its inherent shared knowledge, a conceptual framework is required; one which will embrace the synergy and energy created when individuals aspire to excellence, and are intrinsically motivated to accept challenge in dealing with conflict in order to arrive at new knowledge.

Comparing Group Work with Team Work

Team development includes both enhancing the ability of individuals to contribute to the team, as well as enhancing the ability of the team to function as a team (as distinct from a group of individuals). In effect, the higher level or most productive teams are looking for solutions that no individual could identify, but which a team could. In his use of the term "egoless team," Weinberg (1971) refers to a team in which individuals are able to subordinate their desires to that of the team. This concept of subordination encapsulates the ethos which must underpin the teaching of team competencies in the higher education contexts, aptly termed team-centred learning, as distinguished from teacher-directed or student-centred learning.

In their book *The Wisdom of Teams*, Katzenbach and Smith (1993) describe five levels of group/team and their key characteristics (see Table 1). Much of the multiple contributor work that is currently being conducted within institutes of higher education is not, in reality, team work at all, but reflects the characteristics of the poorest of the five levels of group/team performance described by Katzenbach and Smith (1993), where effective knowledge management practices are unlikely to occur.

We propose that in order to align more with real-world IT professional environments, it is also necessary to take into account team competencies and to explicitly teach how these team competencies can be realised.

In describing effectiveness in project management environments, Frame (1999) discusses levels of competency relating to the individual, team, and organisation.

Table 1. Five types of teams and their characteristics (Katzenbach & Smith, 1993)

Group/team type	Characteristics
Working groups	Members interact primarily to share information, best practices, or perspectives to help each individual perform within their own area of expertise.
Pseudo teams	No interest in shaping a common purpose and interactions detract from each individual's performance without delivering any joint benefit.
Potential teams	Requires more clarity about purpose, goals, or work-products and lacks discipline in approach. Still to establish collective accountability.
Real teams	Small number of people with complementary skills equally committed to a common purpose, goal, and working approach for which they hold themselves mutually accountable.
High performance teams	Meets all the criteria for real teams and has members who are deeply committed to one another's personal growth and success. That commitment usually transcends the team which significantly outperforms all other like teams and reasonable expectations, given its membership.

These levels should be incorporated into the proposed competency framework. Traditionally, higher education predominantly assesses only at an individual level, yet for optimum effectiveness it is necessary to also take into account the competencies of the teams in which those individuals operate.

Although not the focus of this chapter, it is acknowledged that assessment impinges on the learning outcomes for students. Assessment forms part of the learning cycle with students continuing to process information over the duration of the task. However, the depth and kind of learning as an outcome from engaging in any assessment task is related to the nature of the task. If assessment is founded on students completing memory tasks only, then learning is shallow. If assessment is structured around responding to or building case studies, problems and solutions, scenarios and simulations, then learning is deeper, and more meaningful. The latter kinds of assessment foster additional skills, and attitudes not normally acquired in memory only tasks. It would appear that a deep approach is essential to the assessment of team competencies. It would follow that assessment drives the learning, that is, if team competencies are valued, then assessment practices must be structured to give students the opportunities to feel and respond to functioning as a team. Opportunities must be made available to students to acquire and practice team competencies. These in turn must be assessed within the team performance.

Teaching team competencies takes time.

> *It is not possible to wave a magic wand and create a high-performing, self-managed team overnight. A self-managed team needs a culture of lifelong individual and team learning.* (McCann, 2005)

McCann identified four components to team learning as: questioning, valuing diversity, communicating, and learning as an iterative process, which compliment Katzenbach and Smith's (1993) collective accountability, each of which develops over time with practice.

Students learn to be a team by functioning as a team. Designing assessments to include trust and commitment to the welfare of the group is an essential step in teaching team competencies. When there is trust, there will be cohesion and a cohesive team in turn enables students to function productively and effectively. This is not to say there will not be disagreements and debate. There will be, but the outcome will be healthy debates in which members hold the good of the team as their prime concern. The "egoless team" will evolve.

To accommodate the process and the time it takes for the development of team competencies, we suggest that the acquisition of team competencies be included in all years of study in a degree program, beginning with the first year of study. Emerging from the necessary struggles and adaptations of working in teams over an extended period of time should be a culture of team functioning. Implementing assessment to reflect this culture will ensure that teams are built and maintained. When academics also model this same team approach, students have an optimum learning environment in which to learn team competencies.

Team-Centred Learning

It is paradoxical that when referring to team competencies we must also acknowledge the individual competencies of each team member. Although the literature does not clearly identify personal qualities that might contribute towards "teamness," Belbin (1981) has proposed the ideal mix of individuals that would contribute to an effective team, a mix the authors support.

Much of the literature still discusses how leaders of teams can motivate team members into behaviours that will effectively contribute to more effective organisational outcomes (Jay, 1995; Wellins, Byham, & Wilson, 1991), whereas Frame (1999) provides an alternative perspective of team competency, listing the functions carried out by good teams to achieve successful outputs. Although not inferring comprehensiveness, Frame at least provides a starting point in which to teach team competencies to the team members themselves rather than to only team leaders.

Expanding on this output function approach and to further identify characteristics of high performing teams, Gilson, Pratt, Roberts, and Weymes (2000) use an example of a 1995 New Zealand America's Cup syndicate who desired a team with the following characteristics:

- *Works in an environment which encourages every member to make a meaningful contribution*
- *Has a high degree of personal integrity and honesty*
- *Recognises personal goals but not hidden agendas*
- *Continuously monitors and improves its performance*
- *Is fun to be in* (p. 221)

This description is, we believe, exemplar of high-performance teams and one which can be incorporated into teaching team competencies.

IT educators may already be implicitly, mostly unconsciously, engaged as members of teams in addition to their valued and recognised individual roles within higher education environments. In order to teach team competencies, there must first be a recognition of, or a change in their mind set, a concept raised by Senge (1992) to explicitly acknowledge the teams in which they work. For too long universities have rewarded the individual at, what we would claim, the expense of the effectiveness and possible exemplary outcomes of already existing teams—if only they were acknowledged. We propose that the way forward to teach team competencies is first for educators to adopt the principles themselves, and subsequently apply these in their teaching using a team-centred approach. In this way, educators can truly *model* the team competencies they intend to teach, thus accelerating the understanding of all team competencies in the IT student population.

Developing the Mindset of Teams

Whereby the development of team competencies is recommended within a degree program in the university system, the concept can be easily adopted by the secondary system of education. Students can be required to complete assessments in teams instead of groups. They can begin to function within a shared vision and develop the capacity of the team to achieve (Senge, 1992). The types of teams outlined by Katzenbach and Smith (1993) can be applied both vertically and horizontally. For example, teachers in any one year group can begin to develop team competencies by designing assessment task which require students to be a working group (the first level of teams). Their second task could demand they function as a pseudo or potential team. Their final task for the year should enable them to function as a high performance team. This developmental approach provides a pathway of growth as students learn to contribute to, and develop, a shared vision through personal interaction. The synergy emerging from compromisation, arrived through the experience of "creative tension" (Senge, 1992), can be felt by students as they continue to experience assessment in teams over several years.

Alternatively within a secondary school and all school years, assessment tasks in the early secondary years could reflect the team competencies required for working groups, pseudo, and potential teams and the later years reflect real and high performance teams. In this way a stronger culture and a mindset would evolve, making the transition to university smoother with a possible reduction in the struggle and concomitant stress currently experienced by students who work in groups or pseudo teams without the mindset and support from academics who know what teamness really encompasses.

Figure 1. Multi-dimensional team competency teaching model

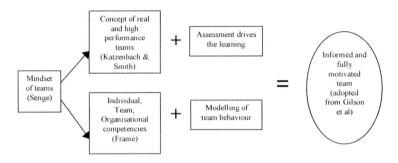

Teaching Team Competency Examples

Teaching team competencies is multi-dimensional and is represented in Figure 1.

To help educate potential IT project managers, the Faculty of Information Technology of one Australian university provides a carefully structured IT project management (ITPM) subject, to provide students with the most appropriate skills and relevant knowledge to prepare them for the workforce, its learning objectives focusing on both project success and the project manager's role in taking responsibility for their projects (Jewels & Bruce, 2003; Jewels & Ford, 2004).

The teaching team responsible for delivering the unit has itself been the recipients of both faculty and university teaching awards for group (team) categories. Usually numbering around eight people, the team comprises of full time academic and administrative university staff, postgraduate students, and sessional (part-time) staff working in project management fields. Over the three years that the unit has been offered, there has yet to be a team member who has willingly given up their position; a testament both of their individual commitment to the goals of the unit and to the "fun" nature of its delivery.

Within the 13-week curriculum for final year IT students a single theme is made explicit by continually referring to a 40-year old quotation: "*A project managers' primary tool is the brainpower of other people who are professional specialists in their own fields*" (Gaddis, 1959).

Most ITPM students will have had earlier experience of group work but many have difficulty in comprehending (and in many cases believing) the statements made by the lecturer in the first week that:

Your most valuable resource in this unit is your fellow students, and

This unit will not be subject to bell-curve marking...you can all get grades of seven (high distinctions)...you are not competing with each other.

In addition to the traditional "hard" skills such as methodologies, processes, and tools, the content of the unit also includes a number of specific team related issues:

- Stakeholder Analysis
- Team Dynamics/Group Conflict
- Conflict Resolution/Personality Type
- Communication Practices
- Organisation Culture
- Knowledge Sharing in Projects

Each week a case incident is drawn from the same single case study used throughout the unit involving a divergent rather than convergent problem (Schumacher, 1977). It requires students to "dig" around and thus construct their own conception of the possible problems and solutions. Students were originally required to address each week's problem on their own, and their individual solutions discussed in a tutorial session where the diversity of the problem solving approaches are made obvious, thus reinforcing the notion that regardless of how well an individual might be able to address an issue, others would be able to provide alternative solutions. More recently, an experiment has been undertaken to allow multiple students to work on weekly problems. Trialing different partners in this manner, allows students to select appropriate partners for this unit's two team assignments, representing 55% of the unit assessment.

Although a formal online discussion forum is available to students in which commonly asked questions are answered by students themselves, this little utilised method is supplemented by informal student discussions.

The teaching team continues to refine its team competency teaching model in terms of modeling its own behaviour, in providing appropriate assessments and in providing team competency content. Unfortunately, there is however still little evidence that students have fully understood the desired learning objectives related to team competency. The ITPM subject is but one unit in a 36-unit course and it might be overly ambitious to expect that any single unit could dramatically influence the mind-sets of students regarding the importance of "teamness."

Summary

A British economist, more than a century ago, said that:

The full importance of an epoch-making idea is often not perceived in the generation in which it is made. ...A new discovery is seldom fully effective for practical purposes until many minor improvements and subsidiary discoveries have gathered themselves around it. (Marshall, 1920)

Although introducing team competency principles into an IT curriculum appears to be a necessity, the ideas implicit within this teaching may not be fully appreciated by students until there are more units embodying the principles into their own subject matter, making it a course core outcome.

This chapter has examined the need for teachers to apply team competency principles to address and accommodate the dynamic, fast paced world in which knowledge management is a feature. A new team-centred pedagogy to team learning has been presented and supported by examples of successful teaching practices. IT educators have a responsibility to their graduates to prepare them to be managers of knowledge in an information knowledge era.

References

Belbin, R. (1981). *Management teams: Why they succeed or fail.* Oxford, UK: Butterworth-Heinemann.

Biggs, J. (2003). *Teaching for quality learning at university* (2nd ed.). Buckingham, UK: Society for Research into Higher Education and Open University Press.

Brown, J. S., Collins, A., & Duguid, P. (1989). Situated cognition and the culture of learning. *Educational Researcher, 18*(1), 32-42.

Drucker, P. F. (1964). The big power of little ideas. *Harvard Business Review, 42*(3), 6-8.

Drucker, P. F. (1993). *Post-capitalist society.* New York: Harper Collins.

Dubofsky, M. (1975). *Industrialism and the American worker.* New York: Crowell.

Ferrán-Urdaneta, C. (1999). *Teams or communities? Organizational structures for knowledge management.* Paper presented at the SIGCPR '99, New Orleans, LA.

Frame, J. D. (1999). *Project management competence.* San Francisco: Jossey-Bass.

Gaddis, P. O. (1959, May-June). The project manager. *Harvard Business Review, 32,* 89-97.

Gilson, C., Pratt, M., Roberts, K., & Weymes, E. (2000). *Peak performance: Business lessons from the world's top sports organizations.* Netley, South Australia: Harper Collins Business.

Grant, R. M. (1997). The knowledge-based view of the firm: Implications for management practice. *Long Range Planning, 30*(3), 450-454.

Jay, R. (1995). *Build a great team.* London: Pitman Publishing.

Jewels, T., & Bruce, C. (2003). *Using a case method approach in an IT project management curriculum: A long look over the shoulder of a practitioner at work.* Paper presented at the Informing Science and IT Education Conference, Pori, Finland.

Jewels, T., & Ford, M. (2004). A single case study approach to teaching: Effects on learning and understanding. *Issues in Informing Science and Information Technology, 1*(1), 359-372.

Jewels, T., & Underwood, A. (2004). The impact of informal networks on knowledge management strategy. In S. Montano (Ed.), *Innovations in knowledge management.* Hershey, PA: Idea Group Publishing.

Katzenbach, J., & Smith, D. (1993). *The wisdom of teams.* Boston: Harvard Business School Press.

Leonard-Barton, D. (1995). *Wellsprings of knowledge: Building and sustaining the sources of innovation.* Boston: Harvard Business School Press.

Marshall, A. (1920). *Principles of economics.* Retrieved August 2, 2002, from http://www.econlib.org/library/Marshall/marP0.html

McCann, D, (2005). *Team learning.* Retrieved March 7, 2005, http://www.tms.com.au/tms12-2c.html

Nonaka, I. (1991). The knowledge-creating company. *Harvard Business Review, 6*(8), 96-104.

Palloff, R. M., & Pratt, K. (1999). *Building learning communities in Cyberspace: Effective strategies for the online classroom.* San Francisco: Jossey-Bass.

Schumacher, E. (1977). *A guide for the perplexed.* New York: Harper & Row.

Senge, P. M. (1992). *The fifth discipline: The art and practice of the learning organization*. Adelaide, Australia: Random House Australia.

Simon, H. A. (1976). *Administrative behaviour: A study of decision making processes in administrative organization* (3rd ed.). New York: Free Press.

Taylor, F. W. (1967). *The principles of scientific management*. New York: Norton.

Toffler, A., & Toffler, H. (1995). *Creating a new civilization: The politics of the third wave*. Atlanta, GA: Turner Publishing.

Von Krogh, G., Ichijo, K., & Nonaka, I. (2000). *Enabling knowledge creation*. New York: Oxford University Press.

Weick, K. E. (1978). *The social psychology of organizing*. Reading, MA: Addison-Wesley.

Weinberg, G. (1971). *The psychology of computer programming*. New York: Van Rostrand Reinhold.

Wellins, R. S., Byham, W. C., & Wilson, A. M. (1991). *Empowered teams: Creating self-directed work groups that improve quality, productivity, and participation*. San Francisco: Jossey-Bass.

Chapter XIII

Cooperative Learning and ICT

Nicoletta Sala
University of Italian Switzerland, Switzerland

Abstract

ICT can promote the cooperative learning that is a teaching strategy where small teams, each composed by students of different levels of ability, use a variety of learning activities to improve their understanding of a subject. Recent studies emphasized that the computer can play a central role in a teaching environment based on cooperative learning. This chapter focuses on an educational experience that analyses 45 high school students' cognitive abilities while they are developing a database that contains their school evaluations and which will be available online. This educational approach used cooperative learning and the "Learning by Doing" environment. The database has been protected with passwords to different levels of priority (e.g., principal, school manager, parents, and students). The project involved three classrooms of the fifth year (students aged 18 to 20) in the Laboratory of System and Techniques of Transmission in a High School in Italy.

Introduction

Information and communication technologies (ICTs) can help the learning environment fortifying the active role of the students in their learning process. In this environment it is possible to combine the constructivist approach and the cooperative learning. Students work together to reach an educational goal and the computers and the information technologies can play a central role in the learning environment. The traditional learning theories are based on a dualism between knowledge and learner. The knowledge exists independently of the learner, and it can be seen as contextualized so that the knowledge can be learned, tested, and applied more or less independently of particular contexts. Teaching is a matter of transmitting this knowledge, learning of receiving it accurately, storing it, and using it appropriately. The use of the ICT to support the learning goes hand in hand with the philosophy of constructivism. The five guiding principles of constructivism are the following (Brooks & Brooks, 1993):

1. Problems must be relevant to the students.
2. Curriculum have to be structured around primary concepts.
3. Students' point of view should be sought and valued.
4. Teachers have to adapt the curriculum to address students' suppositions.
5. Teachers should assess student learning in the context of teaching.

The use of ICT can help the constructivist theory because it is possible to create a "Learning by Doing" environment that also combines the constructivist approach. The computer plays a central role in this environment. An instructional strategy that supports the constructivist approach is cooperative learning (CL) that is a teaching strategy in which small groups, each with students of different levels of ability and use a variety of learning activities to improve their understanding of a subject. CL is not simply a synonym for students working in teams where each member is responsible not only for learning what is taught, but also for helping learn, thus creating an atmosphere of achievement. Cooperative learning techniques:

1. Increase student retention
2. Promote student learning and academic achievement
3. Enhance student satisfaction with their learning experience
4. Help the students develop skills in oral communication

5. Develop students' social skills

6. Help to promote positive race relations

7. Promote student self-esteem

Johnson et al. (1991) suggested the conditions for CL that includes the following five elements:

1. **Positive interdependence:** Each group member's efforts are required and indispensable for group success. The team members have to rely on one another to achieve the goal. If the team members fail to do their part, everyone can suffer consequences.

2. **Individual accountability:** All students in a group are held accountable for doing their share of the work. The group must be accountable for achieving its goals and each member must be accountable for contributing his or her share of the work.

3. **Face-to-face interaction:** Although some members of the group work may be parceled out and done individually, some must be done interactively with group members providing one another using the feedback, challenging one another's conclusions and reasoning, teaching, and encouraging one another. Thus, it is possible to promote each other's success.

4. **Appropriate use of collaborative skills:** The students are helped and encouraged to develop the following social skills—leadership, decision making, trust-building, communication, and conflict management skills.

5. **Group processing:** Team members establish the group goals, periodically control what they are doing well as a team, and they identify the changes that they will make to function more effectively in the future and in a real work environment.

Cooperative learning models are based on the premise that learning is best achieved interactively rather than through a one-way transmission process. In cooperative learning situations there is interdependence among students' goal attainments; students perceive that they can reach their learning goals if and only if the other students in the learning group also reach their goals (Deutsch, 1962; Kibby & Mayes, 1989; Johnson & Johnson, 1994). Cooperative learning can be as simple and informal as pairs working together in a Think-Pair-Share procedure, where students consider a question individually, discuss their ideas with another student to form a consensus answer, and then share their results with the entire class.

Background

The rapid development of ICT technologies introduces novel learning styles which are different from the traditional learning. The learning theories are based on a dualism between knowledge and learner. Knowledge is thought as contextualized so that it can be learned, tested, and applied more or less independently of particular contexts. The teaching is a matter of transmitting this knowledge, learning of receiving it accurately, storing it, and using it appropriately. The use of the ICT to support engaged learning goes hand in hand with the "Learning by Doing" strategy and with the constructivist approach. An instructional strategy that supports the constructivist approach is the Cognitive Flexibility Theory (Spiro & Jehng, 1990; Spiro, Feltovich, Jacobson, & Coulson, 1992). Cognitive Flexibility Theory is called "cognitive flexibility" because it refers to the "flexible" way learners assemble and retrieve knowledge from their brains. Spiro and Jehng (1990, p. 165) affirm: "By cognitive flexibility, we mean the ability to spontaneously restructure one's knowledge, in many ways, in adaptive response to radically changing situational demands...This is a function of both the way knowledge is represented (e.g., along multiple rather single conceptual dimensions) and the processes that operate on those mental representations (e.g., processes of schema assembly rather than intact schema retrieval)." Ideally, adapted to the hypertext learning environment of the World Wide Web and relying on multiple representations of content and diverse case studies, the theory emphasizes the importance of giving learners the opportunity to create their own representations of information so that they can transfer their knowledge and skills beyond their initial learning situation (Scardamalia & Bereiter, 1993). Cognitive Flexibility Theory is best used in designing learning environments that support the use of interactive technologies (e.g., hypertext and hypermedia). Its primary applications have been literary comprehension, history, biology, and medicine. For example, Jonassen, Ambruso, and Olesen (1992) described an application of this theory to the design of a hypertext program on transfusion medicine. The program presented a number of different clinical cases which students had to diagnose and treat using various sources of information available (including advice from experts). The learning environment presented multiple perspectives on the content and also emphasized the construction of knowledge by the learner.

"Learning by Doing" is an approach in the learning where it is possible to gain in the ability to navigate a challenge or problem or even one's life by implementing the learner's own powerful natural process of exploration and discovery. Strategies of "Learning by Doing" are used to encourage learners to apply the knowledge that they have acquired and add to it direct experience. The nature of the activity may be designed by the teacher and the experience may need to be reviewed and analyzed afterwards for learning to take place. An important feature of this approach is the structure devised by the teacher within which learning takes place. Teaching methods can be selected to provide a structure to each stage of the cycle, and to take learners through the appropriate sequence.

To learn developing a project (e.g., creating a hypertext or a hypermedia on a particular subject) is based on collaborative and cooperative learning, which are essential elements of communicative learning within transformational philosophy. Collaborative learning is a philosophy which involves a sharing of authority and responsibility among group members who strive to build consensus and group ownership for the learning. Cooperative learning is a teaching strategy where small teams, each composed by students of different levels of ability, use a variety of learning activities to improve their understanding of a subject. Each member of a team is responsible not only for learning what is taught but also to help the learning, thus creating an atmosphere of achievement.

Johnson et al. (1985) suggested that the use of cooperative learning is useful for classrooms with limited computer access, others emphasize that cooperative learning helps the students to learn with computers, and, at the same time, computers furnish to the students new media to collaborate with others, such as e-mail, networked computers, and sharing of diskettes (Tan, Gallo, Jacobs, & Lee, 1999). Other studies confirm the effectiveness of cooperative learning in higher education (Cooper et al., 1990; Johnson, Johnson, & Smith, 1991; Astin, 1993; Felder & Brent, 1994).

The next paragraph describes a case study where three different samples of high school students (aged 18-20) developed an online database on the collection of their evaluation. They worked using the "Learning by Doing" strategy and in real context and in groups they have cooperated to build their knowledge on hypertext, hypermedia, database, and ASP (Active Server Pages) environment. Thus, their role was active in their learning path.

Cooperative Learning and ICT: A Case Study

The Internet and the World Wide Web can help the school-family communication. The cheapest way to send information to the students' families is through e-mail, but the students' parents could prefer to control their childrens' school evaluations in real time directly at home using their personal computer. This control is possible only if the school organizes a database available online, which contains the students' evaluations. This case study is an example of cooperative database production environment, and the students work towards common goals to produce a database available online. They follow the cooperative learning model where each has a role to assume and contribution to provide for group success. This is an example of computer-supported cooperative learning (CSCL) environment because the students realized a cooperative database. The idea is simple. Class members are organized into small groups after receiving instruction from the teacher. Students become "experts" on a concept, for example, how to realize a relational database, a computer network, and are responsible for teaching it to the other group members, using the Jig Saw method (Aronson, Blaney, Stephan, Sikes, & Snapp, 1978). Groups subdivide a topic and members work together with those from other groups who have the same topic. They then return to their original groups and explain their topic. Cooperative efforts result in participants striving for mutual benefit so that all group members gain from each other's efforts, recognizing that all group members share a common fate, knowing that one's performance is mutually caused by oneself and one's colleagues, and feeling proud and jointly celebrating when a group member is recognized for achievement (Johnson & Johnson, 1994). In this case study, the cooperative process describes "what students are doing" within the educational environment. So, its components must define everything related to the flow of work, such as tasks to be performed, how to know if they are being rightly done, and mechanisms to support the work. A good flow of work definition, in which interdependencies are established, allied with mechanisms to support work in-group, guarantee that cooperation process will be stimulated (Santoro, Borges, & Santos, 1999, 2000).

The Cooperation Model for learning used in this case is shown in Figure 1 (Santoro et al., 2000). The model is based on the objective that one wants to reach, for example, learning a certain concept; and on the process, that is related to the cooperative actions, for example, cooperative design of a database. The objective of the proposal brings all the issues related to group context and culture, which will determine how the process should be implemented in order to stimulate cooperation. It is related to four aspects:

- Previous Knowledge (background knowledge representation of the group)
- Learning Theories (a learning theory should give basis to the learning environment)
- Cooperation Forms (the cooperative way chosen by the group to work)
- Cultural Aspects (the cultural factors, which determine the context on which the group is inserted)

Figure 1. Cooperation Model for learning

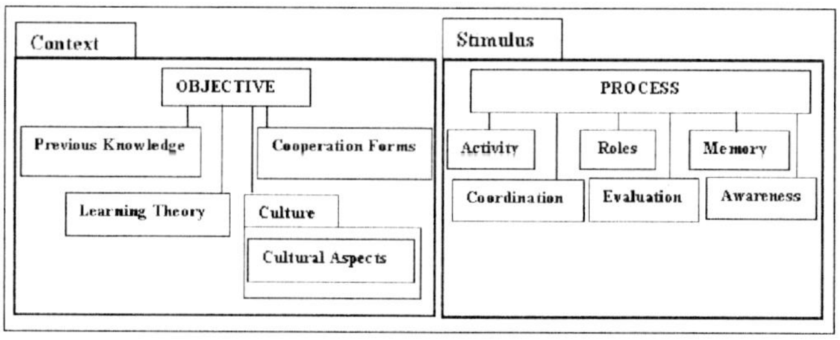

The Process element is related to six issues and is linked to the problem of Stimulus:

- Activity (activities to be developed by the group)
- Roles (functions that group members can assume, which can be different according to process stages; for example, controller of the project or computer graphic expert)
- Memory (storage of everything related to the way activities happen)
- Coordination (related to process controls and help to the learner)
- Evaluation (mechanisms to support the evaluation of learning)
- Awareness (elements responsible to guarantee that people understand and they are conscious of the process)

The characteristics of the case study are shown in Figure 2 (Sala, 2000).

In the school year 2003/2004, a sample composed by 45 students (37 males and eight females, aged 18-20) from three different classrooms (fifth year of the Technical Institute "Cobianchi," Verbania, Italy), worked in 16 groups to realize the database.

In this educational project were established the following educational goals:

- To construct a database in a real work context using the strategy of the cooperative learning
- To use the Internet as archive of information
- To create a client/server application with ASP environment using the WWW

Figure 2. Characteristics of the case study

Project: "Database available online"	Characteristics
Learning environment	Computer-Supported Cooperative Learning (CSCL)
Theory of learning	Constructivist theory
Learning strategy	Learning by doing
Model of cooperation	Project development
Activities	Database development
Domain	Development of the scientific critical thought
Kind of interaction	Face-to-face
Quality of degree of interaction	High
Activities of cooperative work	Coordination of activities (negotiation and decision making, group memory)
Role assignment	Teacher/instructor Student/learner
Implementation/platform	Windows WWW

- To use the "Learning by Doing" as educational strategy and the cooperative learning

The project's characteristics are the following: "To design a database that collects student school evaluations. The database could be available online for different levels of navigation with passwords (e.g., the parents, the administration, the principal, and the teachers)."

Database construction is an analytical task that presents a variety of creative, critical, and complex thinking skills. Students have to decide what information should be included and how to organize the information in the database. Objects, their attributes and their relationships, have to be carefully considered when building a data model. The students then have to look for the information to be captured in the database. The sorting and searching of the database required to answer queries can generate a variety of comparisons and contrasts based on which fields are selected for searching and sorting. These processes require the organization and integration of a domain of knowledge.

The time to complete the project was 40 hours (about a school week). In this period, all teacher activities stopped to develop only this project, which has been divided in three phases.

In phase 1, 16 work groups (each composed by two to three students):

- Discussed together, the database organization (a relational database, shown in Figure 3)

Figure 3. Database organization

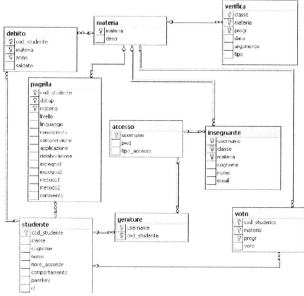

- Established the tables and the "query" to access to the database
- Organized a client/server application

Sometimes adaptations were necessary to promote the participation of a member, in particular to promote the active and equitable participation of all students.

The students discussed and decided the following five users of the database:

- **Parent:** Can access only his or her child's school evaluations
- **Teacher:** Can insert the data of the tests or oral examinations for all his or her students
- **Coordinator:** Controls a classroom and he or she can visualize all information on his or her classroom)
- **Administrative Manager:** For the administrative information on the students and their families
- **Principal:** He or she is the school director that can visualize all classrooms' information
- **Administrator:** Controls the school networks and the database

In phase 2 the students have:

- Researched some information on the Internet on ASP (Active Server Pages)
- Realized the database using cooperative approach
- Created the client/server applications (where client is defined as a requester of services and a server is defined as the provider of services)
- Designed the user interface for the online use of the database

Phase 3 has been dedicated to test the database and to correct it. During the project development, the students put particular care into making the user interface "friendly" by designing:

- The structure of the home page to access to the database online
- The icons, with shape and image which recall the linking function (e.g., a little home recalls the function which permits to go to the "home page")
- The visual interface which involves the choice of minimum point typeface (e.g., Arial 12), the colors, the background, the bottom shape, etc.)

The graphic interface has been thought for an easy navigation to avoid the Conklin's problem "lost in the hyperspace," that is "shipwreck" in the seaside of the information (Conklin, 1987). Elm and Woods (1985) and Oborne (1990) demonstrated that this kind of "shipwreck" is a consequence of the lack of a "clear conception of the relationships within the system." This statement seems to imply the assumption that an easy navigation depends upon the ability on the side of the users to abstract from the system display in order to build a conceptual representation of its architecture.

Inside this educational project were introduced:

- A periodical "time out" that is a break of all activities in the classroom. It is necessary to discuss the students' problems during the project (e.g., the coordination with the components of the group, the interaction between the different groups, the organization of the hypertext).
- A journal of the classroom where the students resume all project activities done in a day (like a "logbook"). It is the "Memory" of the project.

One complex aspect of instruction with cooperative learning is the evaluation and two important questions are:

1.   How should students be evaluated and how should that evaluation be communicated?
2.   How can an evaluation system help modify and refine cooperative learning instructional programs?

These questions guide to design appropriate evaluation methods for cooperative learning activities. To answer the question, (1) some multiple-choice tests were proposed to control the knowledge (e.g., on the ASP, on the database, and on the theory of the computer networks) that the students have attained working in groups. The results of the multiple-choice tests were encouraging because: 66.3% of the students have achieved a good knowledge, which corresponds to the 447 correct answers out of 675 on the technical subjects of the project (e.g., how to create a database). It is important to compare the statistical data of the sample to evaluate the effectiveness of the teaching strategy. Next, Figure 4 shows the histograms about these statistical data.

The effective evaluation of the cooperative learning in inclusive classrooms also focused on both process of the group experience and on the tutor's contribution. For this reason, all students were controlled during their work, observing the social interaction between the group members (e.g., to observe the students' discussions) and how they worked together.

To answer the question, (2) the educational strategy has been organized in two ways. One strategy was to observe the students during their interactions. There are three basic ways students can interact with each other as they learn in a cooperative context. They can compete to see who is "best," they can work

Figure 4. Histograms on the percent of the correct answer

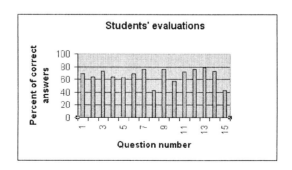

Figure 5. Test to evaluate the teacher's work

Evaluation of the teacher's work	1)	2)	3)	4)
Did the teacher help you on time?	No, with late	Only few times the tutor was on time	Few times the tutor help me in late	The teacher was on time in all occasions
Has been the teacher's helping appropriate?	Never	Few times	Sometimes	On all occasions
Has been the teacher's suggestions exhaustive?	Never	Few times	Sometimes	On all occasions
Has been the project clearly presented?	No, it has not been clearly presented	No, it is has been presented with inaccuracy	Yes, but the presentation had some inaccuracy	Yes, the project has been clearly presented
Has been the teacher's interaction with the groups correct?	No, the teacher never worked with my group	No, because the teacher only sometimes worked with my group	Yes, the teacher interacted with my group periodically.	Yes, the interaction with the teacher has been good

individualistically toward a goal without paying attention to other students, or they can work cooperatively with a vested interest in each other's learning as well as their own.

The results evidenced that the cooperation among students, who celebrated each other's successes, encouraged each other to do homework, and learn to work together regardless of ethnic backgrounds or whether they are male or female, is still rare.

It is important to emphasize that to the question: "Do you like this educational approach?" One hundred percent of the students involved in the project answered "Yes, because I work and I learn at the same time."

The second strategy was to give the students an anonymous test to evaluate the contribution of the teacher that has controlled their works (e.g., the teacher's work strategy, the teacher's interaction with the work groups, and the quality of the teacher's suggestions, as shown in Figure 5).

Students have appreciated the teacher's contribution to the project (only 10% of the students have chosen the columns 1 and 2). The teacher will use the negative data to modify his or her methodology. This feedback is important because all educational process was under control.

It is possibly a question, now: "Is the cooperative approach in the learning different than the traditional educational methods?"

This case study shows that the cooperative is different because inside this approach:

- The educational process is different (there is the presence of a good interaction between students and teachers).

- The students, during the database development, have learned how to use the information technology tools (e.g., create a client/server application, organize a database using real administrative data, use Flash™ for the animation, and to create the home page).

- The role of the teacher is modified (now he or she is a tutor that helps the students to reach the educational goals inside the database development).

- The role of the students is active (they build their knowledge working in a real context).

In particular, active learning involves using knowledge and skills to "generate" a product, such as an essay, a physical artifact, or an information technology product (in this case study a database) which embodies knowledge. This may also involve investigating to create a solution to a problem (Kafai & Resnick, 1996).

Conclusion and Future Trends

The rapid progress in information and communication technology (ICT) brings significant influences as well as a lot of new opportunities in higher education systems. ICT can also modify the traditional education that is based upon a paradigm normally called the "knowledge reproduction model." The students in this paradigm are viewed as passive learners "waiting to be filled" with knowledge. Knowledge is not static, there are multiple sources of knowledge, and students should not be passive learners. Students have to be active in their learning process. Whether it is accepted or not, a fundamental shift is occurring in education as a result of the increasing use of the information and communication technologies (Rath, Rieck, & Wadsworth, 1998). Strange (1995) affirms that this shift is a "cultural revolution" in teaching and learning. Many recent studies demonstrate that cooperative learning provides a variety of educational advantages over more traditional instructional models, both in general and specifically in engineering education. Some researchers, such as Lee and Lehman (1993) as well as Spiro and Jehng (1990), emphasized the active role learners must play in order to learn in hypertext-based learning environments. Learners have to actively interact with the learning environment and contents by browsing, selecting, searching, scanning, and so on. Jonassen (2000) pointed out that when technology is used as a constructivist learning tool, it "can help to transform learning and learners to help them to become independent, self-regulated, life long seekers, and constructors of knowledge" (p. 25).

Tonfoni (2003) states that ICT create interesting multicultural collaborative environments. Cardoso, Pimenta, and Costa Pereira (2003) affirm that the ICT can offer to the teachers several possibilities to develop the traditional teaching model in accordance with the new references for learning, systematized by Hills and Tedford (2003). In the case study, 45 students cooperated developing a database available online that contains the student's evaluations. In this educational project the creativity is present in the active navigation in the Internet to search information and in the creation of the graphics solutions. The "Learning by Doing," comprising the constructivist view of learning, can help to re-define the roles of the ICT in the school. In particular:

- Support of active learning and learning strategies (possibilities of active creations, explorative learning, etc.)
- Insert the interactivity (level of interactivity—reactive, proactive, or mutual concerning the learner and the program)
- Involve the navigation (structure of hypertext/hypermedia)
- Develop attentiveness and motivation (maintaining curiosity, relevant topics, etc.)
- Increase social learning (stimulating discussions between the learners, stimulating to support each other)

Thus, new ICT transforms the learning environments, creating new opportunities for students to design, experiment, collaborate, and express themselves creatively. The future of the world depends on the constructive and competent management of world interdependence as well as interdependence in family, work, community, and societal environments. Students who will dedicate many years in the cooperative learning working cooperatively with students, who vary in ability, ethnicity, gender, and so forth, will be better able to build positively interdependent relationships than students who will have spent many years in a competitive and individualistic learning.

The rapid evolution of information and communication technologies introduces novel learning styles, and cooperative and active learning follows this evolution. The challenge is to study ways to enable "quality" learning through working groups, via the use of information and communications technology (Lim, 2002).

A revolution already exists with the World Wide Web as the primary information and a retrieval tool. New e-learning scenarios can promote different kinds of cooperative and collaborative learning (Gilroy, 2001; Bouras & Tsiatsos, 2002).

The Internet technology also introduces the Web-based education and the distance learning provides a novel learning style where it is necessary to create one unified control model and to enable to reuse of Web-based learning content across multiple environments (Chang, Lin, Shih, & Wang, 2005).

Virtual reality (VR) is another technology that could influence the teaching methods. It permits to create new cooperative environment that involves students in virtual environments. This technology permits to realize new kind of pedagogical software tool for primary school children (Gerval et al., 2002; Popovici et al., 2004). In the architectural education, spaces created in cooperative way by the students using fractal and non-Euclidean geometries will exist and they could be modified with algorithms (Galofaro, 1999). The cooperation in virtual worlds will introduce new sociological problems. The next step of this case study will be to create a virtual reality environment using the "Learning by Doing" strategy and the cooperative learning in a faculty of architecture.

References

Aronson, E., Blaney, N., Stephan, C., Sikes, J., & Snapp, M. (1978). *The jigsaw classroom*. Beverly Hills, CA: Sage Publications

Astin, A. (1993). *What matters in college: Four critical years revisited*. San Francisco: Jossey-Bass.

Bouras, C., & Tsiatsos, T. (2002, August 9-12). Extending the limits of the CVE's to support collaborative e-learning scenarios. In *IEEE International Conference on Advanced Learning Technologies*, Kazan, Russia (pp. 420-424).

Brooks, J. G., & Brooks, M. G. (1993). *In search of understanding: The case for the constructivist classroom*. Alexandria, VA: Association for Supervision and Curriculum Development.

Cardoso, E. L., Pimenta, P., & Costa Pereira, E. (2003, December 3-6). ICT role in higher education development environmental factors. In *Proceedings of the 2nd International Conference on Multimedia and Information & Communication Technologies in Education*, Badajoz, Spain (pp. 148-161).

Chang, W. C., Lin, H. W., Shih, T., & Wang, C. C. (2005, March 28-30). Applying Petri Nets to Model SCORM Learning Sequence Specification in collaborative learning. In *Proceedings of the 19th International Conference on Advanced Information Networking and Applications*, AINA, Taipei, Taiwan.

Conklin, J. (1987). Hypertext: An introduction and survey. *Computers*, *2*(9), 17-41.

Cooper, J., Prescott, S., Cook, L., Smith, L., Mueck, R., & Cuseo, J. (1990). *Cooperative learning and college instruction*. Long Beach: California State University Foundation.

Deutsch, M. (1962). Cooperation and trust: Some theoretical notes. In M. R. Jones (Ed.), *Nebraska symposium on motivation* (pp. 275-319). Lincoln: University of Nebraska Press.

Elm, W. C., & Woods, D. D. (1985). Getting lost: A case study in interface design. In *Proceedings of the Human Factor Society* (pp. 927-931).

Felder, R. M., & Brent, R. (1994). *Cooperative learning in technical courses: Procedures, pitfalls, and payoffs*. (ERIC Document Reproduction Service, ED 377038). Retrieved March 3, 2003, from http://www.ncsu.edu/felder-public/Papers/Coopreport.html

Galofaro, L. (1999). *Digital Eisenman: An office of the electronic era*. Basel, CH: Birkhäuser.

Gerval, J. P., Popovici, M., Ramdani, M., El Kalai, O., Boskoff, V., & Tisseau, J. (2002). Virtual environments for children. In *Proceedings of the International Conference on Computers and Advanced Technology Education (CATE)* (pp. 416-420), Cancun, Mexico.

Gilroy, K. (2001). *Collaborative e-learning: The right approach*. Cambridge, MA: The OTTER Group. Retrieved December 18, 2004, from http://www.ottergroup.com/otter-with-comments/right_approach.html

Hills, G., & Tedford, D. (2003). The education of engineers: The uneasy relationship between engineering, science, and technology. *Global Journal of Engineering Education UICEE, 7*(1), 17-28.

Johnson, D. W., Johnson, R. T., & Smith, K. A. (1991). *Cooperative learning: Increasing college faculty instructional productivity* (ASHE-ERIC Higher Education Report No. 4). George Washington University.

Johnson, D. W., & Johnson R. T. (1994). *Learning together and alone: Cooperative, competitive and individualistic learning*. Boston: Allyn & Bacon.

Johnson, R. T., Johnson D. W., & Stanne, M. B. (1985). Effects of cooperative, competitive, and individualistic goal structures on computer assisted instruction. *Journal of Educational Psychology, 77*(6), 669-677.

Jonassen, D. H., Ambruso, D., & Olesen, J. (1992). Designing hypertext on transfusion medicine using cognitive flexibility theory. *Journal of Educational Multimedia and Hypermedia, 1*(3), 309-322.

Jonassen, D. H. (2000). Transforming learning with technology: Beyond modernism and post-modernism or whoever control the technology creates the reality. *Educational Technology, 40*(2), 21-25.

Kafai, Y. B., & Resnick, M. (1996). Introduction. In Y. B. Kafai, & M. Resnick (Eds.), *Constructionism in practice: Designing, thinking, and learning in a digital world* (pp. 1-8). Mahway, NJ: Lawrence Erlbaum Associates.

Kibby, M. R., & Mayes, J. T. (1989). Towards intelligent hypertext. In Y. B. Lee, & Lehman, J. D. (1993). Instructional cuing in hypermedia: A study with active and passive learners. *Journal of Educational Multimedia and Hypermedia, 2*(1), 25-37.

Lim, D. (2002). *Learning by "doing" and "experiencing": A success story.* Retrieved June 20, 2004, from http://www.uwex.edu/disted/conference/ Resource_library/proceedings/02_41.pdf

McAleese (Ed.). (n.d.). *Hypertext: Theory into practice.* Oxford, UK: Ablex Publ.

Oborne, D. J. (1990). Browsing and navigation through hypertext documents: A review of the human-computer interface issues. *Interactive Multimedia, 1*(1), 3-32.

Popovici, D. M., Gerval, J. P., Chevailier, P., Tisseau, J., Serbanati, L. D., & Gueguen, P. (2004). Educative distributed virtual environment for children. *International Journal of Distance Education Technologies, 2*(4), 18-40.

Rath, A., Rieck, W. A., & Wadsworth, D. (1998). Educator's approaches to multimedia CD-ROM development: Programming processes and curricular concepts. *Journal of Technology and Teacher Education, 6*(2/3), 205-220.

Sala, N. (2000). Multimedia technologies in educational and cognitive processes. In *Proceedings of the Conference in Information System (JCIS 2000)* (Vol. 2, pp. 632-635).

Santoro, F. M., Borges, M. R. S., & Santos, N. (1999). Computer-supported cooperative learning environments: A framework for analysis. In *Proceedings of the World Conference Educational Multimedia, Hypermedia & Telecommunications ED-MEDIA 1999* (pp. 62-67).

Santoro, F. M., Borges, M. R. S., & Santos, N. (2000). Cooperation model for learning: A system of pattern. In *Proceedings of the World Conference Educational Multimedia, Hypermedia & Telecommunications ED-MEDIA 2000* (pp. 978-983).

Scardamalia, M., & Bereiter, C. (1993). Technologies for knowledge-building discourse. *Communications of the ACM, 36*(5), 37-41.

Spiro, R. J., Feltovich, P. J., Jacobson, M. J., & Coulson, R. L. (1992). Cognitive flexibility, constructivism and hypertext: Random access instruction for advanced knowledge acquisition in ill-structured domains. In T. M. Duffy, & D. H. Jonassen (Eds.), *Constructivism and the technology of instruction: A conversation* (pp. 57-76). Hillsdale, NJ: Lawrence Erlbaum Associates.

Spiro, R. J., & Jehng, J. (1990). Cognitive flexibility and hypertext theory and technology for the non-linear and multidimensional travel of complex subject matter. In D. Nix, & R. Spiro (Eds.), *Cognition, education, and multimedia: Exploring ideas in higher technology* (pp. 163-205). Hillsdale, NJ: Lawrence Erlbaum Associates.

Strange, J. H. (1995). A cultural revolution: From books to silver disks. *Metropolitan Universities, 6*(1), 39-51.

Tan, G., Gallo, P. B., Jacobs, G. M., & Lee, C. K. E. (1999). *Using cooperative learning to integrate thinking and information technology in a content-based writing lesson.* Retrieved July 10, 2004, from http://iteslj.org/Techniques/Tan-Cooperative.html

Tonfoni, G. (2003). Cognitive tools for supporting respectful collaboration in multicultural environments: How to envision learning and visualize knowledge. In *Proceedings of the International Conference on Education and Information Systems: Technologies and Applications*, Orlando, FL (489-494).

Chapter XIV

Simulation, Training, and Education Between Theory and Practice

Angela Piu
University of Calabria, Italy

Abstract

This chapter reports the results of a theoretical and practical research work on simulation, both as a teaching strategy that creates a dynamic and experiential situation which enables participants to take on roles in relation to the variables to be tested or modified, and the learning content that the students need to acquire. With reference to the training and educational needs of contemporary society, the theoretical premises underlying simulation are considered and examined in relation to recent findings regarding the process of learning and teaching and the acquisition of knowledge, as well as some recent research results. On the basis of the findings, it appears necessary to reflect on the synergy triggered through simulation. It particularly emphasized the role of simulation in the integration of different skills and types of knowledge, leading to the overcoming of the compartmentalization of knowledge and its fragmentation into discrete subjects or disciplines. Questions remain open regarding the role of ICT in the whole simulation process.

Introduction

The change in the concept of education that emerges from the contemporary pedagogical literature is closely related to a number of social, economic, and cultural factors, as well as the enormous growth of knowledge that has accompanied advances in new technologies. In other words, the way we acquire knowledge has been radically altered by the rapid development of technology and, in particular, by information technology, which facilitates the circulation of ideas and knowledge to every corner of the globe, and the management of information and knowledge (de Kerckhove, 1991). The effect of all this on education can be seen in the new kind of relationship that can be established between the learner and the information to be learned. It is mediated through technologies which are becoming more and more sophisticated and interactive, giving the learner increasing opportunities for immersion; that is to say, opening the way for real involvement and interaction, both physical and intellectual, in virtual worlds (Levy, 1997).

While in the past, education could be viewed, by and large, as the adaptation of the individual to external situations, today we can see the emersion of a concept of education focusing on the subject and his or her awareness in every single aspect: physical, emotional, cognitive, and ethical. The concept is in harmony with the idea that learning abilities are not closed and pre-codified, but depend on the decision of the subject to consciously develop them, with his or her need of finding the right key to understand and interpret a text or situation, and even alter it. This on going relationship, which will continue to change and evolve throughout the learner's lifetime, enables the learner to develop his or her logical capabilities and critical and interpretive faculties but, above all, the ability to make decisions.

In such a scenario, there is an urgent need to pay close and constant attention to the contexts in which education takes place. These strategies, as modalities for the realization of educational processes, become points of reference to the extent that they make it possible for the effective development of all aspects of the personality of each individual allowing him or her to grow in a unique manner. This implies a revision of the following traditional ideas: structure of education, learner and teacher relationships, and even the concept of learning itself, as well as teaching practices. In conclusion, we must challenge and, if necessary, reject traditional ideas about learning, in order to ensure the growth of new approaches to learning that respond, in a more adequate way, to the educational needs of the contemporary world.

Main Themes

Learning Theory: An Ecological Perspective

In order to guide and interpret learning processes, it would be opportune to consider firstly a general theory of learning which takes account of the context, culture, and content without neglecting the individual identity and social and ethical aspects. Neither behaviorist nor cognitive theories are recognized as a reliable guide on which to base a program with a social validity and educationally valuable (Pontecorvo, 1999). The first theory seems to be more suited to the concept of learning which privileges passive learning, in the sense that sees learning as the consolidation of a response which, being part of the organism under observation, is reinforced and thereby "learned" through the appropriate mechanisms used to reinforce the desired outcome. In this way, the role of the environment is underlined and aspects such as the subjective experience of the individual learner are neglected. Cognitive theory, on the other hand, has laid a primary emphasis on the acquisition, manipulation, and the importance of abstract symbols. Both theories seem, therefore, inadequate to describe the dynamics of what actually occurs in the interplay between a subject and the environment. Despite paying lip service to the interaction between the two poles (the individual and the environment), both theories emphasize one of the two poles while excluding the other (Bornfenbrenner, 1986); on some occasions veering toward the external environment, on others, exclusively focusing on the internal mental processes of the individual without any social context consideration. In other words, the learner is totally decontextualized.

The theory of experiential learning, on the other hand, stresses the dynamic nature of the learning process and the reciprocal relationship acting between the individual features, the environmental influences and the behavior in the learning process (to be understood properly they have to be holistic). The individual learner is considered as a dynamic entity, containing as many cognitive elements as affective and motivational ones, acting within the environment but at the same time, changing the environment through a two-way process of reciprocal interaction (Kolb, 1984).

The environment, in this way, is not defined as an objective world, but as it appears and is perceived by the individual. The perception of the environment by each subject depends on the personal experience in a precise and immediate context, and extends outwards to other situations, in which there may never be any direct participation. Above stimuli do have an influence on the culture or subculture—social institutions and so on—the subject is immersed in (Bornfenbrenner, 1986).

There is, in other words, an interdependence between a person and the environment. This being the case, learning can no longer be considered a process whereby the individual is the passive recipient of information, but it is rather a process of construction, an active dialogue between an individual and the environment, which transforms both (Kolb, 1984).

Learning is, therefore, active, constructive, and flexible. It is a cognitive process, which requires the active participation of the learner. There is an interaction between the subject and the context involving not just the intellect but also the emotions and affections. In other words, it is an extremely complex process with a multiplicity of interconnected variables. In order to synthesize the above analysis the variables outlined can roughly be divided into two groups:

- Cognitive, knowledge, and abilities the learner brings to a specific learning task and corresponding strategies used to tackle it.

- Non-properly cognitive attributes having a significant influence on the performance of an individual (i.e., they can be behavioral, affective, and emotional).

Constructive, Active, and Flexible Learning

Recent psychological research concerning the acquisition of knowledge looks at learning as a process of construction, during which new elements are included in the *corpus* already in the learner's possession (Anderson, 1990). Knowledge is, therefore, constructed rather than recorded or merely received, and this building process is influenced by the way in which the existing information is structured.

Previous knowledge, in whatsoever way it is organized, represents the basis and hook for further acquisitions, which are connected with what is already in the long term memory of the individual and is organized into comprehensive units or schemata. These schemata guides the new information in the acquisition process, by checking and re-elaborating what is perceived or learned to give it meaning. They are, in other words, expectation structures that influence the process and products of cognitive activity (Pontecorvo, 1983). The concept of schemata is used to highlight two fundamental psychological elements: dynamics and continuity. The former refers to the dynamic character of knowledge acquisition, which takes place through the use, modification, and re-organization of structures which elaborate experience and are, in turn, influenced by them. The latter concerns the continuity between the old and new information, between what is remembered and what is learned. Ausubel (1995) claims that, in order to determine this continuity, meaningful learning must take place; if this does not occur, the new information once absorbed will remain isolated, that is to say, it has not been grafted successfully onto the body of existing knowledge. Many researchers have stressed the pivotal role played by the individual's cognitive strategies, which select and guide the learning process (Boscolo, 1994).

The strategic connotation of learning is brought out by one of the key concepts used to describe it: cognitive strategy. This term is used to describe the method used to achieve an objective, to oversee the cognitive functions involved in the learning process, such as the codification, storing, and transformation of information. The use of a strategy implies the attempt, which, to a certain extent, is consciously guided to adapt cognitive processes to the task required. The learner, in this sense, is not only the person who has stored a certain amount of knowledge, but is also the person who can recover the information when required; in other words, subjects must adapt their learning to objective, difficulty, requirements, and so on. Brown and Campione (1981) made a distinction between two types of activity, which are often interdependent and give rise together to the so called "meta-cognitive sensitivity"; this basically means that knowledge must be relative to the kind of cognitive elaborations which are appropriate to a given circumstance. The first activity concerns the learner's knowledge regarding his or her own cognitive abilities and the characteristics of the learning situation, and is seen as meta-cognitive. It can be considered static in the sense that once acquired it is always available to the learner. The second refers to knowledge pertaining to self-regulating mechanisms (i.e., the checking processes that the individual uses when engaged in learning or problem solving).

At last, self-regulation is manifested through meta-cognitive abilities or skills which predict the outcome of actions or events, verify the results of an action and coordinate the attempts at learning or problem solving.

Motivation in Learning

During the last decade, learning acquisition research has given increasing emphasis to the reciprocal relationships between cognition, emotion, and behavior. Moreover, school motivation has become an interactive process involving student, teacher, group, or class.

Although articulated in different ways, the theory of intrinsic motivation, that of causal attributions and the theory of auto-efficiency have a number of common characteristics, which take into account the interrelation between individuals and the environment. They seek to explain motivation in terms of a complex process involving cognitive, emotional, and behavioral aspects. The theory of intrinsic motivation has a number of aspects marking the range of human motivations. The theories of attribution and auto-efficiency, on the other hand, explain motivation mainly in terms of cognitive processes, that is to say expectations, aims, intentions, and self perceptions. They attribute more importance to successful behavior without providing any explanation of the content of motivation, or to other typical human reasons leading individuals' actions (Messana, 1999).

According to many researchers, individuals learn more effectively when they have intrinsic reasons for doing so. Consequently, there is no need for external incentives as the learning itself provides the incentive. This "effectance" motivation constitutes a source of energy which gives rise to the kind of behavior through which individuals are able to understand and master their environment. This experience is sufficient on its own to maintain and justify efficient behavior.

A further contribution to the study of intrinsic motivation is offered by those psychologists who, in order to explain human behavior, use concepts such as intention, volition, autonomy, and choice. Many researchers devoted their attention to the concept of auto-determination (i.e., people's ability to conduct their lives according to precise choices). Intrinsic motivation is based here on the need for auto-determination; commitment drives behavior rather than hope of reward or fear of punishment. Individuals, in this sense, feel motivated when they perceive themselves to be in control of their actions—this is called "locus of causality."

Besides uncertainty, curiosity, and the individual's need for self determination, other internal events, such as causal attributions, seem to play an important role. Attributional theory, for example, states that each individual seeks to discover and understand the causes of events and tries to find answers, or, in other words, attributions of causality. This theory assigns an important role to thought, unlike the theory of curiosity in which the crucial dimension is represented by the level of uncertainty produced by various thoughts regardless of their content. Weiner (1986) demonstrated that cognitive reactions to success and failure allow us to predict which behavior is orientated towards success. In order to understand motivation, attributional theory considers thinking essential to distinguish the nature of the causes because each causal dimension produces a number of psychological consequences. The attribution of the result of each cause determines a different perception in every case and influences the expectations of the individual as regards possible future results.

According to the theory of auto-efficiency, on the other hand, the perception of one's own ability and competence plays a central role, as it functions as a factor in motivation and behavior. Expectations of success increase if a person considers him or herself capable of completing the task, and attributes a personal value to success. The individual's perception of his or her own capabilities has a positive (or negative) influence on the person's willingness to participate in an activity, as well as the level of commitment he or she would devote to it. Bandura

(1996), who closely analyzed personal conviction in one's ability to organize and carry out a task, introduces the concept of auto-efficiency. In this concept, motivation is defined as a process through which goal directed behavior is partly initiated and sustained by personal expectations of a successful outcome, partly directed by a sense of efficiency in carrying out the work, and partly controlled by the individual's own evaluation of his or her progress towards the final aim.

Simulation

Results coming from studies on the understanding of the learning process and the difficulty of providing adequate and suitable training and education for the changing requirements of contemporary society, force educational psychologists to carry out experiments to find more open and flexible teaching methods. New strategies aim to develop cognitive areas traditionally neglected by the school curricula, but playing a crucial part in the education of each individual. These new strategies, moreover, can help to overcome the atomization of knowledge, by using different disciplines for communicative and goal related tasks in order to come to a better understanding of the surrounding world. There is the need, in other words, of methodologies able in providing practical, interactive and exploratory teaching strategies, simultaneously combining cognitive and social aspects.

Simulation is a dynamic activity which enables participants to tackle real problems and propose solutions. It is a group activity letting students learn to work together, be guided by the rules of the group and respect each other. It is an excellent vehicle for acquiring and building knowledge (i.e., students can acquire strategies and techniques), the importance of which has been largely neglected in the classical classroom environment. Moreover, by combining the interventions of different disciplines in the execution of simulation tasks, it can help overcome fragmentation of knowledge, which is an increasing danger as subject areas become more specialized. Unlike more traditional teaching methods, simulation activities present students with real and meaningful problems they have to face and solve by cooperating with each other and sharing what they learn with each other. It can develop over time and lead students to a growing awareness of, and confidence with, the world around them in that it encourages them to make connections between their own and different situations (Bornfenbrenner, 1986).

In conclusion, the idea behind a constructive and participatory teaching approach used in simulation is that real learning happens more effectively when it is collaborative and active and when students are presented with meaningful tasks (Piu, 2002).

Construction and Creation of Knowledge in Simulation

The realistic context of a simulation, even if constructed artificially, requires participants to employ all their cognitive and emotive faculties. It provides a source of direct and immediate gratification, enabling the subject to become a protagonist, to play an active role and to recognize the importance and relevance of the undertaken learning process (Meyers & Jones, 1993). Many factors are involved in the process: understanding why there is a need to find out something before investing time and energy in doing so; becoming aware of the usefulness of the knowledge acquired; understanding knowledge as a dynamic process within which no questions can be considered definitively closed, but rather open to modification, adaptation, and, where applicable, verification. Moreover, simulation activities favor the increase in individual autonomy, since the participants are encouraged to view themselves as responsible for their own actions and for their own lives. At last, each person tackles the simulation task by drawing on his or her previous knowledge gained from personal experience and learning in formal and informal contexts. In this situation, two key processes take place: firstly (in order to find answers), the participants have to apply relevant abstract concepts, and secondly, they have to reflect upon their own actions and thoughts. In this way, elements of experience can become integral parts of the abstract conceptual framework, and modify the previous intellectual and emotional background of the individual (Baker, Jensen, & Kolb, 1997).

The didactic value lies, therefore, in the opportunity of activating an ongoing dialogue between the mental processes of analysis and synthesis; it is difficult to separate these two operations, or, what is better, they are complementary and closely interwoven. This interweaving opens the doors to abstraction. It offers the students the chance, within the laboratory of the simulation, to create a concept which is tried out in a concrete situation and later extrapolated and tested in other situations. This putting into practice helps students to better understand the concept and apply it.

The task to be faced in simulation, in fact, requires the students to bring into play the schemata of knowledge already at their disposal and use them either to assimilate new information or, if a cognitive conflict arises, to review and adapt the previous schemata. The student's previous knowledge, however organized, is reinforced or modified in relation to the problem at hand. The student is placed in a situation where a cognitive conflict or a social cognitive conflict is present. Students are then forced to deconstruct their previous ideas and, in order to find a solution, they have to modify and reorganize them on the basis of the challenge set up within the group. From the above experience it can emerge the awareness for the students of having had a false concept and can induce them to seek not only where the lacunae are, but also to examine the logical steps they used to construct that concept. Learners, while finding themselves in the situation where their concepts no longer work, are encouraged to dismantle the conceptual stereotypes and throw out the meaningless phrases, thereby creating a space in which new concepts can emerge and be developed and refined. By starting from known though incomplete elements, the student can gradually build a new awareness, under the guide of the tutor and the support of the peer group.

Nonaka (1997) claims that the creation of knowledge is a spiral process between tacit and explicit knowledge. Tacit knowledge includes all those cognitive elements—schemata, beliefs and points of view, abilities, mental habits—underlying one's perception and understanding of reality. They may come into play in the changed environment created by a simulation exercise. If bits of tacit consciousness remain unrecognized (i.e., if they are taken for granted without being articulated and brought into the light), the simulation may be ineffective. For this reason, it is necessary the identification and revelation of tacit knowledge through the working in the group, so that the group in its entirety learns from the knowledge of each individual and vice versa. Furthermore one has to evaluate whether the uncovering and sharing of tacit knowledge is sufficient, or whether it is necessary to integrate those elements with external knowledge to take the learning process a stage further. Once the integration has been achieved, the process of forming tacit knowledge begins again. What is important is that implicit assumptions are made explicit and articulated, tested and shared, and subsequently reabsorbed into the renewed cognitive map.

Problematic Situation and Cultural Unit

Research has highlighted that the mere acquisition of a competence or skill through the learning process is not sufficiently rooted, unless the learner familiarizes with the new skills, by applying them in different but related contexts; (i.e., new knowledge will be ephemeral without an adequate internal grounding and referencing and a clear idea of its applicability in specific contexts).

The role of problem solving in simulation can help students engage in decision making and come up with solutions which would be difficult to find "off the peg" or from theory alone. In problem solving simulations, subjects can:

- Carry out work on the introduced concepts, checking the reliability of the main elements of the given problem in the situation

- Formulate conjectures and hypotheses on the basis of the information in their possession and forecast, with reasonable accuracy, a series of possible outcomes

- Critically analyze the concepts and relations in the simulation and develop and put forward, at least, two possible courses of action to be taken, with concrete predictions as to their consequences

One of the pay-offs of simulation is that, in favoring an interdisciplinary approach, it helps to overcome the narrow frontiers of single disciplines and discrete categories. In a simulation task different disciplines (e.g., language, mathematics, and science) can and must be brought together for the common goal to provide a solution to real problems. The arid distinction between one topic and another one, with its consequent hierarchical approach to learning tends to privilege some aspects of knowledge while neglecting or ignoring others, as well as to stifle the learner's initiative by rendering mental activity static.

In simulation tasks, on another hand, different topics can integrate, complementing one another, and reinforcing one another in a dialectical manner for the educational, cultural, social and professional benefit of the students. They can provide them with practical skills, such as the ability to make decisions and self reflection and to work in a group in a supportive and creative way. This does not mean that each discipline does not have its own area, concerns, grammar, syntax, lexicon, methodology, and so on, which have to be respected; by bringing different disciplines together to solve real problems, students can incorporate them into their own understanding and appreciate their intrinsic value. In this way, it is possible to bring together different sectors of knowledge, science, and education, even if there is a movement towards further specialization, in order to form a synthesis and create a unitary and humanistic knowledge (Laeng, 2001).

Developing Motivation

Simulation can help develop intrinsic motivation, in particular the desire to learn. Stipek (1996) divides activities helping in developing motivation into three groups: (1) activities of intermediate difficulty and multi-dimensional tasks, (2) new and unexpected situations and simulation of real events, and (3) tasks which require a higher order of thought. Activities of intermediate difficulty and multi-dimensional tasks can provide students with the opportunity of finding satisfaction through the preparation of a finished product. New and unexpected situations and simulations of an event can create suspense as regards the outcome.

Finally, tasks which require a higher order of thought, such as problem solving, allow students to develop a critical and self critical approach and make informed judgment.

Besides developing intrinsic motivation, simulation can provide students with a continuous feedback, not from above, but in the form of the results seen through the eyes of the individual and the group. These results emerge over the long term moving from satisfaction with achieving a particular task to an overall increase in confidence in one's ability. The more one achieves successful results within the simulation group, the greater the overall pay-off. In other words, feedback on the work of the group can sustain and increase self respect, encourage the desire to learn and provide intrinsic motivation to carry out tasks both within the groups and in other learning situations.

This form of self-control, which simulation can build up, leads to greater meta-cognitive sensitivity in that it encourages self analysis. By reflecting on their results, students become more self aware, and therefore more autonomous, and carry forward into the future and the next task an enhanced sense of their own abilities.

Research Experiences

Two main research activities were carried out.

1. An experimental cognitive research project (Piu, 2002) was undertaken in the province of Cosenza on a sample of high school students, as part of the students program, during the academic year 1999/2000. The aim of the project was to establish the students' answer to simulation and especially: to what extent they saw it as a useful learning tool, how much they were involved into group work, to what extent simulation helped their self awareness and self esteem, and so on. Taking into consideration the latest psychological and pedagogical research findings, a questionnaire was drawn up. Under the supervision of a tutor, who was a graduate in Economy, the students were collected in groups (from six to 15 students for each group) and were involved in simulation tasks such as setting up and running business and social enterprises. Young Enterprise Europe was the European umbrella organization. The project was coordinated in Italy by a non-profit foundation called IG students. The students taking part in the experiment were responsible for the election of their peers to various roles such as marketing director managing director, sales manager, personnel manager, and so on. First of all the students set up a company charter and decided on its aims and ethos; in the second phase they decided on a service or product to market and, in the final phase, they determined production costs and times and materials to be used; at last they produced a business plan, which they exposed in local fairs, before competing with other students' simulated business proposals at a European level.

From the enquiry at the end of the experience, it emerged that 44% of the students felt very involved, and 54% fairly involved in the projects in which they worked on. Their commitment is evidenced by their attendance to meetings (it was 97% of the whole sample for the programmed meetings), but it is also worth mentioning that 78% of the interviewees were involved much more the required number of hours. The above results lead to the conclusion that the project had a keen response from IG students; 98% of them felt in fact that the experience was very interesting. Some students were involved in producing goods, others in producing services, but what appealed to everyone was having worked in a group. A special remark is needed for some factors, which many participants cited as important in the survey: 23% mentioned the possibility of combining theory and practice, 20% appreciated the chance of expressing their own way of seeing reality and situations, and 21% found positive the opportunity to address real problems.

At last, 59% of the students considered the experience a way of learning which was much closer to reality than the lessons usually attended at school. As a result, 90% of the interviewees felt they acquired new knowledge and 83% of them still remembered at the end of the experience what they learnt, because the approach offered them the opportunity to integrate new information with pre-existing one.

It can be interesting to observe another significant result: many students stated they would make use of the skills acquired during simulation in the future, even in different contexts from the experienced ones. Probably the above result can be explained with the 85% of students claiming they acquired a great self awareness with respect to their own actions (i.e., they were persuaded they developed skills of anticipation and forecasting). With respect to motivation, on another hand, it emerged that, despite the fact that only 42% of students stated they learnt something and understood their own potential, great part of the students declared their desire to be involved in further initiatives, even if such a commitment could imply no school gain.

2.   A simulation experience was carried out with teachers in primary and junior high school in the "Don Milani" school in Crotone, during the academic year 2002/2003. Unlike the previous enquiry which involved students, in this project the teachers were the participants. Main aim of the experience was to enable teachers to better understand the limitations in the "teacher" role during simulation (i.e., the danger of imposing decisions on the group) and to learn about the students' perspectives, by putting themselves in the students' position. In the course of the experience, simulation exercises were used to create a protected area, in which to experiment and learn communication strategies in complex environments (Fregola, 2003). The

following considerations emerged: simulation is perceived by teachers as an activity encouraging students to carry through an activity until it is completed; the knowledge and decisions taken by the group in terms of expectations, strategies, and working practices needed to be made explicit and incorporated in the practice, so that their importance could be evident to participants; articulation of the choices is a necessary condition for internal communication and, at a later stage, also outside the group. It emerged that group decisions must clearly be defined and agreed by all; finally, the result is in direct proportion to the motivation of the group as a whole and of its individual components. Faced with a structurally complex task, group members understood the inadequacy of working by standing alone and the need of working together and build up a collective awareness.

Conclusion

The results reported in this chapter lead us to state that simulation is an important educational tool. Nevertheless, further research is required not only to confirm and verify what has been found and to extend the findings to other contexts, but also to find out, in a more complete manner, how simulation can be better used in a school environment (i.e., which tasks are most suitable, the right size of group, the need for continuity, the level of supervision and so on). Finally, much work has to be done and many questions still remain open, particularly there is a need for further experiments to confirm the benefits of simulation work across the curriculum for students.

Future Trends

To achieve the aims mentioned above, further research is needed to verify the added value that simulation can offer in terms of developmental methodologies, and, especially, to find the best ways to put theories into practice. In the author opinion the need for practical actions in the following two key areas is evident:

1.   In order to test the relationships between the materials, interaction, motivation, and contextualization as well as students' progress in terms of development of cognitive abilities and skills, there is a need for students' assessment at different stages and at the end of the programs.

2. Simulation can be used for systematic and global evaluation of teaching-learning experiences? Until now two roles can be recognized: (1) process monitoring, to verify the development of single units of teaching and learning, (2) overall evaluation, for the verification of methods, processes, projects and cognitive and behavioral results.

At last the influence of ICT on simulation experiences has to be analyzed.

Two main ways of intervention are hypothesized: (1) ICT use for the monitoring of the processes, (2) ICT use for the creation of special environments leading people involved in the experiments to interact with them, so letting researchers better analyze single elements and factors in the process under observation.

References

Anderson, J. R. (1990). *Cognitive psychology and its implication*. New York: Freeman.

Ausubel, D. P. (1995). *Educazione e processi cognitivi*. Milano: Franco Angeli.

Baker, A. C., Jensen, P. J., & Kolb, D. (1997). In conversation: Transforming experience into learning. *Simulation and Gaming, 28*(1).

Bambrough, P. (1994). *Simulations in English teaching*. Philadelphia: Open University Press.

Bandura, A. (1996). *Il senso dell'autoefficacia*. Trento: Erickson.

Boscolo, P. (1994). Adattabilità e flessibilità nell'apprendimento. In B. Vertecchi (Ed.), *Formazione e curricolo*. Firenze: La Nuova Italia.

Bornfenbrenner, U. (1986). *Ecologia dello sviluppo umano*. Bologna: Il Mulino.

Brown, A. L., & Campione, J. (1981). Inducting flexible thinking: The problem of access. In M. P. Freedam, J. P. Das, & N. O'Connor (Eds), *Intelligence and learning*. New York: Plenum Press.

De Kerckhove, D. (1991). *Brainframes, mente, tecnologia, mercato. Come le tecnologie della comunicazione trasformano la mente umana*. Bologna: Baskerville.

Delors, J. (1998). *Nell'educazione un tesoro*. Roma: Armando.

Ellington, H., Gordon, M., & Fowlie, J. (1998). *Using games & simulations in the classroom.* London: Kogan Page.

Fregola, C. (2003). *Riunioni efficaci a scuola.* Trento: Erickson.

Kolb, D. A. (1984). *Experiential learning: Experience as source of learning and development.* Englewood Cliffs, NJ. Prentice Hall.

Laeng, M. (2001). *Unità della cultura e costruzione di concetti scientifici.* Lecce: Pensa.

Levy, P. (1997). *Il virtuale.* Milano: Raffaello Cortina.

Messana, C. (1999). *Valutazione Formativa e Personalità.* Roma: Carocci.

Meyers, C., & Jones, T. B. (1993). *Promoting active learning.* San Francisco: Jossey-Bass.

Nonaka, I., & Takeuchi, H. (1997). *Creare le dinamiche dell'innovazione.* Milano: Guerini e Associati.

Piu, A. (2002). *Processi formativi e simulazione. Fondamenti teorici e dimensioni operative.* Roma: Monolite.

Pontecorvo, C. (1983). Concettualizzazione e insegnamento. In C. Pontecorvo (Ed.). *Concetti e conoscenza.* Torino: Loescher.

Pontecorvo, C. (1999). *Manuale di psicologia dell'educazione.* Bologna: Il Mulino.

Stipek, D. J. (1996). *La motivazione nell'apprendimento scolastico.* Torino: Sei.

Weiner, B. (1986). *An attributional theory of motivation and emotion.* New York: Springer-Verlag.

Section V

Chapter XV

E-Teaching Scenarios

Manfred Schertler
University of Erlangen-Nuremberg, Germany

Abstract

In this chapter a modern approach to e-teaching scenarios at the university level is introduced that focuses on the teacher. This approach covers content-related and communicational components of an e-education scenario. Content creation and delivery via Internet, as well as teacher-learner communication is shown from the point of view of the teacher. The content related part of an e-teaching scenario uses the well-known variety of computer-assisted training applications. The communication part refers to all aspects of teacher-learner and learner-learner communication within e-teaching scenarios. Based on elementary communication patterns and an easy-to-use technical infrastructure a set of reference communication processes for e-education is created and carried out depending on the chosen teaching method. To prove the technical feasibility of the concept the whole e-teaching process is supported by prototypic software solutions.

Introduction

Many new media technologies create concepts to find new ways of teaching and learning. Nevertheless, these concepts often cannot be implemented in successful educational scenarios (Kerres, 1998). The new technologies that should solve pedagogical problems in a revolutionary way are not developed for use in education from scratch. New technologies are mostly designed for economic or technical settings whereas pedagogical goals cannot be reached equally (Euler, 1999).

Recent research in the field of e-learning primarily deals with learner focused concepts. Tasks, actions, and roles of teachers often are only implicit parts of these concepts. First of all, new teaching and learning technologies meet several different predispositions and attitudes of teachers. Some teachers hope for better instruction using technology. Others fear acceptance, usage, and integration problems. E-education scenarios call for teacher activities that focus on supporting, consulting, and moderating learning processes more than imparting knowledge (Mandl & Reinmann-Rothmeier, 2001). Knowledge transfer in Web-based e-learning scenarios can be conferred almost completely on computer systems. Teachers design and produce the required learning material in advance supported by special authoring systems. But besides knowledge transfer, particularly the communication processes between teachers and students, determine the success of Web-based educational programs at the university level. Most e-learning platforms and applications on the market support at least basic communication functionalities. Nevertheless, the main focus resists on the production and distribution of contents, but well structured and complex content alone cannot reach modern pedagogical goals like soft skills or decision-making abilities. Only by discussion, using, and working with the new acquired knowledge these goals can be accomplished.

In this chapter a teacher focused e-learning approach for higher education scenarios is pinpointed. First we show how learning theory, motivational aspects of didactics, and teacher's attitude influence our concept. Then we define e-teaching scenarios and illustrate the main ideas with two examples. After that we discuss the effects of content-related and communication-related aspects of the concept. Finally we summarize the most important insights and sketch possible further developments.

Background

Learning Theory

In the beginning of computer-based training, the prevailing learning theory was behaviorism. Behaviorism is restricted to observations of learning behavior that is influenced by external forces. Even many modern e-learning programs cannot deny their behaviorist roots as still many computer-assisted training programs are based on behaviorist ideas. Within e-teaching scenarios, behaviorist learning modules help teachers to communicate basic principles of a subject to a target group that is very heterogeneous concerning educational requirements.

In contrast to behaviorism, the cognitivist approaches emphasize internal process of learning that lead to a certain individual behavior. This theory takes a look at information processing within the cognitive structure of students and analyses decision making, implementation, and application of logic. Individual internal processes interfere with a suitable e-teaching strategy.

Different learners have different learning preferences and requirements that different e-teaching strategies have to consider and satisfy. The structure of learning material also adds to teaching success as teachers try to match this structure with the supposed cognitive structure of their students. Examples for this structuring are linear learning path for beginners and complex learning networks for advances students. The presentation and interaction modules of an e-teaching scenario should be designed accordingly.

But constricted cognitive approaches also disobey the complexity of human behavior as they reduce it to information processing. Cognitivism does not feature emotions, situations, or feelings (Kerres, 1998). The constructivist learning theory tries to cope with these shortcomings. It also hopes to solve the problem of inactive knowledge. Knowledge is called inactive when it cannot be used outside the learning context. Teaching by constructivist principles means to guide the students to construct their own knowledge and to be aware of the situational context this construction takes place. A successful learning process depends on individual activity and former experience. Multimedia technology can help to stimulate constructivist learning processes (Issing, 1998).

Motivational Aspects of Didactics

Motivation plays a key role at the beginning of each e-teaching scenario. While a teacher designs and carries out an e-teaching scenario, he or she always has to keep students' motivation on a high level. Curiosity effects lead to high initial motivation but in most cases this level of motivation is difficult to perpetuate (Kerres, 1998).

There are two basic types of learning motivation:

- **Intrinsic motivation:** Learning behavior is founded and motivated by the individual wants of a student. This motivation can only be influenced by the teacher in an indirect way. He needs to connect a Learning Object with possible effects on the life situations of his students.

- **Extrinsic motivation:** As soon as external stimuli come into play, the learning behavior is determined by extrinsic motivation. Extrinsic learning goals cover graduation, certification, securing the own employment, or gathering status symbols. Learning out of extrinsic motivation feels labori-

Figure 1. Teacher attitude

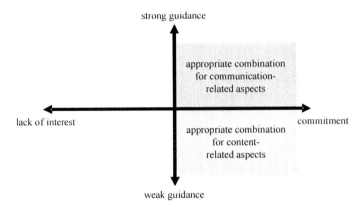

ous and demands more communication with the teacher. To maintain a certain level of extrinsic motivation the teacher has to increase his motivational actions all the time and always is in danger of over-saturation.

One important goal in education is to transfer extrinsic into intrinsic motivation, because intrinsic motivation leads to better learning outcomes.

Teacher's Attitude

A teacher's attitude influences learning success in class. Two dimensions characterize teacher attitude (Döring, 1989):

- **Emotion:** A teacher's attitude toward students referring to emotion can be described on the one hand as appreciation or commitment and on the other hand as disregard or lack of interest.
- **Guidance:** Teachers who lead their classes very strictly are contrary to teachers who allow students to work on their own responsibility.

These two dimensions can specify every teacher's attitude. Figure 1 displays the appropriate combinations for e-teaching scenarios concerning both content-related and communication-related aspects of a scenario.

E-Teaching Scenarios

Definition

E-teaching scenarios help university teachers to apply information and communication technology when it leads to the highest benefit compared to conventional e-learning solutions. In a complex technical environment, teachers need support to successfully change their role from conveying knowledge to accompanying students in their learning processes.

E-teaching scenarios consist of two parts of computer supported teaching:

- A *micro-didactical part* focuses on course contents. It uses the well-known variety of computer based training applications like drill and practice exercises, tutorial applications, and simulations, for example business games.

- A *macro-didactical part* refers to all aspects of teacher-student and student-student communication within e-learning networks. In addition to the need for content students also demand intellectual exchange, individual advice, and personal guidance. Based on elementary communication patterns a set of reference communication processes for distance education is created. A reference communication process suggests which communicative actions the participants of a communication scenario should perform.

Scenarios that emphasize merely the micro-didactical part run the risk of creating inactive knowledge that cannot be used outside the learning context. Only if content from the micro-didactical part of e-teaching scenarios is combined with communication processes of the macro-didactical part in a reasonable way the students are able to construct applicable knowledge on their own.

Figure 2 shows how micro- and macro-didactical elements of e-teaching scenarios work together. Depending on the purpose of each application within the whole e-teaching process the technical solutions support either networking features or represent stand-alone systems.

The skill gap module as well as the course management platform and the learner information system are based on PHP/MySQL technology. As a result, data can easily be distributed between these system modules and access by standard Web browsers is facilitated. Information from a syllabus or from the skill gap module constitutes the basic conditions of an e-teaching scenario. Learners have access

Figure 2. Overview e-teaching scenario and applications

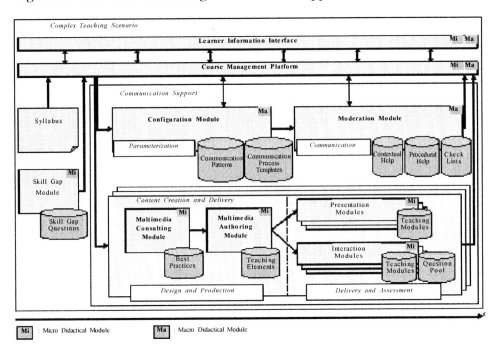

to all the required scenario information using the learner information interface. The communication platform handles all communication acts between learners and teachers. Every communication sequence is prearranged within the configuration module and executed within the moderation module. Both modules are implemented using Java to ensure that teachers and students are not limited to only one technical platform. The only requirement is an up-to-date Java runtime environment.

Content is created using the multimedia consulting and authoring modules which are stand-alone systems running on Windows platforms. Students gain access to the content via presentation and interaction modules both implemented with standard markup languages like HTML and SMIL. A Web browser and the RealPlayer are needed to work with the modules.

Examples

Tele-tutorials at universities usually serve as knowledge distribution scenarios. They are based on a one-to-one relationship between teacher and student. Students work with e-learning software and teachers support them when problems occur. The micro-didactical part features presentation and interaction sections as shown in Figure 3.

Figure 3. Micro-didactical part of a tele-tutorial

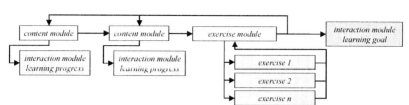

After each content module the student can test his or her learning progress with an interaction module. A comprising exercise at the end of a content domain checks the overall learning success. Another interaction module concludes the tele-tutorial and verifies whether a student has reached the educational objective or not.

Students and teachers communicate with each other using e-mail and several synchronous channels in case of substantial comprehension problems (see Figure 4).

Screen-sharing and shared-application systems enable the teachers to interact even more closely with their tele-students. Misunderstandings can be prevented as both teacher and student look at the same screen content and use the same micro-didactical elements (Schoblick & Schoblick, 2001).

E-teaching scenarios that focus on communication (like tele-case studies) try to give consideration to increasing requirements of the modern professional world (e.g., thinking in networks, personal responsibility, and creativity). Case studies teach students to use their knowledge to cope with real life problems (Kaiser, 1983; Warner, 2003).

A typical *tele-case study* consists of several steps (Bodendorf & Schertler, 2000). First, an overview of the case and the influencing factors is given. Then the case, its major facts and circumstances, and possible questions to be

Figure 4. Macro-didactical part of a tele-tutorial

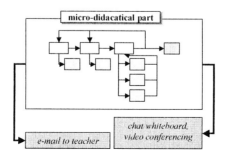

Figure 5. Micro-didactical part of a tele-case study

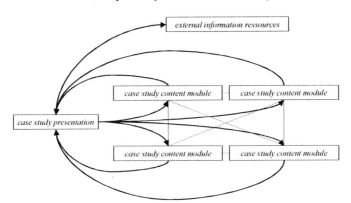

answered by the students are presented. After that students analyze the case information and gather additional information from various sources, for example the Internet. Each student develops a solution for the case. As all students are divided into teams, each team combines the individual solutions of its members and presents the team solution. Finally, all team solutions are discussed among the students and together with the teacher and maybe with a company's representative.

The micro-didactical elements of a tele-case study are shown in Figure 5. As for the different case study phases the micro-didactical part represents the case presentation and background information activities.

Case presentation and background information are supported via discussion forums and e-mail. The individual and team solutions access a further discussion forum. The group solution and final discussion phases utilize more complex and above all synchronous communication channels (see Figure 6). Both phases depend on a lively discussion ambience for which the teachers' moderating skills are vital.

Content-Related Aspects

Presentation Modules

Modern e-courses for knowledge distribution feature a broad variety of content types. Basic elements of these presentation modules are text, picture, and audiovisual items. Hypertexts for example are text only modules; pure anima-

Figure 6. Macro-didactical part of a tele-case study

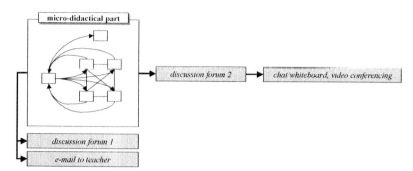

tions consist of only picture elements. Instructional films are an example for the use of nothing but audiovisual elements.

In most e-learning presentations however authors combine different types of media items to create multimedia contents.

Table 1 lists selected examples of multimedia presentation modules.

Narrated slide shows combine the presentation slides of a lecturer with his or her spoken comments. Each slide is synchronized with the according part of the audio file. A lecture on demand (LoD) is characterized as a complete reproduction of a real time lecture event. The basic idea is to provide the students with lecture content at any time and any place. This is done by recording video and audio streams of lectures, editing the recordings, and linking additional teaching resources (slides, annotations, diagrams, animations, questions, exercises, tests, ...) to the lecture video. These teaching resources together with recorded lectures build up the LoD offered to the students (Schertler & Bodendorf, 2003).

Interaction Modules

Interaction modules are included in e-teaching scenarios to supervise the students. From a didactical point of view three different stages of control are applicable:

Table 1. Examples for multimedia presentation modules

Content types	Examples
text elements, picture elements	pictures with textual annotations
text elements, audiovisual elements	educational movie with subtitles
picture elements, audiovisual elements	narrated slide show
text, picture, and audiovisual elements	lecture on demand

- **Learning progress:** Interaction modules that control learning progress, go along with corresponding presentation modules. The whole syllabus is subdivided into different learning objectives and these objectives are broken down into small learning targets. Every interaction module tests a number of learning targets and therefore describes the current learning progress of a student. As soon as a student is able to correctly pass a certain learning progress interaction module, he or she is ready to approach the next part of the syllabus.

- **Learning objectives:** On this stage, interaction modules check whether a whole learning objective is achieved by a student. These interaction modules mark the end of a knowledge distribution process and support the teachers' decision how far a content domain is finalized. In addition to tests on the learning progress stage interaction modules can set up assignments that examine contextual knowledge, evaluation capabilities, and analytical skills as well.

- **Learning success:** At the end of an entire e-teaching scenario the learning success is determined. Learning success regards not only knowledge distribution but also communication-related aspects of e-teaching.

In the following section, two exemplary software applications are presented that support the teacher in designing LoD presentation modules and interaction modules for the first two stages of didactical control.

Software Tools

Tool: Lecture on Demand Authoring System

To produce LoDs in an efficient way, a simple-to-use authoring system has been developed (Schertler, 2002). It features, among other things, import and playback of Real Video files, import of Web-compatible additional multimedia material, on-the-fly synchronization of video and additional material, integration of subtitles, integration of Internet link collections, and integration of meta-data. Figure 7 shows the main window of the authoring system.

The technical solution is based on an XML application and W3C recommendation called synchronized multimedia integration language (SMIL) (W3C, 2004). SMIL can be processed and displayed by standard RealPlayer software. The authoring system uses SMIL to display and synchronize the different media elements within one system environment. Students only need a standard, free of charge RealPlayer as a front-end to control the synchronous presentation of the video and audio streams together with the additional multimedia material

Figure 7. Screenshot lecture on demand authoring system

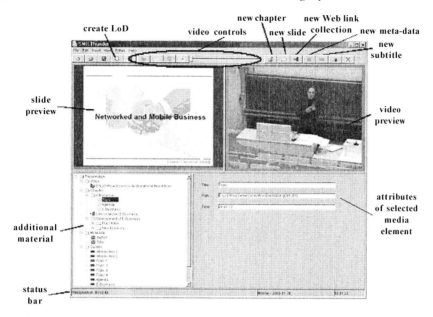

(presentation slides, subtitles, Internet link collections). The video stream is positioned in the upper left corner of the LoD presentation, the presentation slides are displayed on the right. The navigation area with the ordered list of slides (including the control information) is located below the video area. Figure 8 gives an impression of a LoD presentation from the user's view.

Tool: Online Test System

The online test system allows teachers to create and carry out exams via the Internet. Every online test consists of several closed-ended questions that are characterized by their type (for example multiple choice or classification), the level of the learning target (knowledge, comprehension, application, or problem solving), the process time, and the difficulty of the question (easy, medium, or hard). When a teacher wants to create an examination, he selects the desired percentage of each question type, level of learning target and difficulty of the exam as well as the overall process time and the system composes the online test (see Figure 9).

After the teacher has made possible adjustments the test is submitted to the students who answer the questions within a secure network. At the end of the test, the system calculates the number of points reached by each student and marks the exam.

Figure 8. Screenshot SMIL-based LoD presentation

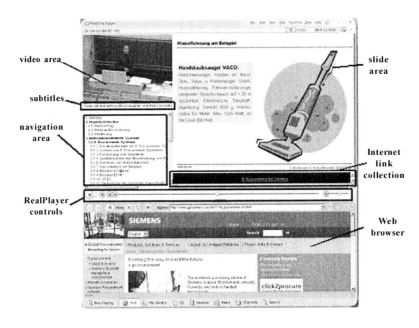

video area

subtitles

navigation area

RealPlayer controls

slide area

Internet link collection

Web browser

Figure 9. Screenshot online test system

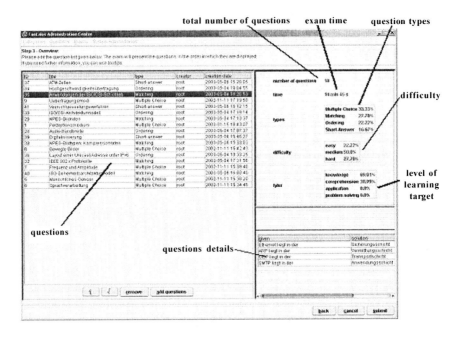

total number of questions   exam time   question types

difficulty

level of learning target

questions

questions details

Communication-Related Aspects

Scheduled Communication

It is a well-known fact that communication plays a major role in successful e-education scenarios (Berge & Collins, 1995). Most of the available e-learning software environments offer at least some kind of communication support. But the focus of e-teaching still is on producing content and distributing course material via the Internet. Alongside well structured and preprocessed content, it is necessary to discuss, apply, and work with new knowledge to build up the competencies that students need to face the challenges of their professional and private life (Salmon, 2001).

Our approach to put emphasis on communication in contrast to the mere conveyance of content is the so called scheduled communication in e-teaching scenarios. Scheduled communication is a concept that is mainly based on a tight time structure (schedule) of an e-teaching process. The term "scheduled" refers to a precise and detailed placement of learning and teaching acts within one e-teaching communication process. The schedule has the objectives to prevent being "lost-in-e-learning," to simplify organization of group learning processes, to carry out communication processes in a more systematic way, and to facilitate allocation of supporting tools with teaching or learning activities.

E-learning scenarios need a tight over-all organization. Disordered communication processes lower learning success and motivation to go on with a course. A schedule of default actions supports target-oriented processes and learning flows.

Communication Processes

A critical success factor for every learning process is the appropriate correlation between communication and educational purpose. A theoretical background to fulfill this task can be found in the media synchronicity theory (Dennis & Valacich, 1999) and the task media fit model (Buder, 2000). Both theories help to overcome missing functionality of existing systems to guide and moderate communication processes (Bodendorf & Schertler, 2004).

Communication process designers concentrate on managing a structured support of learning processes as well as on a purposeful mapping of communication tools. One major goal is to define basic communication processes and to use the definitions to configure communication channels. The teacher or moderator needs to set parameters for each channel according to the current task in order to avoid too restricted or too open communication processes.

In a communication process participants attend partially or completely moderated courses. Courses are based on certain teaching methods and consist of recurring learning phases. As courses can be handled like communication processes these learning phases can be denoted as communication patterns. Each pattern within one process supports a specific task which is characterized by a typical communication situation. To facilitate a certain task each pattern is linked to the communication channels that ensure a worthy exchange and acquisition of knowledge.

Examples

The communication process of a *tele-tutorial* starts with a warm-up phase that is used to clarify the learning objectives (see Figure 10). In order to motivate the students several appealing communication tools like instant messaging clients with smiley support or whiteboards are used. In the next phase the students learn by using presentation and interaction modules and communicate with their teacher to discuss comprehension problems. The corresponding communication pattern is called review. Within a tele-tutorial the review pattern is carried out in a one-to-one relationship between teacher and student using videophony and whiteboard tools. Checklists give hints to create a convenient communication atmosphere. The content distribution and exercise phase ends after a prefixed time. In the last process phase all participants are invited to join a discussion resuming the most important topics of the tutorial outline.

In the first phase of a *tele-case study* communication process students use a chat and a whiteboard tool to check preliminary case aspects with the teacher. During the case presentation a forum is used to post comprehension questions. In case of misdirected forum contribution the teacher ensures the topical affiliation and reassigns the contribution to the correct discussion thread. Another forum is used to exchange and review background information among

Figure 10. E-teaching scenario—Tele-tutorial

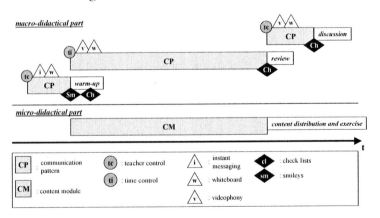

all students. This phase as well as the following one is student controlled, the students define the moment when actions have to be finished. In the structuring, assessment, and decision phase communication tools are used to create individual and team solutions. To enhance synchronous and asynchronous discussions no restrictive moderation functions like floor-control are applied during structuring and assessment. Only bad word and cry filters secure decent communication. A bad-word filter compares each message with a list of forbidden expressions. In case of a bad-word violation the system refuses to send the message. The cry filter blocks words written in capital letters. To keep the discussion topic focused the size of a contribution is limited (e.g., to 200 characters) to prevent individual students from taking over the discussion. A minimum time delay between contributions of one person is set (for example to one minute) so each participant has to wait a few moments before posting again. This prevents users from sending only fragments of messages. These users often try to control a conversation by unnecessarily increasing their number of contributions and segregating other participants. After the decision phase, which is time controlled to force the students to work together properly, the team solutions are presented and discussed, the teacher comments on the solutions, presents real life aspects of the case environment, and sums up the whole case study.

Figure 11 shows both micro- and macro-didactical elements of a tele-case study. The case resources (articles, Internet links, …) are accessible to fulfill information needs until the final decision phase is over.

Figure 11. E-teaching scenario—Tele-case study

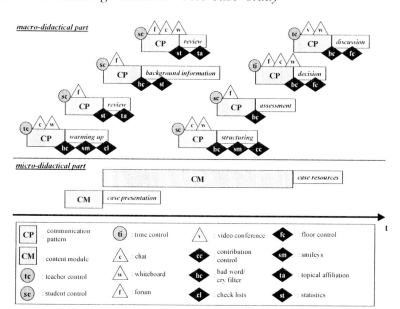

Software Tool: Communication Platform

A technical infrastructure for scheduled communication connects teachers and students. At the beginning of an online course the teacher uses the communication platform to configure the current communication scenario. Scenarios consist of a combination of communication patterns within a communication process. The teacher is able to define new processes or to use predefined templates for a specific course configuration. Each template is assigned to a category (for example general presentation, case studies, management games, project work, and so forth) to be easily detected by an inexperienced teacher.

The following steps define a communication process:

- **Choose communication patterns und define pattern sequence:** The teacher chooses the communication patterns he or she likes to design the communication process with (e.g., warm-up-pattern, presentation pattern, discussion pattern, etc.). The sequential order of the patterns is similar to a workflow definition within a workflow management system.

- **Define attributes of communication patterns:** Each communication pattern has specific characteristics to fulfill its tasks in the over-all communication process. The teacher determines the trigger type, which enables teachers and/or students to switch to the next phase and communication pattern in the process. Possible triggers are teacher control, student control or time control. Additionally, the teacher can compose help texts and work instructions for each pattern. Based on the theoretical background the system also suggests reasonable communication channels for the current pattern.

- **Assign communication channels:** As mentioned before, each pattern comprises suggestions of communication channels that suit the tasks of a pattern best, but the actual decision of assigning a communication channel to a communication pattern is incumbent on the teacher.

- **Define attributes of communication channels:** The selected communication channels are provided with moderation functions and an additional help text from the teacher.

After a communication process is completely defined it is given a convenient name and saved as a template to use and re-use in several courses.

Figure 12 shows a demo screenshot of the user interface of the communication platform.

A menu bar is located on top of the screen. Menu items include login and logoff functions, course and participant information and help options referring to the

Figure 12. Screenshot communication platform

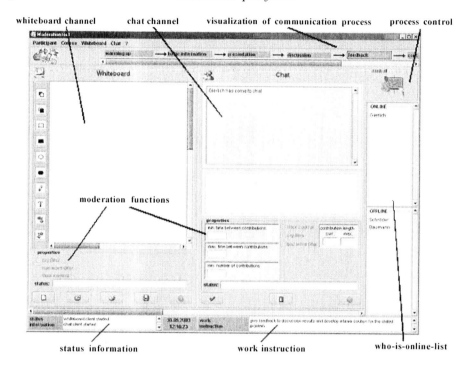

communication channels of the current communication pattern. Beneath the menu bar the communication process of the current course is displayed, the active pattern is highlighted. The major part of the user interface features the automatically displayed communication channels. Figure 12 for example shows a whiteboard combined with a text chat. In the lower part of the screen a status information area and the work instructions are provided. On the right side the control status (learner, teacher, or time control) is displayed. This area fulfills either a mere information task (in case of teacher or time control) or offers a pattern control button to indicate a desired pattern switch. In addition the user interface comprises a who-is-online-list that shows all participants of a course and their online status.

Conclusion

Research activities in the area of Web-based education focus on approaches which put main emphasis on the needs and requirements of students. Teachers face new tasks like consulting, escorting, and moderating within learning processes. In many cases teachers feel overstrained with this change of their professional self-image. As a result teaching outcomes are not as high in quality as they could be. This chapter sketches an approach to point out the teachers' perspectives in e-education processes. E-teaching scenarios support teachers to reveal the full potential of modern educational technology.

Teachers transfer tasks like motivation, knowledge distribution, and learning progress control onto computer-based presentation and interaction modules. These modules are incorporated into communication processes consisting of reusable communication patterns and supported by aligned communication channels. Software tools support every phase of an e-teaching scenario. In addition to the system prototypes presented in this chapter, there is also a skill gap management tool, a multimedia consulting system, and a course management platform have been developed within the scope of this research project (Schertler, 2004).

Future Trends

As the main field of application for this research project has been teaching and learning at universities the e-teaching scenarios and communication processes represent mainly needs and demands of university staff and students. To transfer the research results to other educational environments like primary or high school, one possible future development will be able to create suitable scenario types as well as appropriate communication processes for these environments. Possible scenarios cover teacher-centered classes as well as group or team working.

Another very important aspect for future developments is the involvement of mobile technologies. Knowledge distribution, exercise, and application can reach an even higher level when implemented in mobile e-teaching scenarios. On the one hand mobile devices relieve students from learning attached to a certain place as they can receive information in the form of multimedia streaming content via pocket personal computers or mobile phones. One technical scenario for a mobile streaming application is the so called "lecture to go." Based on the idea of lecture on demand distribution a recorded lecture is stored on a streaming server. A mobile client with player software is used to receive the lecture recordings (see Figure 13).

This scenario is highly useful for students who want to access lecture content independently from time and place. The penetration of the market with pocket personal computers like the one shown in Figure 13 is steadily moving on. Together with mobile networks like WLAN and UMTS high quality mobile streaming is already possible and competes with stationary streaming solutions. Mobile e-teaching scenarios on the other hand enlarge the scope of applicable

Figure 13. Lecture to go

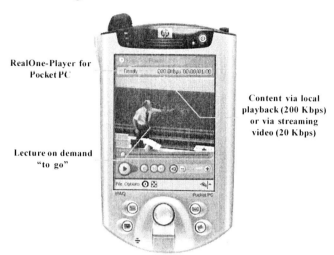

RealOne-Player for
Pocket PC

Content via local
playback (200 Kbps)
or via streaming
video (20 Kbps)

Lecture on demand
"to go"

pedagogical methods. Distributed business games, project work, and case studies not only deepen the students' knowledge but also improve various other skills like team work, communication abilities, and conflict resolution.

Distributed case studies for example benefit from mobile learning in various ways. Students can access vital case information via their mobile device at any time and any place. They can share thoughts and ideas with fellow students who are also equipped with mobile clients. If tutors provide a more dynamic learning environment tasks can be assigned to the students according to their current location.

References

Berge, Z. L., & Collins, M. P. (1995). *Computer-mediated communication and the online classroom*. Cresskill, NJ: Hampton Press.

Bodendorf, F., & Schertler, M. (2000). Media-based cooperative teaching between university and industry. In E. Wagner, & A. Szucs (Eds.), *Research and innovation in open and distance learning, Book of essays 1st (EDEN Research Workshop)*, Prague (pp. 88-90).

Bodendorf, F., & Schertler, M. (2004). Communication management and control in distance learning scenarios. In *Proceedings of Information Science and Information Technology Education* (Joint Conference), Rockhampton (pp. 279-288).

Buder, J. (2000). *Wissensaustausch und Wissenserwerb in Computerkonferenzen: Der Einfluss des Metawissens*. Doctoral dissertation, University of Tübingen.

Dennis, A., & Valacich, J. (1999). Rethinking media richness: Towards a theory of media synchronicity. In *Proceedings of the 32nd Hawaii International Conference of Systems Sciences (HICSS-32)*. Los Alamitos: IEEE Computer Society (CD-ROM).

Döring, K. W. (1989). *Lehrerverhalten*. Weinheim: Deutscher Studien-Verlag.

Euler, D. (1999). Multimediale und telekommunikative Lernumgebungen zwischen Potentialität und Aktualität: Eine Analyse aus wirtschaftspädagogischer Sicht. In I. Gogolin, & D. Lenzen (Eds.), *Medien-Generation* (pp. 77-98). Opladen, Germany: Leshe & Budrich.

Issing, L. J. (1998). Lernen mit Multimedia aus psychologisch-didaktischer Perspektive. In: G. Dörr (Ed.), *Lernen mit Medien: Ergebnisse und Perspektiven zu medial vermittelten Lehr- und Lernprozessen* (pp. 159-177). Weinheim, Germany: Juventa.

Kaiser, F. J. (1983). *Die Fallstudie: Theorie und Praxis der Fallstudiendidaktik*. Bad Heilbrunn, Germany: Klinkhardt.

Kerres, M. (1998). *Multimediale und telemediale Lernumgebungen*. Munich: Oldenbourg.

Mandl, H., & Reinmann-Rothmeier, G. (2001). E-Learning: Lernen mit neuen Medien. *WechselWirkung, 6*(23), 12-19.

Salmon, G. (2001). *E-moderating: The key to teaching and learning online*. London: Kogan Page.

Schertler, M. (2002). *Produktionsumgebung für videobasierte E-Learning-Pakete* (Working Paper). Nuremberg: University of Erlangen-Nuremberg.

Schertler, M. (2004). *Telemediale Lehrarrangements*. Doctoral dissertation, University of Erlangen-Nuremberg.

Schertler, M., & Bodendorf, F. (2003). Production environment for Web-based video lectures. *World Conference on E-Learning in Corporate, Government, Healthcare, & Higher Education, 2003*(1), 2401-2408. Retrieved from http://dl.aace.org/14161

Schoblick, R., & Schoblick, G. (2001). *Netmeeting*. Poing, Germany: Franzis.

W3C. (2004). *Synchronized multimedia*. Retrieved from http://www.w3.org/AudioVideo/

Warner, C. (2003). *The case study method. HBS Handbook 2002*. Retrieved from http://www.harbus.org/news/2003/02/18/AdmitWeekend/The-Case.Study.Method-372561.shtml

Chapter XVI

Distributed Virtual Reality Learning Environments

Sam Redfern
University of Galway, Ireland

Micheál Colhoun
University of Galway, Ireland

Jordi Hernandez
University of Galway, Ireland

Niall Naughton
University of Galway, Ireland

Damien Noonan
University of Galway, Ireland

Abstract

In this chapter we discuss the emerging technologies of collaborative virtual environments (CVEs), and outline their suitability for improving the pedagogical support provided by online learning environments. We provide a critique of current approaches to online learning (ranging from Web-based to video-conferencing), and argue that they are generally poor with regard to support for complex task-based interactions, as required by modern approaches to collaborative learning, as well as being weak in terms of supporting sociability and community, which are powerful mechanisms for combating isolation. We present and discuss our own prototype CVE learning environment, using this discussion as a mechanism for further exploring the issues involved in online learning and online community in general. We present and discuss our virtual campus architecture and our model for complex task-based synchronous and asynchronous interaction.

Introduction

In today's information age, the demand for distance education (DE) has never been greater. With fewer traditional undergraduates (aged 18 to 22) enrolling for third level education, universities are now catering to the new "non-traditional" students. Having greater responsibilities and obligations within their lives, these students have greater expectations and requirements of the educational programs they partake in (Beller, 1998; Pallof & Pratt, 1999; Bernard, de Rubalcava, & St-Pierre, 2000). The different requirements of these non-traditional students demand a much more accessible and flexible framework for delivering education; it is not surprising; therefore, that DE programs are rapidly gaining in popularity.

Remarking on the currently pervasive model for DE, in which the only human-to-human interactions are the occasional instructor-student correspondence, Beller (1998) notes:

> *Under this model, distance learning is essentially self-learning, and requires great will power and self discipline on the part of the student as well as suitable learning skills. Such studies often suffer from an inferior public image and/or low popularity compared to studies conducted at traditional universities, either due to low-quality academic materials and poor academic control, or because of the difficulty of dealing alone with complex learning materials. The relatively low rate of success of these distance courses, and the even lower rate of those completing their studies and obtaining degrees, have contributed to their poor image. (p. 3)*

It is clear that, with this correspondence model, the process of learning has several problems that have damaged the credibility of these institutions. While the augmentation of such educational programs with modern multimedia technologies may improve the efficiency of content delivery, extensive studies on these DE programs continue to outline specific problems of isolation, dropout rates, procrastination, poor communication channels, and motivation.

To create a successful learning environment, designers must address the importance of the degree of social interaction that occurs within the physical campuses of modern universities. Emphasis needs to be put on technologies to support these strong interpersonal relationships, and promote cooperation and collaboration within this community. This approach places a new responsibility on instructors to facilitate and nurture the interpersonal relationships within the community: instructors must have an active role in transferring the student from the passive teacher-centered individual learning to the interactive learner-centered collaborative learning community (Haythornthwaite, Kazmar, Robins, & Shoemaker, 2000). This socially interactive model has been shown to be as effective as, if not more effective than, the face-to-face classroom environment. When compared to the older "one-way" correspondence model, it has been shown to generate much greater degrees of student satisfaction, motivation, learning, and quality of education (Hiltz, 1997; Kimery, 2000; Smith, 1999; Stacey, 1999; Beller, 1998; Pallof & Pratt, 1999).

Online Learning Environments

The traditional one-way model of DE course delivery fails primarily because of the lack of support for social interaction, involving both student-instructor and student-student communication. The constructivist approach sees learning not as an isolated individual act, but a collective result of social interaction. New knowledge is constructed by "anchoring" accumulated knowledge to the alternative points of view, understanding, and experiences of others (Strommen & Lincoln, 1992). To implement such a pedagogical model requires the building of a community of socially interdependent scholars: a learning community. While it may be possible for this to happen in a relatively natural and unplanned way in traditional "face-to-face" education, to do so in a DE context requires that software packages explicitly focus on the subtleties of developing strong, supportive, and trustful social relationships. In order to provide an effective collaborative learning community, we must look beyond the capabilities of currently deployed computer-mediated communication (CMC) tools, and address the provision of more highly developed means of mediating the collaborative learning process.

The online communication tools commonly used to support DE provide for both asynchronous and synchronous instruction. Common asynchronous tools include e-mail, listserv, and Web bulletin boards. Synchronous tools include chat rooms, application sharing (including whiteboards), and tele- and video-conferencing. Other tools, such as streaming video, Web pages, online tests, and computer-based training (CBT) systems are for use by single users, and as such are not really communication tools. Asynchronous tools have an important role in the "anywhere, anytime" paradigm of distance education that makes it attractive to many people in the first place. Many students also report that they feel more at ease with participation when they have time to construct their arguments.

Despite the acknowledged strength of CMC as a platform for DE, a number of deficiencies in its use as a means of interpersonal communications are discussed in the literature. These deficiencies limit the transmission of interpersonal and social information, including the restriction of "social presence," diminished social-context cues and restricted number of channels, particularly nonverbal modes of expression (Chambers, 1999; Redfern & Naughton 2002; Hernandez, Noonan, Redfern, Colhoun, Naughton, & Collins, 2003). The crucial requirements for community and richer interpersonal communication are very often badly supported by online tools: we cannot see the facial expressions or body language of colleagues as we conduct discussions; we cannot hear voices or tones of voice to convey emotion. Even as far back as the late 1980s, Nipper discussed the need to create a sense of "synchronous presence" to reduce the social distance between participants; indeed, this need for social connection is a goal that is probably just as important as content-oriented goals for a course (Nipper, 1989).

In addressing how new technology can make teaching more effective, Kimery (2000) makes several observations concerning the cohesiveness of collaborative groups and their degree of learning. Kimery set out in spring 1998 to deliver an undergraduate course online to increase enrolment. His initial findings were less than encouraging. Of the 30 students enrolled, only half participated in interactive discussion. Even after assigning a sizeable grade to online participation, several students still avoided posting any meaningful material. After several months he concluded that *collaboration* had not yet taken place. Kimery defines four classes of groups that are differentiated by their learning effectiveness: Pseudo Groups; Traditional Groups; Co-operative Groups; and Collaborative Groups. In "pseudo-groups," group members are unmotivated to interact, and as a result, perform below the capabilities of even the group's weakest link. In "traditional groups," interaction takes place but the group has the sole objective of completing the assignment. A "cooperative group" has developed collaborative skills that allow the group to perform better than their strongest link. The final group, the "collaborative group," is defined as a high performing collaborative group that is performing far ahead of the members' potential performance. Further useful work on cell-based learning is due to Tiessen and Ward (1999).

Collaborative Virtual Environments

Collaborative virtual environments (CVEs) are computer-enabled, distributed virtual spaces or places in which people can meet and interact with others, with agents and with virtual objects. CVEs vary greatly in their representational richness from 3D virtual reality to 2D and even text-based environments. To date, CVEs have primarily been used for military and industrial team training, collaborative design and engineering, and multiplayer games.

Most significantly, CVEs represent a shift in interacting with computers and communications technology in that they provide a space that contains or encompasses data representations *and* users *and* virtual tools (Snowdon, Churchill, & Munro, 2001)—the concept is that the information space is inhabited by its users. During the early days of CVEs (in the early 1990s), researchers put most emphasis on simulating face-to-face co-presence as realistically as possible. More recently, it has been realized that this is not enough for genuinely useful computer-supported cooperative work (CSCW), and indeed not necessarily even required. The CVE research community is actively pursuing a number of research directions, each of which is directly relevant to the use of CVEs for DE purposes:

1. Work artifact collaboration. In "real world" domains, collaborative work involves the interleaving of singular and group activities: this requires considerable explicit and implicit communication between collaborators. Individuals need to negotiate shared understandings of task goals, of task decomposition and sub-task allocation, and of task progress. It is important that collaborators know what is currently being done and what has been done in context of the task goals. Shared work artifacts are increasingly being embedded within CVEs. By making the actual work take place within the CVE, collaborators can be aware of each other's activities. The work artifacts become not only the subject of communication, but also the medium of communication: as one user manipulates an object, changes are visible to other users (Benford, Snowdon, Colebourne, O'Brien, & Rodden, 1997; Snowdon, Churchill, & Munro, 2001).

2. "What You See Is What I See" (WYSIWIS). Conversational and action analysis studies of traditional collaborative work have shown the importance of being able to understand the viewpoints, focuses of attention and of action of collaborators (Büscher, O'Brien, Rodden, & Trevor, 2001; Hindmarsh, Fraser, Heath, & Benford, 2001).

3. Chance meetings. Informal and unplanned meetings with colleagues are rarely provided for in collaborative tools, yet they are known to be crucial to the work of many workers, particularly knowledge-workers.

4.   Peripheral awareness is increasingly seen as an important concept in collaborative work, as evidenced in ethnographic studies (e.g., Heath & Luff, 1996). It is clear that team members involved in parallel but independent ongoing activities need to be able to coordinate and inform their activities through background or peripheral awareness of one another's activities.

5.   Non-verbal communications are known to have a strong effect on how utterances are interpreted. Research into alternative input mechanisms for capturing this type of information from the user has been underway for some time.

6.   The "designing for two worlds" principle: as people work in virtual environments, they are never fully immersed in it but are always partially in the real world too.

CVEs clearly have the potential to enable innovative and effective distance teaching techniques, involving for example debate, simulation, role play, discussion groups, brainstorming, and project-based group work. The emphasis can be placed on the human-to-human interactions as common understandings are negotiated and developed across differences of knowledge, skills, and attitudes.

It is often stated that a virtual social space for students to congregate in is essential to distance courses (e.g., Harasim, Hiltz, Teles, & Turoff, 1996; Berge & Collins, 1995). However, the modern thinking in CSCW would suggest that it is better if an environment is designed in such a way that collaborators naturally meet as they go about their work, rather than having to explicitly log on to a social environment. This can be achieved by designing virtual environments that offer the means to access appropriate information and task-related tools as well as communication tools. If these things are not provided, then the CVE is merely a graphically-rich communication tool—not unlike teleconferencing and videoconferencing—which will lose out on the ability to act as a place, foster community, and enable important collaborative work principles such as work artifact collaboration, chance meetings, and peripheral awareness.

Communities: Physical and Virtual

It can be argued that communities, *conceptually*, can exist as social networks of people with shared interests constantly in the process of social interaction (Preece, 2000). Unlike the spatial constraints of neighborhoods and villages in the communities of our physical world, online social networks have no spatial dimension and they can easily extend across the entire globe. In a physical community, the community is usually based on shared socio-economic status, ethnicity, gender, and mostly a shared geographical location. Online communities, on the other hand, are based on the shared interests and aspirations of their members. Software platforms that provide the communication services of e-mail, Web cams, teleconferencing, chat, bulletin boards, and so on, take the approach that online communities are, to large extent, social conceptualizations.

In the broader context of developing social community, such platforms can never develop any temporal sense of social history or culture within groups of its users. The central issues at the core of a community's development require some form of metaphorical representation that promote the persistence of a social community, and does not require the immediate presence of its members. These representations act as a permanent record of the social activities of a community. Aside from the immediate content of the community's social interactions, computer-based communication systems provide little tangible evidence of a community's existence, and one may be prompted to ask: in the (temporary) absence of a community's members, what gives that community definition?

Communities in the physical world have the additional provision of a shared physical space. A community's spatial surroundings and the social connotations that can be inferred from them can have a strong influence on the activities taking place within that community (Dieberger, 1999; Harrison & Dourish, 1996). Humans do not view diverse spaces in an objective manner, but subjectively associate their spatial settings with learned social connotations. In this respect, a community's definition (consisting of people, purposes, and policies) is metaphorically projected onto its surrounding space. These *spaces* infused with social meaning then become *places*. It is these *places* that will give a community a sense of persistence in the absence of its members.

A useful mechanism for creating and sustaining an online community is to allow participants to be involved in its development (Palloff & Pratt, 1999; Huxor, 2001; Raybourn, 2001). Typically this might involve the posting of home pages providing personal information for colleagues to see. However, recent research suggests that involvement in the development of the core environment itself may be far more powerful. By focusing solely on work effectiveness, we risk missing out on social richness—this has indeed been a problem with technologies such as video conferencing, which typically provide spaces for interaction but not social places as meaningful platforms for communication: social behavior is engendered by other important aspects of an environment beyond the mere provision of a shared coordinate system (Harrison & Dourish, 1996). We would argue for the provision of purely social environmental artifacts to increase the sense of place and to help engender persistent and evolving meaning into the workspaces provided.

Virtual Reality Teleworking Communities

Our Virtual Reality Tele-Working Communities (ViRTeCo) project has been underway for the past two years, and is now nearing completion. The primary objective of the ViRTeCo project has been to develop a prototype CVE software platform that supports virtual e-learning communities and other socially-focused tele-working applications.

Figure 1 illustrates the core public spaces in the ViRTeCo virtual learning environment. Perhaps the most important design consideration was that we should promote the likelihood of context-sensitive chance meetings while minimizing the amount of navigation time and effort required by users. At the centre is the entrance hall. This is the arrival point for all users of the system. Four activity-themed public spaces are accessible from the entrance hall:

- The Mail Room
- The Offices Portal
- The Lecture Halls Portal
- The Library and Projects Portal

By designing an environment with thematic sections, we have attempted to create a virtual campus whose appearance aids navigation by enabling students to easily identify the purpose of each section. Just as Clark and Maher (2001)

Figure 1. The public spaces in the ViRTeCo virtual learning environment

focused on context and experience through their design models by creating a place for learning, we have modeled our environment with thematic relevance, allowing students to experience a sense of "place" while interacting and collaborating.

The Mail Room is an information drop-off and collection point, themed in the style of a cyber-café. Students are required to use the mail room for the collection and submission of work assignments: this helps to ensure that a critical mass of users visit the ViRTeCo environment at specific times. Users will tend to meet each other in the mail room at the start and end of work assignments, thereby facilitating context-sensitive chance meetings.

As well as containing a large public seating "seminar" area facing a large presentation screen, the Offices Portal provides an elevator to teachers' and students' private offices. We have used the elevator metaphor throughout our designs wherever we need to imply a one-to-many relationship (where a single doorway leads to many destinations). When a user accesses an elevator, they choose from a list of destinations from this point (similar to a real-life elevator). We thus have the flexibility of providing an unlimited amount of private spaces such as offices and project rooms.

The Lecture Halls Portal is a large public space, allowing large of amounts of users to congregate around the time of scheduled online lectures. It also provides portals (elevators) to the scheduled (synchronous) lectures themselves. These are facilitated using third-party software.

The Library and Projects Portal provides access to structured information repositories and, via a portal (elevator), to private project rooms. Once created for a specific group of participants and for a specific purpose, a project room never needs to be destroyed. Each time a meeting is held in the room, the current state of work artifacts and collaborative documents will be recalled automatically.

The structured information repositories, which are accessed via the bookshelves in the library portal, could be described as populated, interactive threaded bulletin boards (see Snowdon et. al [2004] and Höök, Benyon, and Munro, [2003] for discussion of the current thinking regarding inhabited information spaces). They are used for any structured information storage purpose, for example course content storage and annotation, external course links, personal favorites, and bookmarks. Navigating information in a structured 3D way is known to provide powerful memory recall mechanisms. When a user navigates inside a "book," they are presented with a navigable multi-story building. As they browse through, interact with, and annotate the information stored, they meet other users studying precisely the same topics as themselves. This concept of context-sensitive chance meeting is precisely what may happen in a real-world library. Floors and sub-floors represent subtopics within the overall building topic (similar to root

Figure 2. Collaborative work using a shared Windows application

threads in a bulletin board). Floors and sub-floors that are near each other store information that is semantically related.

Figure 2 depicts an interactive, multi-user collaboration work tool that visitors to an information repository can make use of. These are the mechanism by which information is presented (typically via an embedded Web-browser connected to a standard URL) and document-centric collaboration can occur (typically via a shared Windows application work-tool). In the information repositories, and throughout the whole ViRTeCo environment, interactive work-tools are provided abundantly. This allows interaction to occur between users wherever and whenever they happen to meet. Work-tools may appear as, for example, whiteboards, computers, or presentation screens. Our work-tool client/server software allows users to interact via collaborative Web browsing, Windows application sharing, or whiteboard-like sketching, while remaining embedded in the shared environment.

Non-Verbal Communication

In traditional face-to-face communication, we use our bodies to express both conscious thought and subconscious emotions. We use it voluntary and involuntary, and there is a vast range of social signals that we transmit visibly by our body language. Non-verbal communication involves facial expressions, body posture, limb gestures, orientation, and activity (e.g., Salem & Earle, 2000). In the media of virtual environments, embodiments have progressively taken on more spatial 3D human-like representation. In terms of representative embodiment in cyberspace, these 3D "avatars" are ideal visual interfaces.

In ViRTeCo, our avatars currently have 16 joints, each with three degrees of freedom in that they can be rotated around their respective X-, Y-, and Z-axes. In terms of promoting a participant's social personality, avatars must not only be capable of displaying a unique visual appearance, but must also be capable of displaying unique human-like behaviors. This suggests specifying a high-level scripting language that individual users can create/edit to generate new behaviors for their avatars. An XML-based specification was an ideal choice for serializing the kinematical data structures that define these animations: we refer to our specification as gesture markup language (GML). Our motivation is two-fold: we believe the virtual body to have great potential for improving remote communication, and also for enriching the virtual workplace from a social perspective.

A crucial aspect of non-verbal communication is facial expression. Several virtual environments research teams are investigating the automatic production of facial expression through the processing of digital images from Web-cams. With few exceptions, current approaches to automated analysis of users' facial expressions focus on a set of five prototypic "universal" expressions (anger, disgust, fear, happiness, sadness). In daily life, prototypic expressions occur relatively infrequently, and emotion is more often communicated by changes in one or two discrete features, such as tightening of the lips in anger. An alternative approach, therefore, which is growing in importance, is to identify the movement of key facial features over multiple image frames. For communication purposes in virtual environments, it has been shown that comic-style caricature faces may be more effective than photo-realistic faces, since they can produce exaggerated and therefore less ambiguous movements; also, they allow the strong graphical definition of important features and the omission of irrelevant ones. ViRTeCo uses this approach to render direct mappings from the motion cues extracted from Web cams, rather than producing stock animations based on facial expression estimations. This provides much more individualized results and is not be hampered by incorrect recognition of expressions.

Conclusion

E-learning, which is a specific type of tele-working, has enjoyed rapid growth in recent years. Despite the improvement that it offers to many learners over traditional face-to-face education, it still suffers from many of the same problems as did the distance education correspondence courses that it has replaced. For the most part, e-learning has simply automated the one-way communication model of distance education through the use of static Web sites. One of the main problems continues to be isolation and consequent procrastination and lack of motivation. Technologies such as chat-rooms, Web forums and Web-casting are recently improving this in a somewhat ad-hoc manner: however, a new paradigm for e-learning is on the horizon: a truly integrated and complete virtual university, in which human-to-human communication, collaborative project work, and social community are fully supported.

The ViRTeCo project, and a small number of others like it around the world, are producing the first prototype environments, and are teasing out the technical, social and work process issues that need to be addressed for this new style of software to become a mainstream reality.

Future Trends

When you consider that widespread use of the Internet first started less than 10 years ago, the rapid changes in business practices, global digital communications, and the lifestyle possibilities fuelled by it are quite remarkable. Closely related to these technologies are the rapid growth of the virtual, dispersed organization and the huge increase in tele-working. According to a recent survey by the *Economist*, more than 80% of 237 senior executives surveyed worldwide expect to have tele-workers or remote workers in the next two years, up from the 54% who have them now. The modern information society is beginning to provide the opportunity for flexible work practices and liberation from geographical and temporal restrictions. However, the technologies for appropriately supporting dispersed work practices are still in their infancy.

The technological basis for a virtual reality approach to work is already in place in the games industry, where massively multi-player virtual reality gaming has enjoyed enormous growth in the past five years. It is through use of these same technologies, combined with the thoughtful and appropriate application of computer-supported co-operative work (CSCW) theories, that the next generation of tele-working and e-learning technologies can be provided. We expect to see technologies similar to ViRTeCo appearing in the tele-working and e-learning marketplace within the next few years: the recent upsurge in patent filing in the CVE arena would underline the truth of this.

Acknowledgment

The support of the Informatics Research Initiative of Enterprise Ireland is gratefully acknowledged.

References

Beller, M. (1998). The crossroads between lifelong learning and information technology: A challenge facing universities. *Journal of Computer Mediated Communication, 4*(2). Retrieved October 26, 2005, from http://jcmc.indiana.edu/vol4/issue2/beller.html

Benford, S., Snowdon, D., Colebourne, A., O'Brien, J., & Rodden, T. (1997). Informing the design of collaborative virtual environments. In *Proceedings ACM GROUP Conference* (pp. 71-80).

Berge, Z., & Collins, M. (1995). Computer-mediated communication and the online classroom in distance learning. *Computer-Mediated Communication Magazine, 2*(4), 6-13.

Bernard, R., de Rubalcava, B., & St-Pierre, D. (2000). Collaborative online distance learning: Issues for future practice and research. *Journal of Distance Education, 21*(7), 260-277.

Büscher, M., O'Brien, J., Rodden, T., & Trevor, J. (2001). "He's behind you": The experience of presence in shared virtual environments. In E. F. Churchill, D. N. Snowdon, & A J. Munro (Eds.), *Collaborative virtual environments: Digital places and spaces for interaction* (pp. 77-98). London: Springer-Verlag.

Chambers, M. (1999). The efficacy and ethics of using digital multimedia for educational purposes. In A. Tait, & R. Mills (Eds.), *The convergence of distance and conventional education: Patterns of flexibility for the individual learner* (pp. 5-16). London: Routledge.

Clark, S., & Maher, M. L. (2001). The role of place in designing a learner centred virtual learning environment. In *Computer Aided Architectural Design Futures Conference*.

Dieberger, A. (1999). Social connotations of space in the design of virtual communities and social navigation. In A. Munro, K. Höök, & D. Benyon (Eds.), *Social navigation of information space* (pp. 35-52). London: Springer-Verlag.

Harasim, L., Hiltz, S. R., Teles, L., & Turoff, M. (1996). *Learning networks.* Cambridge, MA: MIT Press.

Harrison, S. & Dourish, P. (1996). Replacing space: The roles of place and space in collaborative systems. In *Proceedings of the ACM Computer Supported Cooperative Work Conference* (pp. 67-76).

Haythornthwaite, C., Kazmar, M. M., Robins J., & Shoemaker, S. (2000). Community development among distance learners: Temporal and technological dimensions. *Journal of Computer Mediated Communication,*

6(1). Retrieved October 26, 2005, from http://jcmc.indiana.edu/vol6/issue1/haythornwaite.html

Heath, C., & Luff, P. (1996). Convergent activities: Collaborative work and multimedia technology in London Underground Line control rooms. In D. Middleton, & Y. Engestrom (Eds.), *Cognition and communication at work: Distributed cognition in the workplace* (pp. 96-130). Cambridge: Cambridge University Press.

Hernandez, J., Noonan, D., Redfern, S., Colhoun, M., Naughton, N., & Collins, D. (2003). Collaborative virtual environments and the virtual campus. In *International Conference on Multimedia and ICTs in Education 2003*.

Hiltz, S. R. (1997). Impacts of college-level courses via asynchronous learning networks: Some primary results. *Journal of Asynchronous Learning Networks*, *1*(2). Retrieved October 26, 2005, from http://www.sloan-c.org/publications/jaln/v1n2/v1n2_hiltz.asp

Hindmarsh, J., Fraser, M., Heath, C., & Benford, S. (2001). Virtually missing the point: Configuring CVEs for object-focused interaction. In E. F. Churchill, D. N. Snowdon, & A. J. Munro (Eds.), *Collaborative virtual environments: Digital places and spaces for interaction* (pp. 115-139). London: Springer-Verlag.

Höök, K., Benyon, D., & Munro, A. (2003). *Designing information spaces: The social navigation approach*. Springer: London.

Huxor, A. (2001). The role of the personal in social workspaces: Reflections on working in AlphaWorld. In E. F. Churchill, D. N. Snowdon, & A. J. Munro (Eds), *Collaborative virtual environments: Digital places and spaces for interaction* (pp. 282-295). London: Springer-Verlag.

Kimery, E. (2000). Developing online collaboration. In A. Aggarwal (Ed.), *Web-based learning and teaching technologies: Opportunities and challenges*. Hershey, PA: Idea Group Publishing.

Nipper, S. (1989). *Third generation distance learning and computer conferencing*. Retrieved June 20, 2001, from http://www-icdl.open.ac.uk/mindweave/chap5.html

Pallof, R., & Pratt, K. (1999). *Building learning communities in cyberspace: Effective strategies for the online classroom*. San Francisco: Jossey-Bass Publishers.

Preece, J. (2000). *Online communities: Designing usability, supporting sociability*. Chichester, UK: John Wiley & Sons

Raybourn, E. M. (2001). Designing an emergent culture of negotiation in collaborative virtual communities: The DomeCityMOO simulation. In E. F. Churchill, D. N. Snowdon, & A. J. Munro (Eds.), *Collaborative virtual environments: Digital places and spaces for interaction* (pp. 247-264). London: Springer-Verlag.

Redfern, S., & Naughton, N. (2002). Collaborative virtual environments to support communication and community in Internet-based distance education. *Journal of Information Technology Education, 1*(3), 201-211.

Salem, B., & Earle, N. (2000). Designing a non-verbal language for expressive Avatars. In *ACM Collaborative Virtual Environments Conference* (pp. 93-101).

Smith, R. B. (1999). Experiments comparing face-to-face with virtual collaborative learning. In *Computer Support for Collaborative Learning Conference* (pp. 558-566).

Snowdon, D., Churchill, E. F., & Munro, A. J. (2001). Collaborative virtual environments: Digital spaces and places for CSCW: An introduction. In E. F. Churchill, D. N. Snowdon, & A. J. Munro (Eds.), *Collaborative virtual environments: Digital places and spaces for interaction* (pp 3-17). London: Springer-Verlag.

Snowdon, D., Churchill, E. F., & Frécon, E. (Eds.) (2004). *Inhabited information spaces: Living with your data.* London: Springer-Verlag.

Stacey, E. (1999). Collaborative learning in an online environment. *Journal of Distance Education, 14*(2), 14-33.

Strommen, E. F., & Lincoln, B. (1992). Constructivism, technology, and the future of classroom learning. *Education and Urban Society, 24*(4), 466-477.

Tiessen, E., & Ward, D. (1999). Developing a technology of use for collaborative project-based learning. In *Computer Support for Collaborative Learning Conference* (pp. 631-639).

Chapter XVII

The Meaning and Development of KM in E-Learning According to the CARID Experience

Marco Pedroni
University of Ferrara, Italy

Abstract

Knowledge management and e-learning have many common elements: both are based on information and knowledge exchange, but the most important element marking this relation is the structure of the knowledge, necessary issue in order to organize and efficiently share the stream of information. CARID, the Academic Centre for Didactic Research and Innovation at the University of Ferrara, has developed a particular method for the representation of knowledge contexts and the support for information streaming, all based on indexes and expansible concept maps.

Introduction

In order to apply Web technologies to learning, and to offer e-learning courses, two strategies can be followed (Frignani, 2003).

The first is a traditional strategy and consists of reproducing the methods of "face-to-face" training by means of the Internet. This strategy allows the creation of a virtual classroom, that is, an interactive learning situation that maintains the traditional relationship between teacher and students in a class. The virtual classroom is based upon synchronous interaction, and makes use of tools like chat-lines, audio-conferences, video-conferences, the remote sharing of a blackboard, or other software tools. Of course, this method implies the availability of a wide range of Web transmissions for both teachers and users, who are also required to respect a specific timetable. The basic feature of the virtual room is that it represents a substitute for traditional school, with the advantage of avoiding transport problems. It is best used when a group of people cannot arrange a meeting in the same room because of prohibitive expenses or for other reasons. On another hand, the replacement of a real classroom, besides implying high costs of transmission and the use of very expensive specific software, cannot really reproduce true communication like in a real classroom. All in all, the traditional strategy of applying Web technologies does not represent any remarkable development in the learning process, it does however, allow organizational problems to be solved.

The second strategy, also called pure strategy, implies a review of the method according to the opportunities offered by technological innovation. This strategy can include a development of synchronous interaction methods, which gradually distance themselves from the model of the traditional classroom; yet, it will mostly deal with asynchronous interaction. This kind of interaction is based upon the principle of the non-sharing of a timetable among interlocutors, so it is completely different from a real classroom situation where teacher and students share both place and time. This implies the need to create, by means of studies on methods and technologies, specific interaction strategies based upon the use of asynchronous communication tools, among which the simplest and best known are mailing, newsgroups, and forums.

As shown by above examples, asynchronous interaction can represent a replacement of traditional methods too. For example, the use of e-mail is not very different from the methods used at the beginning of remote distance training, which were based on mail. In this case, being cheaper and quicker, such replacement improves and optimizes the traditional method without damaging communication, as opposed to the virtual classroom with respect to a real classroom. The development of communication technologies however, especially the advanced management technologies of Web interaction, breaks new ground to some kind of well-developed didactic collaboration, which is interesting for research and goes beyond a simple replacement of traditional "face-to-face" or remote learning. In other words, advanced interaction on the Internet allows many opportunities that would otherwise be impossible, and improves traditional learning, going beyond the simple improvement of technical elements or the solution of organizational problems. The analysis of these opportunities, which is part of a research on methods and technologies carried out by CARID (*Centro di Ateneo per la Ricerca e l'Innovazione Didattica e l'Istruzione a Distanza dell'Università degli Studi di Ferrara*—University Center for Didactic Research and Innovation and for Distance Learning), highlights the essential relationship between e-learning and knowledge management, which is the key for understanding the development of the research in this field. Summarizing such is the meaning of the well-known sentence by Clark Aldrich of Gartner Group, who, in February 2000, said: "I don't know if e-learning will wind up as a subset of knowledge management, or knowledge management is going to be a subset of e-learning in two years, but it will be one or the other" (Cavalli, 2004).

Knowledge Management

The coming of digital technologies in the field of institutional and entrepreneurial management has totally changed—and is still changing—the relationship between management and its accumulated knowledge reservoir.

Computer technologies entered the field of work mainly through the introduction of management software: in the '60s, '70s, and '80s, managers and employees gradually started to use the newborn computer science in the fields of accountancy, store management, personnel management, and marketing. At the same time, the first management database appeared, in which all data concerning applications was stored in a structured way. Each management application, often developed in Cobol, was equipped with its own database structured within Cobol itself, through the Data Section. The first database management systems were the first tools to store data not directly linked to single applications, yet they were available for any application by means of specific software libraries called "drivers." This was another revolutionary idea for data sharing and transmission within corporate. Data contained in the DBMS could be used both in the same context where it was created, and in other contexts managed by different software procedures. For example, accountancy data could be used for marketing management, and storeroom data could be used for production management. Main result of such data exchange was that management was able to make use of data from all departments, in order to make comparisons and have more information available for decisions and development of new strategies. This context saw the development of Decision Support Systems, i.e., software tools aimed at supporting company management in decision making by means of the analysis of data stored in the company database. At this point, knowledge become an essential part of management, and will be considered as such by managers and employees.

Decisions in dealing with current situations and problems can also be based on experience gained from the past. From this point of view, company data storage systems become especially important. In a company in step with technological development, such data cannot be erased or stored in places where they cannot be used anymore, as happened with paper-based information and documents. Data had to be filed in such a way that it could always be used, so, in the '80s, the idea of data warehousing became more widespread. All this reinforces and enhances the concept of knowledge, making it constantly available to users in support of problem analysis and decision making. Knowledge has therefore acquired an intrinsic value for management, and has become an important source of value to companies and organizations. It can therefore be considered as an indicator of its overall worth along with its infrastructure and financial standing. This undoubtedly revolutionary idea is the essence of the use and diffusion of knowledge management and reflects its importance as a practical, multi-faceted activity within a company.

The effect of knowledge acquisition is not limited to acting as only a support system for controlling the activities and decision making in a company. One element that is becoming more and more important, especially in working contexts featuring high turn-over, is the transmission of knowledge within personnel management. This issue has two main elements. On the one hand, operators at any level constantly need information and training, that is, they need to draw from the common knowledge reservoir to update and increase their personal knowledge and to adapt their activity to new methods and technologies, as well as to company aims. On the other hand, some method of recording an individual operator's knowledge becomes necessary especially when, for what-ever reason, he leaves the company, as this prevents discontinuity, the repetition of mistakes, and a general loss of experience and knowledge within the company. As a consequence, it is necessary to establish a connection between the company's acquired knowledge reservoir and the training and knowledge—or rather tacit knowledge—among operators.

Tacit knowledge (know-how) is knowledge, experience, practical abilities, memories of operating, decision making, and control processes as a whole, that are not supported by any document, but simply transmitted among operators through verbal communication or when directly working together.

As stated by I. Nonaka and H. Takeuchi in *The Knowledge-Creation Company*, "Tacit Knowledge is personal, hard to communicate: it is embedded in individual experience and regards one's own feelings, ideals and values" (Nonaka & Takeuchi, 1995).

The authors highlight four main stages within the tacit knowledge transmission process:

1. **Socialization:** Knowledge transmission between operators working together: in this stage, during which technical abilities, experiences, and concepts are shared, knowledge basically remains tacit. The transfer of knowledge is carried out like an apprenticeship, or "training on the job": that is, through observation, imitation, and practice. This calls for an atmosphere of confidence that is necessary for the sharing not only of experiences, but also feelings and conceptual abstracts.

2. **Externalization:** Tacit knowledge is turned into explicit knowledge that can be documented and filed and available on demand, regardless of the presence and direct support of those who have the "know-how." In this stage, language plays an essential role but is often not able to thoroughly and clearly explain what is required. Rhetorical figures and references to already existing models are thus needed. This is the most important and complex stage in the creation of new knowledge that generates new concepts that, in turn, will generate new products or a new organizational set-up.

3. **Combination:** The processing of explicit knowledge in order to produce or discover new knowledge to be used for management. In this stage, existing knowledge is gradually integrated within in a wider body of knowledge, and this may well lead to the production of new knowledge. Communication is either direct or via analogue and digital documentation, and draws on company files.

4. **Internalization:** Metabolization of a company's explicit knowledge and its transformation into tacit knowledge. Completion of this stage is necessary for a positive evaluation of the whole process, in that the result is the learning of new abilities that fit the needs of the company. In the assimilation stage, experience gained during the above mentioned stages of knowledge transformation develop a personal worth in the form of tacit know-how and conceptual schemes. Assimilation is triggered by learning, or by direct experience, or by the use of explicit knowledge, verbalized or recorded on documents or computers. It represents a stage of personal enrichment and of knowledge metabolization, resulting in an increase of human capital.

It is thanks to this model, according to Nonaka and Takeuchi's theory, that the sharing of tacit knowledge becomes the "inferential engine" of the new knowledge that results from processing knowledge and experiences within the company. Thus, it is clear that the information system of a company can be the key tool to structure and crystallize tacit knowledge, as well as the means of conveying stored knowledge to all staff.

The role of knowledge therefore follows a natural evolution: from an uncertain and barely measurable factor, mostly linked to individual operator experience, ability and culture, it becomes an essential element, an evaluation parameter for the company, and the object of studies, research and organizational activities.

From KM to E-Learning

Knowledge management means a well structured management of company knowledge, its processing, and its use to support activities such as analysis, decision making, product control and processes. E-learning deals with methods and technologies for knowledge transmission and management of remote learning (both in time and place), through the use of the Internet. What is the relationship between the two fields?

According to these premises, the answer is clear: knowledge management has to make use of e-learning in order to transform knowledge sharing in a process which is not occasional or subjected to temporary needs or to operational decisions, but structured and marked by continuity and specific monitoring and control procedures. E-learning needs to draw from the body-general of knowledge, and it needs to be explicit or made explicit through knowledge management, so that its content can be used immediately or made suitable for later training sessions.

A Web-based communication system therefore, be it in-house or between the company and its stakeholders, must integrate both disciplines, the boundaries of which will tend to disappear as documents and information sharing becomes more and more widespread in all business areas.

The method of asynchronous e-learning thus proves to be an innovative strategy in relation to traditional teaching and synchronous interaction. Knowledge structuring, that is, the organized filing of information and documents within a body of knowledge managed by digital tools, requires a previous analysis and decision regarding the correct placement of the subject to be introduced into the system. Such a decision cannot be easily and successfully made in an interactive context, be it real or virtual, characterized by synchronic time-sharing, because it requires a specific reflection. In other words, in a virtual or real classroom it is difficult to work together on a structuring scheme, or on a knowledge map regarding the subject discussed, or even to dispose of tools to immediately dissect and log concepts interventions, according to their reference fields. Therefore when dealing with any given issue, it is impossible to state something like "What I am about to say must be inserted in this position within the knowledge context we are talking about" first.

In the stage of e-learning communication management, a continuative, progressive organization of documents and information implies the use of a core-system of knowledge management. This aims at supporting didactical process by combining the functions of indexing and mapping subjects, managing the data warehouse (that is, the body of historical records of contents transmitted and received through the network) and, in part, the Learning Management System (the platform on which content modules, or Learning Objects, are installed and supplied, and on which the activity of users is registered). In an index-based environment, the Learning Object, which supports the specific function of content's transmission, becomes an integrated part of a library of different kinds of documents that is ever-growing thanks to didactic interaction. Integration of Learning Object in a knowledge map, in the form of an index or concept map, implies his contextualization in knowledge environment.

The main contribution of knowledge management technologies to the field of e-learning is the implementation and management of a structure meant to contextualize information and document exchange. This structure links content modules to contributions coming from didactic interaction, such as oral tests, answers, interventions, upload, and information about links, it also registers and shows their relationships. With regard to this, it is worth highlighting the importance of the relationship between structure and Learning Object: the main difficulty in the production and re-use of content modules in e-learning courses is the contextualization stage, or rather the creation of content by combining and relating Learning Objects from different sources and featuring different degrees of granularity. Of course, the opportunity of gathering and separating Learning Objects according to their granularity and to knowledge contextualization structure, and placing them within such structure, allows the problem of Learning Object integration in a specific context to be solved. The result is an architectural knowledge system that places contributions and accurately shows the relationships between them. Its adaptability also allows knowledge mapping expansion and restructuring, to replace content media, and to show their logical links.

The CARID didactic methodology is based on a progressive organization of knowledge that draws from content contributions, thus combining the fields of e-learning and knowledge management. Such a method allows a steady growth of organized knowledge within a structure always available and open to all course users.

In detail, when CARID students enter in site's reserved didactic interaction areas and choose, within a topic, the knowledge management function (named Cosmo), the browser shows a page containing the specific arguments' index, and a little closeable box supporting Cosmo's functions (Figure 1). All the documents (queries, answers, contributes, attachments, links to Web pages, Learning Objects) related to every specific topic are reachable clicking on his title (Figure 2). Arguments related to other topics, according to a hierarchical structure, have a folder icon before the title: the clicking on the folder shows the complete list of documents related to that topic and all his hierarchical dependencies (Figure 3); obviously, the click on the first folder shows all index's included documents, in the subject order.

The student can add a new contribution clicking on the "Intervento" button (visible only after direct click on a title, not after choosing a folder, Figures 2 and 3). It opens the editing environment (Figure 4), or read a previous contribution while clicking on its title (Figure 5).

Figure 1. Cosmo: Carid KM system—Index: A generic topic index concerning didactics of communication and a box with main functions the user can access for each subtopic

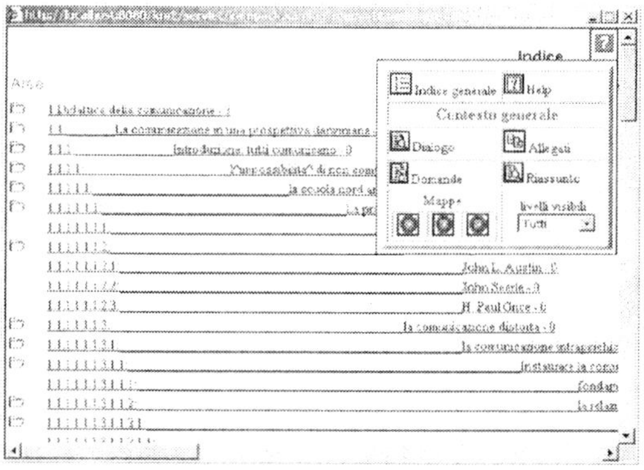

Figure 2. Cosmo: Carid KM system—Filing contributions on a single argument: The choice of a topic opens the relative dialog environment and the click on question mark button opens and closes the functions' box

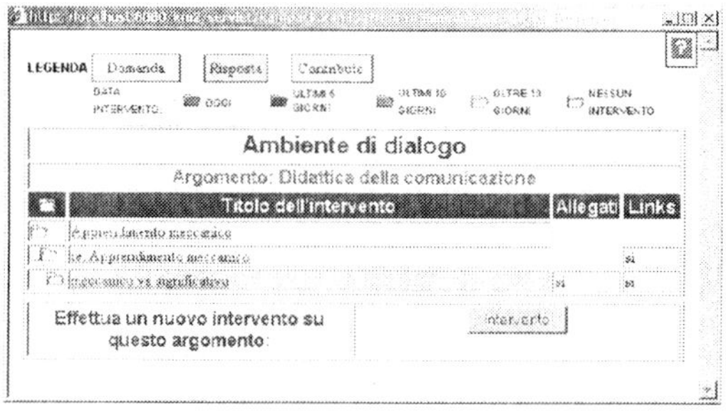

Figure 3. Cosmo: Carid KM system—Filing contributions on parent arguments and his dependencies: Clicking on folders in the topic index opens the dialog environment on the corresponding argument and his dependencies (they are listed in the first column)

Figure 4. Cosmo: Carid KM system—Adding contributions: After choosing an argument, the user can insert a formatted contribute, comprehensive of attachments and links

The above features belong to a structured environment supporting the forum functionality: moreover, Cosmo allows automatic composition of documents by collecting all contributions ordered by general index. In other words the composition of a real and printable "book" of contributions is possible. Representation of knowledge isn't restricted, besides, by tree structures: also not-hierarchical relations between arguments can be represented in Cosmo graphical environment, through automatic drawing of conceptual maps (Novak, 1984) (arguments are nodes of these maps, and clicking on the nodes, or on the colored areas, has the same effect as clicking on titles and folders in the index page). Cosmo allows composition of three kinds of maps, called "Indexed," "Hierarchi-

Figure 5. Cosmo: Carid KM system—Reading contributions: In dialog environment, the choice of a contribute opens the reading environment, which shows the list of queries, answers and contributes derived from the first intervention

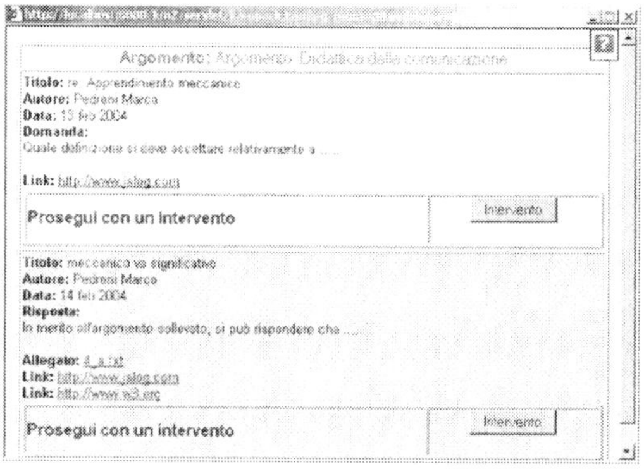

cal circles," and "Concentric circles" (Figures 6, 7, 8). The use of these maps is especially meaningful, because it makes context comprehension easier: navigating among documents with the use of maps has a side-effect on students' minds, the continuous visualization of relations between single parts of context and entire knowledge, and consequently an easier contextualization of learned contents (Rogers, Rutherford, & Bibby, 1994).

Moreover, being maps rebuilding an automatic operation, it's possible to carry out and represent every map while beginning from every node-argument: in this way, more maps' configurations are available for student's context and topic understanding.

The Frontiers of Research

According to the method described above, the most important feature in the combination of e-learning and knowledge management is a structure which contextualizes information and document exchange. Its adaptability allows users to expand and modify its structure. In this paper, we are not going to deal with problems regarding who has the right to modify the structure: on one hand, the supervision of a content expert is necessary, on the other hand the learner can build up an organized knowledge context in order to test his or her own learning. These issues imply a specific, detailed analysis of didactic methods that can be

Figure 6. Cosmo: Carid KM system—Indexed conceptual map: It is like a traditional index, but it supports relations' name. It can also represent a not-hierarchical relations (in this figure, functions box is open). The click on the topics has the same effect of clicking index topics of Figure 1.

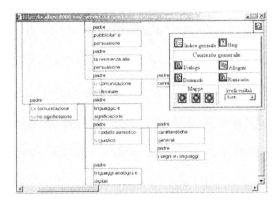

Figure 7. Cosmo: Carid KM system—Conceptual map with hierarchical circles: Grey areas show distribution of hierarchical dependencies of every topic or subtopic. These maps, developed in SVG language, are scalable, click-sensitive, (both areas and nodes) and animated (grey areas can rotate on central node)

implemented in a learning environment on the Web, based on knowledge indexing and mapping.

The studies carried out by CARID focus on the development of a conceptual map, from a graphic image of a knowledge context (able, as opposed to index, to show non-hierarchical relationships regarding the subject discussed), to a document conveying the content; alternatively, in e-learning context, to a learning instrument in itself. Conceptual maps have a clear didactic purpose, and

Figure 8. Cosmo: Carid KM system—Conceptual map with concentric circles: This kind of map shows hierarchical dependencies from a parent topic to its descendants through click-sensitive yellow areas, and other relations through chords joining nodes.

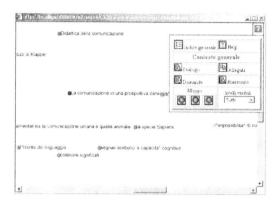

are essential for the student to learn the main relationships among subjects, through a constant analysis of contributions and Learning Objects (Novak, 1998). Yet, as shown by many reports on the use of maps presented by Novak, the same way of representing knowledge can be applied also to micro-structural levels of communication, in which the object of the map is a body of statements and relationships that make up a sentence. As a result, the production of conceptual maps tends to evolve as they turn from graphical schemes of knowledge context ontology (that is, designs and concepts in written form) to a graphic language especially suited to a digital screen (the latter proving to be inadequate to support documents whose style resembles that of traditional paper-based documents. Reading from a screen is not very handy, and many documents sent through the internet are specifically formatted to be printed).

The map may not only be used as a support for information and document exchange, but also as a document jointly edited by the e-learning interlocutors, aimed at conveying contents directly, and characterized by a gradual improvement in its structure. It starts from the representation of a knowledge context, goes into details without continuity solutions, up to the expression of contents related to each sentence of the traditional document. Of course, such map is not a static ontological document such as a simple drawing, but rather a dynamic document, featuring structural information, that is, parts of content and relationship, that are included in a tool such as the Database or in a document written in structured XML marker language. Its display depends on the use of tools for image reengineering, such as style sheets that perform a transformation from XML to SVG (Scalable Vector Graphic) language that comes from XML itself.

Moreover, dynamic reconstruction allows countless modes of context representation and writing all linked to the creation of multiple style sheets. The development of conceptual maps from medium support to knowledge carrier leads to a new definition of the idea of document; it goes beyond the limits of content and formatting inseparability, of direct editing, of editing sequentiality and singularity (Web interaction allows multiple users to work at the structure of the conceptual maps simultaneously), and of univocal representation.

Moreover, shared use of a dynamical environment for conceptual maps' editing and graphic rebuilding allows new features in order to apply constructivist methodology in didactical environments for learning communities (Trentin, 2001). Common and interactive modification and enlargement of maps' structure by learning community's members is certainly an interesting and meaningful way of applying constructivist theory in learning contexts, and this feature can also be used, in perspective, for the sake of improving evaluation methods both for students' learning and for didactic process.

Conclusion

In the management of the e-learning method, based on knowledge management and implemented in the interactive environment developed in-house, CARID faced problems of a cultural nature. The use of such an interaction method calls for an effort involving all the participants in the training process, quite like the introduction of knowledge management techniques in a company. This difficulty calls for training that allows interlocutors to share a successful method to compile documents, contributions, and communication, that can constantly evolve, to enhance the relationship between expert teachers on content, tutors, and students and, in the future, to allow the development of the common writing of structured documents, as well as of an ontological research on the subjects discussed.

The necessity of cultural effort of learning processes stakeholders, emerging from CARID's experience and testified from many other experiences in Italian universities and research centers, implies, by e-learning development's side, the need for a correct and continuous communication in order to provide complete explications about e-learning methodologies, technologies and trends to teachers, tutors and students. Otherwise, efficiency and efficacy of e-learning instruments, especially those which don't derive from traditional learning methods, and don't look like them, are "a priori" compromised.

In the particular case of CARID's Cosmo environment, the share of knowledge management methods and technologies between learning and working contexts allows on one hand a joined development and a joined experimentation of this learning system by different kinds of organizations, and on another hand a better comprehension, by all interlocutors, of meaning and didactic potentialities of such a system. It follows that it's easier, in working environments characterized by non-formal and continuous learning processes, to apply a knowledge management-based learning methodology, which is reusable within the real working context. On the other side, in formal learning environments, interactive knowledge management has to be explained, as learning method, both to students and teachers: it implies a greater effort by technologist and pedagogists, aimed to persuade them of knowledge environment features' utility and to teach the correct use of Cosmo's environment.

At last it has to be noted that CARID's research structure is conscious of the difficulties (technological, methodological, and especially cultural) deriving from the beginning of innovation processes in the different learning contexts, but believes that a real evolution of didactics, and in particular of e-learning, is necessarily related to net-communication, implementation of interactive instruments as Cosmo, and cooperation with contiguous scientific sectors as knowledge management and knowledge representation.

References

Cavalli, L. (2004). La convergenza del knowledge management e dell'e-learning. *E-Learning and Knowledge Management*, *I*(5). Roma: Nuovo Studio Tecna Editore.

Frignani, P. (2003). *Apprendere in rete*. Lecce: Pensa Multimedia.

Nonaka, I., & Takeuchi, H. (1995). *The knowledge-creating company: How Japanese companies create the dynamics of innovation*. Oxford: University Press.

Novak, J. (1998). *Learning, creating and using knowledge: Concept maps and facultative tools in schools and corporations*. Mahwah: Lawrence Erlbaum Associates, Inc.

Novak, J. D., & Gowin, D. B. (1984). *Learning how to learn*. Cambridge: University Press.

Rogers X., Rutherford A., & Bibby, P. (1994). *Models in the mind, theory, perspective, and applications*. Cambridge: University Press.

Trentin, G. (2001). *Dalla formazione a distanza all'apprendimento in rete*. Milano: Franco Angeli.

Section VI

Chapter XVIII

Semantic Web and Digital Libraries

Giorgio Poletti
CARID (Academic Centre for Didactic Research and Innovation),
University of Ferrara, Italy

Abstract

An analysis of the reality surrounding us clearly reveals the great amount of information, available in different forms and through different media. Volumes of information available in real time and via the Web are concepts perceived as closely related. This perception is supported by the remark that the objective of the Web was the definition and construction of a universal archive, a virtual site in which the access to documents was possible with no limits of time or space. In this digital library, documents have to be equipped with logical connections making possible for each user the definition of a reading map that expands according to the demand for knowledge gradually built up. This perspective is pointing now in the direction of the Semantic Web, a network satisfying our requests while understanding them, not by some magic telepathic communication between browser and navigator, but rather a data warehouse in which documents are matched to meta-data,[1] letting specialized software to distinguish fields, importance, and correlation between documents. Semantic Web and library terms have an ever increasing close relationship, fundamental for the progress and the didactic efficiency in knowledge society.

Introduction

Research for the creation of the Semantic Web requires structured information and the definition of the rules allowed for the cataloging of documents. This idea of a network cannot be separated from the concept of technological independence; the progress of communication has to face two problems: firstly the risk of obsolescence of instrumentation capable of reading the data from mass memory support, secondly the need for a multi-channel information distribution. The idea of the obsolescence of instruments for reading data establishes a connection with a verified fact: backups have a "life" longer than the instruments reading and managing original data. Even if not concerned with classic mass memory back-ups, one can think about LPs; today many of us have a lot of them in perfect condition but it is becoming more and more difficult to find turntables and their spare parts.

The multi-channel idea is highlighted by the fact that people have access to information by way of computers, telephones, palm, or interactive TV, and as a consequence there is a variety of forms of documents, one for each type of medium; therefore it is necessary to think in terms of content, structure, and description of the document. We can state that we are trying to add to the independence from space and time limits, also the independence from restrictions connected to the user instruments. One example of this requirement is obtained from news programs offered by some television networks; the same service is available on the Internet, through television and cell phones. It is obvious that news must remain unchanged into the three different systems, so that they are stored in such a way (e.g., title, text, and source) that the software understanding their particular structure is able to visualize them onto the requested service.

At the basis of this line of development is certainly the marker language XML (eXtensible Markup Language) that has flexibility as one of its strong points, which makes it independent of hard and software platforms, so enabling the definition of data easily comprehensible because it has the required specifications to restrict the logical layout but does not pre-determine in any way the possible manner of their description.

The Semantic Web

The introduction to the document presenting XML on the W3C site says:

XML is a layout of a simple and very flexible text derived from SGML (ISO 8879) language. Originally planned to meet the challenge of large scale electronic publication, XML is also carrying out an increasingly important role in the exchange of various data on the Web and in every other environment.

In practice, the strength of XML, emerging in this context, is in its being a meta-language, conceived to be easily implemented and carried out and allowing the interoperability between two documents. In the XML register and in the prospective of the complete realization of a fundamental Semantic Web are the RDF and OWL languages, for which, on February 10, 2004, two official recommendations were issued by W3C. It will be easier to understand the importance of the above statement by reading the definitions recorded in the official documents at the beginning of the description of these languages:

- **RDF:** The resource description framework is a multifunctional language used to represent the information on the WEB.

- **OWL:** Ontology Web language is programmed for the applications that have to analyze the information content instead of presenting the same information to humans. OWL offers a supplementary vocabulary with conventional semantics.[2]

The steps bringing us to the Semantic Web pose a question: How can the final user make use of all this? Tim Berners-Lee seems to have no doubts: "when people see how it works, they will understand its strength."

The Semantic Web will allow:

- *Successful research*, we will search by concept and not by terms; nowadays when we insert a term into a search engine we expect to find documents connected to the concept that we associate with that term. If we search the word "grid," we could mean the electrical term, but the Web will also indicate geography and sport sites.

- *Simple sharing of data* that will aggregate together, keeping their information characteristics enabling us to correlate the documents and their contents to generate new ones, to work towards *knowledge management*.

The concept of digital library, in a semantic context, is closely related to the concept of meta-data and to its more elaborated version, "super-meta-data."[3] A new meaning of *Digital Preservation* concept soon arises; one which widens its research fields to an information structure depending on the accessibility of documents, developing data into a digital key and into the standard concept of consultation.

The digital library and the Semantic Web are in reality very similar, they are different concrete forms of a single idea, almost similar to that of the writer Italo Calvino imagining a city in which its wonders are books: "Do not take pleasure in the seven or seventy-seven wonders of a city, but in the answer to your question" (Calvino, 1972).

"The Web was designed as an information space, to be useful not only for human to human communication, but also for machines which would be able to participate and help. The most relevant obstacle to the fulfillment of this target has been the structure of information on the Web; it was designed, in fact, for human consumption, and even if it was derived from a database with well-defined values for each field, the structure of the data was not evident to a robot browsing the Web. The Semantic Web approach looks to languages for expressing information in a machine processable form instead. The Semantic Web is a Web of data, in some ways similar to a global database" (Berners-Lee, 1998).

The Semantic Web is essentially an extension of the Web as we know it, or, what is better, a return to the original meaning of the Web (Figure 1).

A Semantic Web allows for simpler man-machine communication matching each piece of information with a description of its meaning and a communication transforming itself into cooperation. What has been said on the Semantic Web can be translated into the field of e-learning, where the resources for learning are present in different contexts and media.

The pupil, like the teacher, before activating a cognitive process needs to collate significant material, so it is essential to have a semantic key which permits access to the contents.

In the above context, a central concept becomes the *interoperability of data*, which has to lead to the *integration of the applications*.

We are witnessing the research and implementation of an infrastructure that supports Web pages, but also simply databases and their services, like information coming from other electronic systems such as mobile telephones and palm-tops. This evolution brings with itself new languages that are giving great impetus to new technologies. The current state of the art makes it possible to easily find information on the Web, even if there are some problems with the congruence between the information we find and what we wanted to find. It is more difficult, instead, the transfer of data and information between different applications. In this case making information "machine-understandable"[4] is the first priority (i.e., e-learning and the management of Learning Object).

Figure 1. A concept map from Tim Berners-Lee's original World Wide Web proposal, a hypertext system called the "Mesh," presented in 1989 (http://www.cybergeography.org/atlas/conceptual.html)

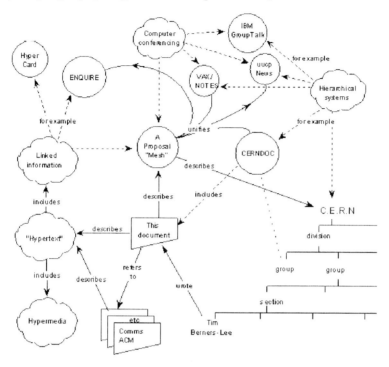

Therefore, the Web has as its principal core, the development of the value inherent in its technology. Becoming a site of shared data and information that can be processed by either users or groups of users, in an automatic mode, through assigned instruments. The Semantic Web already has in place the methodology and technology capable of giving solutions and improvements to the interoperability processes on the Internet. The Semantic Web does not have as a principal target the definition of new models for structuring and memorizing information but rather the coordination, across the Web, of existing technologies which make other technologies useful for the desired aim.

The final objective ultimately becomes the definition of a decentralized system allowing the definition of interconnections without the necessity of human intervention. The Semantic Web is one of the W3C's[5] main lines of research, and a specific group has been established for this aim: "*The Technology and Society Domain*," which works at the point of intersection between Web technology and public policy, and whose main objective is the growth of the current Web infrastructure. The role of this research group is specifically the development and confirmation of the Semantic Web criteria:

- RDF core
- Web ontology

The work developed for the Semantic Web is based on:

- XML to define *ad hoc* layouts for data labeling
- RDF to portray information in a flexible manner
- OWL for the formal description of the semantics applied to the framework of Web documents to make them processable by automatic applications; the Semantic Web requires extremely well-structured ontologies. This requirement comes from the need to have at our disposal strict definitions for the concepts of:

  - Class
  - Connection
  - Characteristics (or attributes)

Ontologies in the Semantic Web will have to allow the various communities the power to model, structure and give meaning to the terms and meta-data in use, on one side making easier standardization and on the other the efficient use of meta-cognitive processes.

The Semantic Web, in other words, has to work on the turning of *"machine-readable"* information into *"machine-understandable"* information.

The Digital Library

Digital library in the context we are analyzing here has the main aim of closely correlating the concepts of meta-data and Semantic Web dealt in up to now. The digitization of paper, or analogical, documents is certainly an important vein of research considering the potential loss of information, and therefore culture, because of the fragility of documental support (e.g., just think of parchment). Such research, to be effective, must be supported by a parallel research dealing with the preservation of documents in a framework that is independent from the instruments that have to access the same documents. These lines of research have been initiated from the consciousness that a conservation process is significant for the determination of the relevance of data extraction to their aim of use and to the creation of flexible meta-data management systems devoted to the determination of standards for the conservation and long-term access to documents.

Traditional libraries are directly involved in the above considerations. They are the places where knowledge is recorded, where the inherent value worth is not the bulk of knowledge, but knowledge organization and its maintenance. No less important is the idea that a library has always been a support element in the learning process; now the advent of e-learning leads us to ask how this tool, extremely limited in terms of space and time, can still be a tool and an equally efficient document back-up in contexts which are free from limits of time and space.

Studies, research and developments in this field pointed exactly in this direction; they allowed the dislocated use of these resources and, paradoxically, where this was made possible increased the number of people who could make use of the "*real*" libraries for consultation. This fact is not totally unexpected since the possibility to have a "semantic" certainty concerning a document makes it easier to go where it is preserved. The need of developing an infrastructure for information preservation in a digital form brings with it a series of problems which demanded groups such as RLG[6] and OCLC[7] to initiate a general research project. At the beginning of 2002 they defined a proposal for the creation of a framework of digital document deposit, a model that could be easily adapted to the documental structures of various libraries.[8] This fact is witnessed by the great number of digital libraries that have sometimes been transformed into digital prototypes. It must be remembered here that more often they gave rise to research projects in specific disciplines or interdisciplinary environments.

The most interesting field of research concerns the organization and definition of tools and the organization for access to digitized documents or to meta-data of analogical documents.

It must not be neglect the organization, preservation and interchange of "*born digital*" documents, which are the principal way through which researchers exchange documents related to the state of the art of their research and their relevant results; as one can imagine it is the case of the great majority of books and documents printed in the last decades. The definition of digitized systems and digital data conservation is important to the extent it is possible to define new information from previous existing data and information. If today society aims to continue preserving documents that science and arts produce, from books to paintings or film, it will be necessary to be equipped with a filing infrastructure that technology can achieve and sustaining. A final uncertainty that is interesting to underline, among the others that emerge in the context of digital libraries in relation to Semantic Web and information technology, is the problem of access to the information.

The problem of the access to information goes beyond the concept of OPAC (Online Public Access Catalogue), an acronym that defines, in a general way, electronic library catalogues supplied for public access to information concerning the resources in a library, to put forward the definition of a GII (Global Information Infrastructure).

An information infrastructure has, as its objective, to make information accessible (and more generally documents) in any form through given applications. The definition of codes, records, and standards simplifies this course towards interconnection and interoperability along with the growing diversification of media present in libraries that are increasingly being transformed into virtual libraries ("*multimediateche*"). The problem of the access to content, increasingly more displaced and "uncontrolled," brings with itself, as an "*alter ego*," the right to intellectual property; we are in a context in which ownership possession is replaced by access, so disrupting the perspectives governing the law in this field. Even if this is not an argument that can be examined closely here, we should keep it in mind as contextual to the development of technology and methodology. The problem of a relationship between the access to knowledge and the right to intellectual property is stronger in groups who train in e-learning or new technology and have to supply an accessible library where the learning process can be developed.

New and more recent projects assign to digital libraries a role which play on the balance between allowing people access to the information in an intelligent manner and following up on the work of cataloguing and preserving documents in traditional analogical and digital forms. The concept of infinite easy access is not always equal to the concept of availability; that is only a part of its meaning. The concept of easy access also includes the technology necessary to read the software required for its "reading." A W3C team is not only working on defining the concept of easy access in relation to the Web but on determining a standard which is pertinent to those who want to make the Web contents more accessible. The definition of a knowledge infrastructure needs expansion and, in some parts, reformulation of the concepts of the library and digital library which will allow the development of all the potential that computer science research has made available, in its works on the automation of information, during last years. In particular, the digital library will be a field of verification, research and development of filing systems and administration of information, systems of knowledge management, of files and interoperable systems, semantic and ontology systems, building new learning, and extrapolation of knowledge.

Semantic Web, Learning Object, and Digital Libraries: Being a Teacher in the Knowledge Society

The universe continually evolving under the stimulus of new philosophies and technologies for the recording, the cataloguing, the management, the use, and the distribution of information, must face the problems, the techniques, and the technologies that are involved in the planning and the production of multimedia instruments for knowledge sharing. To face this challenge means to have cultural instruments. The culture of knowledge management has become an interdisciplinary theme of our society that cannot leave the role of the teacher unchanged. To teach in the knowledge society means to guide the search for knowledge through ontologies (Davies, Fensel, & van Harmelen, 2002) and semantic meanings.

What contribution can be given from the teacher in this process? What benefit can be drown from these technologies and methodologies? What new abilities are demanded? The sharing of knowledge and its structuring becomes a stimulus for learning. The teacher must have a good knowledge of technologies, but also of the languages and the logic that govern them, for example, XML and RDF (Daconta, Obrst, & Smith, 2003). The spread of this approach to knowledge must bring the teacher to analyze his or her role in according to three levels of problems in communication:

- How much exactly the symbols of the communication can be transmitted
- How much precisely the transmitted symbols transfer the desired result
- How much the desired meaning truly leads to behavior in the desired sense

A first contributions teachers must give is concerned with the analysis of the instruments of knowledge exploration so that, when dealing with the problems of communication they can answer to three criteria:

- Efficiency
- Difficulty of use
- Significance

With the *efficiency* criterion the analysis of the various performances can measure what the instrument offers in terms of time of access, reading facility of the contents (quality of the witnesses and the diagram), and use on various instruments without substantial modifications of structure. Still, on this point, they influence the ergonomics and the significance of the man-machine interface and the communication metaphor. The criterion of *difficulty* of use measures the impact between man-machine interface and the average level of use of the navigation system on the side of the user. Such an indication, measured if it is possible by analyzing sample users, defines the eventual difference between the expected result and the obtained result. The *significance* measures the precision of the meaning that is transmitted through various components of the site, how it is perceived and understood by the users, and what gaps in development are found. At last, the contribution and the relationship a teacher must have and can make understandable firstly with the library and then with the digital library is important. The connection with the Semantic Web is deep here.

A great work has been made in this direction and there are seven points of development for this medium which are objectives of the W3C; they can also be used as guidelines for the changing role of the teacher (see http://www.w3.org/Consortium/Points/):

- **Universal Access:** The Web is the universe of network-accessible information (available through computer, telephone, television, or networked refrigerator, ...). Today this universe benefits society by enabling new forms of human communication and opportunities to share knowledge. One of W3C's primary goals is to make these benefits available to all people, whatever their hardware, software, network infrastructure, native language, culture, geographical location, or physical or mental ability.

- **The Semantic Web:** People currently share their knowledge on the Web in human language, understandable only to other people. On the Semantic Web ("semantic" means "having to do with meaning"), we will be able to express ourselves in terms that our computers can interpret and exchange. By doing so, we will enable machines to solve problems that we find tedious, to help us find quickly what we're looking for: medical information, movie review, book purchase order, etc. The W3C languages RDF, XML, XML Schema, and XML signatures are the building blocks of the Semantic Web.

- **Trust:** The Web is a collaborative medium, to be only read like a magazine. The first Web browser was in fact also an editor, though many people think today of browsing primarily as viewing, not as interacting. To promote a more collaborative environment, we must build a "Web of Trust" offering confidentiality, instilling confidence, and making it possible for people to take responsibility for (or be accountable for) what they publish on the Web.

- **Interoperability:** Twenty years ago, people bought software only working with software from the same vendor. Today, people have more freedom to choose, and they rightly expect, software components to be interchangeable. They also expect to be able to view Web content with their preferred software (desktop browser, speech synthesizer, Braille display, car phone, ...). W3C, a vendor-neutral organization, promotes interoperability by designing and promoting open (non-proprietary) computer languages and protocols that avoid the market fragmentation of the past. This target is achieved through industry consensus and encouraging an open forum for discussion.

- **Evolvability:** W3C aims for technical excellence but is well aware that what we know and need today may be insufficient to solve tomorrow's problems. W3C therefore strives to build a Web that can easily evolve into an even better Web, without disrupting what already works. The principles of simplicity, modularity, compatibility, and extensibility guide its own designs.

- **Decentralization:** Decentralization is a basic principle of modern distributed systems, including societies. In a centralized system, every message or action has to pass through a central authority, causing bottlenecks when the traffic increases; for this reason the number of central Web facilities is limited, so reducing the vulnerability of the Web as a whole. Flexibility is the necessary companion of distributed systems, and the life and breath of the Internet, not just the Web.

- **Cooler Multimedia!:** Who wouldn't like more interactivity and richer media on the Web, including resizable images, quality sound, video, 3D effects, and animation? W3C's consensus process does not limit content provider creativity or mean boring browsing. Through its membership, W3C listens to end users and works toward providing a solid framework for the development of the Cooler Web through languages such as the Scalable Vector Graphics (SVG) language and the Synchronized Multimedia Integration Language (SMIL).

Using these guidelines, we can state what the teacher will need:

- **Universal Access:** The teacher will have to develop strategies so that every student can autonomously reach information and develop new knowledge, consistently with the materials and the instruments he or she will have at his or her disposal.

- **A Semantic Knowledge:** The teacher will have to develop strategies for transmitting and sharing information; furthermore he will guide the student to an understanding of the structure of the knowledge making possible the construction and sharing of new knowledge.

- **Trust:** The teacher will have to develop collaborative strategies allowing students to maintain their own autonomy and to grow together, in the awareness of learning. For organizing their knowledge the Web will be an effective instrument.

- **Teaching Interoperability:** The teacher is no longer perceived as the only direct source of knowledge; therefore, as already happened with books, it is important that new teaching strategies assigning the teacher the role of one of the possible knowledge sources, can be developed. The creation of Learning Objects will make visible the concept of interoperability.

- **Evolutionary Ability:** The teacher, beyond content, must teach the principles of simplicity, modularity, compatibility and extensibility: all what makes knowledge structured, dynamic and continually growing.

- **Decentralization:** It will be an important acting principle of the teacher. The teacher must be able in managing the information flows happening inside a class without necessarily becoming the point through which they have to pass.

- **Cooler Multimedia!** Which students have not wished for more interactive materials and multimedia supports. The teacher must equip the classroom with materials to place side by side with books, taking advantage of all the potential that the new instruments put at students' disposal.

At last Semantic Web, Learning Objects and Digital Libraries ask the teacher to become a new professional: tutor and multimedia project manager. Tutor as regards supporting and educating the student to learn how to learn; multimedia project manager for developing new competence in the definition of the structure and use of new materials for learning.

Conclusion

The new world which is outlined in the evolutionary course of technology for information management finds a concrete form in applications based on ontology (OWL language). Semantic Web is applied and implemented very similarly to traditional libraries also if these environments seem to have little in common.

At a first glance, information technology and cultural assets seem worlds separated by large gaps. On the contrary it has been shown how similar the two worlds are and how their aims are convergent and their problems are comparable.

The growing attention towards such themes has much greater value as it shows the need of structuring knowledge and not just to diffuse it with new materials.

At last the conceptual change in the role and function of the teacher must be remembered.

New knowledge and skills are needed in fact in knowledge society.

Future Trends

Technology and methodology supporting Semantic Web and digital library have shown their limits and problems. If we think about the 10 years age of the Web we can agree on its growing suffering, i.e., the problems it is experimenting are the natural consequence of its growth. The Semantic Web seems to answer these problems, the maturity structure of knowledge. The library, as a metaphor for the Internet, and the digital library with it, has to independently carry out the methods of information construction to answer the growing demands for documents conservation and accessibility. This technological and cognitive innovation surely will not leave unchanged anyone in the knowledge society. In particular everyone will need effective materials (Hendler, 2002) and through knowledge in order to draw the maximum benefit from the new opportunities offered by the Semantic Web.

The acquisition of these new abilities will be a challenge for teachers in the next few years. Teachers will transform their role into that of a new professional; they will teach students to navigate through knowledge and to be guided by their own educational needs. Furthermore they will teach to manage knowledge and doing it according to an ontology.

Digital libraries as places of structured information, Learning Object models of knowledge and the semantic approach supported by the Web will be the natural travel companions of teachers, supplying methods that will help mankind to grow culturally and humanly.

Therefore, it's a matter of deciding what we want to invest in: either narrow, specific abilities, strongly integrated with technology, or a progressive development that, without renouncing to technological aspects, will put in the right perspective the abilities and the needs of the students (Longo, 2001).

References

Antoniou, G., & van Harmelen, F. (2004). *A Semantic Web primer*. Cambridge, MA: MIT Press

Berners-Lee, T. (1998). *Semantic Web road map*. Retrieved September 30, 1998, from http://www.w3.org/DesignIssues/Semantic.html

Daconta, M. C., Obrst, L. J., & Smith, K. T. (2003). *The Semantic Web: A guide to the future of XML, Web services, and knowledge management*. Indianapolis, IN: Wiley Publishing.

Davies, J., Fensel, D., & van Harmelen, F. (2002). *Towards the Semantic Web: Ontology-driven knowledge management*. Indianapolis, IN: Wiley Publishing.

Hendler, R. (2002). Integrating application on the Semantic Web. *Journal of the Institute of Electrical Engineers of Japan, 122*(10), 676-680.

Calvino, I. (1972). *Le città invisibili*. Torino: Einaudi

Longo, G. O. (2001). *Homo technologicus*. Roma: Meltemi Editore.

Endnotes

[1]   By meta-data we mean the description or definition of data; the description of the data given by meta-data functions with an intelligent interpretation of a group of data.

[2]   Ontology can be defined accordingly to Gruber with the following sentence "an explicit and formal specification of a shared conceptualization"; the underlining idea is "machine-readability" of ontology.

[3]   The concept of "super-meta-data" is very near digital data object (DDO) definition; it is an object that includes information concerning the layout of the schema allowing the reading and understanding of meta-data, it organizes the information on the object not included in the meta-data (e.g., version of the object) and gathers and organizes information coming from documents differing in content, structure and source.

[4]   A Learning Object can be defined as a re-usable concept unit for e-learning. For an LO to be re-used it is necessary that its presentation is separated from its content and it is possible if data are created in specifics forms. SCORM is one of these forms (see http://www.adlnet.org).

5   W3C (World Wide Web Consortium) develops technology for the interoperability (specifics reference guides, software and development instruments) to lead the Web towards a full development of all its potential. The official W3C site is http://www.w3.org.

6   Research Libraries Group is a non-profit organization supporting researchers and Web specialists in expanding access to research material contained in libraries archives and museums. RLG intends to promote digital conservation of documents for long-term access. The official site of the organization is http://www.rlg.org.

7   Online Computer Library Center is a non-profit organization involved in the research to let people access more and more world information and gradually reduce information costs. Their official site is http://www.oclc.org.

8   The correlation and the state of progress of this research and the project "infrastructure of information" are available on the site http://www.digitalpreservation.gov.

Chapter XIX

Media Selection from the Teacher's Point of View

Donatella Persico
Institute for Educational Technology-National Research Council, Italy

Abstract

Teachers, trainers, and educational designers often face the problem of choosing the most suitable media for achieving their educational purposes. To solve this problem, they need to take into account both the variables at play in the educational setting and the characteristics and potentialities of the media available. This chapter discusses the criteria for media choice, with particular attention to the point of view of the individual teacher who makes decisions on the basis of the educational strategies he or she deems most appropriate and, given that schools usually have limited resources, must favor techniques for material retrieval and reuse rather than new development.

Introduction

Choosing which media to use in a learning process is a crucial phase of educational design. Teachers, trainers, and designers of learning material all face the problem of identifying the most suitable media for conveying a message, for facilitating understanding of a concept, and for acquiring and consolidating skills of various kinds. The problem may be tackled intuitively or set within a systematic design methodology: in any case, solving it successfully is vital, as inappropriate choices may undermine the outcome of the learning process. Consequently, media selection criteria have been the subject of many research studies conducted over the past 50 years and more (Reiser & Gagné, 1982; Boud & Prosser, 2002; Romiszowski, 1988; Laurillard, 1993; Kirkwood, 1994). During this period, the focus has shifted towards emerging technologies. In the '50s and '60s, audio-visual media attracted great interest. In subsequent decades numerous studies sought to determine the potential and limits of the computer in education. Finally, since the '90s, communication technologies have become the main focus. At the same time, there has been a similar shift in the approach adopted to tackle the problem of media choice, especially with the changes in perspective brought about by the evolution of learning theories. For example, Reiser and Gagné's (1982) review of media selection methods considers learning models mainly pinned to a behaviorist approach whereby the aim, when choosing the medium, is to make the imparted stimulus as effective as possible. By contrast, more recent studies (Bates, 1991; Collins et al., 2000; Boud & Prosser, 2002) have tended towards a framework in which the educational functions of different media are not limited to optimal message conveying but embrace the performance of learning activities within a constructivist perspective. In other words, media are today seen as tools which designers of educational projects can use for constructing environments that foster and facilitate the learning process.

Most studies of media selection criteria have been carried out from the viewpoint of distance education because, when geographical distance separates the provider and the beneficiary of learning, adopting media is almost unavoidable. This chapter will instead focus on media choice by teachers in the school context.

Selecting Media: The Variables at Play

In distance education, decision making in instructional design is based on the following "variables" (Figure 1):

Figure 1. Variables at play when choosing media in educational design

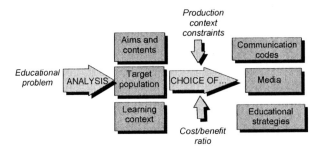

- Aims and contents of the educational process

- Characteristics of the target population (size, age, motivation, prior competence, time constraints, etc.)

- Limits imposed by the context in which the training is to take place (training
  setting, tools and resources available, etc.)

- Constraints of the production context, i.e., the resources available to solve
  the educational problem

Important as it may be, media selection is only one of the decisions to be made
and it goes hand in hand with the choice of the most suitable strategies for
reaching the learning goals. Considerations about the cost/benefit ratio often
influence these decisions.

The same applies in the school setting, though the situation is slightly different.
Educational problems tend to be less content-dependent and more education-
oriented because meta-cognitive skills are considered more important than mere
content acquisition or skills development. The school curriculum sets out the
learning goals and the contents to be taught, but teachers have ample room for
maneuver to focus on one topic rather than another, and to concentrate efforts
on higher level types of objectives, such as problem solving abilities, expressive
skills and meta-cognitive competences. The target population is the class to be
taught. It has fairly homogeneous characteristics, but individual features must be
taken into consideration to maintain motivation and interest. The limits of the
setting usually consist of classroom logistics, scarcity of resources and time table
constraints. These may place strong limitations on teachers' creativity. Finally,
the constraints of the production context are very tight too. For an individual
teacher, producing purpose-made learning material is not always a plausible
option: reuse of existing learning resources is often a more realistic possibility.
In most cases, the best option is to buy off-the-shelf products after doing a cost-
benefit study.

This points to the need for up-to-date, comprehensive documentation services that provide reliable and detailed information about commercial and open source materials. These kinds of services already exist in several countries (see, for examples, http://www.u-learn.it/page.php?ID=Information). In Italy, since 1985, the Institute for Educational Technology has run a documentation service about educational software: the BSD (Biblioteca del Software Didattico—Educational Software Library—Web site at http://www.itd.ge.cnr.it/bsd). The BSD collects educational software for all subjects and school levels (it has almost 4000 titles) that can be tried out by the teachers on the BSD premises. Alternatively, the online service offered by the BSD (Servizio Documentazione Software Didattico—SD2—Web site at http://sd2.itd.ge.cnr.it/BSDindex.php), provides detailed information about this software and its use. Another example is provided by Mosaico (Web site at http://www.mosaico.rai.it); a service established by the Italian National Television Company, that makes a database of around 6000 short films freely available to schools. Some of these services have gradually evolved into something more than mere sources of information: they have become virtual meeting points for teachers who want to share ideas, discuss and reflect on experiences in the use of educational material, exchange software enhancements, etc. Examples can be found at http://www.shatters.net/celestia and http://mathforum.org/. Some of these virtual meeting places are full-fledged communities of practice (Wenger, McDermott, & Snyder, 2002) that have proved to be very promising for the professional development of several kinds of practitioners, including teachers (Schlager & Fusco, 2003).

Media and Communication Codes

If, on the one hand, media selection is influenced by the above-mentioned variables, on the other hand the potentialities of the various media available must be taken into account. Since the list of existing educational tools is very long and doomed to become obsolete quite quickly, the model herein proposed does not address single tools, but rather the three basic communication codes of text, audio and video, plus computers and communication technology.

Text

When speaking of text, we refer to language written or printed on some kind of physical support (paper, slides, boards, but also TV or computer screen). Text is often accompanied by images that, although using a completely different symbol system, can be considered an integral part of the text component. Text is relatively simple to use and is cheap and easy to produce and exploit. It is fairly flexible in that it can be used in whole or in part, not necessarily in sequence, and it respects the user's reading pace. However, text reading may induce a rather passive attitude. Teachers will need to prevent this by making sure that reading is varied with practice and critical thinking about the key aspects presented.

Text, Educational Aims, and Contents

The static and permanent nature of text make it particularly fit for dealing with complex, abstract contents, like mathematical formulae, that require time and concentration to be grasped. This code also lends itself to the presentation of intrinsically static concepts (e.g., description of objects with a complex structure). Images play an especially important role here, both by aiding understanding of abstract concepts, through schemes, graphics and diagrams, and by providing precise descriptions of concrete objects, through photos and illustrations. If we take as a reference point the taxonomy of learning objectives proposed by Bloom (Bloom, 1956), cognitive objectives are probably those that are best pursued using this communication code.

Text, Target Population, and Learning Context

In the school context, the book and blackboard (or its direct descendants) occupy the lion's share of media used; books in particular play a key role in individual study. The use of print is so deeply rooted in schooling that it has even influenced the way knowledge is organized and communicated in education. This is the reason why, according to some (Maragliano, 1994), the school world strongly resists new technologies, because it senses that taking them onboard means revising its image and dramatically changing its culture. The use of text does not need any special classroom layout: it can be used anywhere as no special devices are required. Using text-based material does require a target population with adequate reading ability and reasonable learning autonomy.

Text and Production Context

The spread of text processing applications has made it simple to produce, modify, print, and reproduce printed material. Nowadays, virtually anyone can produce a document of near professional quality with a minimum of effort. It is worth remembering that texts produced for other than educational purposes can be profitably used in various subjects. In particular, the use of authentic material is fundamental to promote constructivist learning: historical sources, real-life problems, social, demographic, and scientific data can be the starting point for collaborative inquiry learning. The development of the Web has given an enormous boost to the availability of this kind of documents. The Internet is even influencing the way some school subjects are being studied and learnt: in fact, one of the most important meta-learning techniques that teachers should aim to develop is that of retrieving, evaluating, and selecting sources of information.

Audio

Audio is fundamental in face-to-face communication but it is also widely employed by many low-tech and high-tech media, from radio to voice chats over the Internet. It is often found in conjunction with text or video, though there are situations in which it is best used alone, for example for communicating with listeners that are unable to see or read. This is the case not only in education for the blind but also in situations where the sense of sight is temporarily engaged in another activity (e.g., examining specimens under a microscope). As with text, the use of lengthy audio sequences has a tendency to lead the user towards passive message reception. It is therefore up to the teacher to set up learning activities where students will not be tempted to indulge in passive attitudes.

Audio, Educational Aims, and Contents

Audio plays a key role in contexts where sound is the main objective of study, (e.g., in music education or in teaching a foreign language). The advantages this communication code offers include its suitability for informal, captivating, and motivating communication, which means it is often used to communicate ideas and feelings. To put it in Bloom's terms, audio is clearly more suited than text to the pursuit of goals in the affective domain. Using audio can also help to enliven a presentation and to make the communication process more immediate and varied. It can be used to present the views of an expert in his or her own voice, lending the message greater authority. Some interesting historical documents, such as political speeches and declarations, are easily accessible in audio format. The downside of audio is that it is volatile and not well suited to complex, intricate content, neither is its use appropriate where there is a high risk of misinterpretation.

Audio, Target Population, and Learning Context

Audio is easy to use, it imposes no limits on schooling and reproduction systems are cheap and widespread. Consequently, the target population that can be reached with this communication code is potentially enormous. However, it is not recommended if the students have specific problems in comprehending the oral message (e.g., if they speak a different language or suffer from hearing difficulties).

Audio and Production Context

Recording sound and storing it on a computer is fairly straightforward, and equipment costs are within the schools' reach. Furthermore, retrieving audio documents from the Internet or from the wide range of existing multimedia encyclopedias is pretty easy nowadays. Finally, for those subjects that intrinsically require the use of audio, such as language learning, a plethora of educational software exist that integrate both recording and reproduction of a wealth of archived material.

Video

Video is seldom used by itself, being commonly coupled with audio. It places almost no prerequisites on the part of the viewer and reproduction tools are very widespread and cheap. Students enjoy watching a video more than studying on paper, but this should not induce teachers in the belief that video alone can support the achievement of higher order educational objectives, such the ones that can be reached with experiential learning. Indeed, video, like audio, tends to lead the viewer towards passive message reception. Video is particularly suited to introducing a topic and stimulating curiosity in a given subject, or even to starting up a discussion on problematic matters but, if the learning objectives include higher level skills such as developing know-how or favoring critical thinking, watching a video can only be one phase of a more complex learning itinerary.

Video, Educational Aims, and Contents

The dynamic nature of video makes it especially suitable for describing processes that evolve over time:

- Recreating a slice of real life, especially when the setting is difficult to reach (e.g., showing how Eskimos live)
- Investigating phenomena or mechanisms that are intrinsically dynamic (e.g., simulating a complex mechanism like the workings of a watch)

- Reconstructing dynamic models of phenomena that are difficult to see in real life, possibly at other than natural speed or natural size (e.g., movement of planets or cell reproduction)

- Simulating complex emotive situations (human behavior in interpersonal relationships)

In addition, the media-richness of the communication channel (Collins et al, 2000) makes audio/visual communication very involving and therefore particularly suited for pursuing goals in the affective sphere.

Video, Target Population, and Learning Context

For its potential in motivating and involving the viewer, video can be used with a wide target population; indeed it is a classic means of mass education. Effective use in the school context, however, requires a suitable setting: some schools have a special video room with a large-screen projector and sound system. Individuals can make personalized use of video on small screens; in this case, however, quality may be lower and therefore unsuitable for long sequences.

Video and Production Context

It is quite rare for an individual teacher to embark on the production of professional quality audio-visual material. It would call for professional equipment, skills, and costs way beyond the means of the average school. A wide range of video clips are accessible from multimedia software and the Web, while longer material is easy to obtain from specialist resource centers.

Video is also used in learning processes that do not entail passively watching a video sequence. An example is when teachers film students while working on a task in order to record essential phases of a learning process. In this case, professional quality is not essential because the video serves as a basis for reflection on performance or on cognitive strategies. Documenting the learning process is also very useful for assessment purposes and to get parents involved in discussion concerning their children's progress. Alternatively, a video may be the outcome of a project carried out collaboratively by a group of students. For example, a class may study the local environment with the aim of producing a video that illustrates that environment. In this case, the quality of the video itself is completely overshadowed by the potential advantages gained from undergoing the learning process. However, given that learning paths of this kind are demanding both for the teacher and the students, it is vital to weigh up the benefits against the resources needed to implement such a project. A third example is when videoconferencing systems are used to put classes in contact with distant experts or with other groups of learners. In this case, the use of video is usually inspired by social-constructivist learning theories and is integrated with textual communication. These last two ways to use video are dealt with in more detail in the following chapters, because the environments that best support these approaches are computer based.

Computers

In the following, we will speak generally about the computer bearing in mind that this is a terminological simplification: the word computer usually refers solely to the hardware component of this instrument, but it is the software that determines the way the tool is used.

Computers are multimedia tools, (i.e., they are capable of integrating closely the three communication codes: text, audio, and video). For example, if the computer is employed as a support for a presentation, specific software can be used to combine text, audio, and video according to the above described criteria. But the role the computer plays in education goes far beyond that of a simple multimedia support for presentations, thanks to two characteristics of this tool: interactivity and connectivity. For the sake of presentation, in this section we will refer to the computer chiefly as an interactive, stand-alone educational tool; while the potential of connectivity will be explored in the next section, entitled "Computer Networks."

Computers and Interactivity

Interactivity allows the user to play an active role in the learning process. Early applications, mostly inspired by behavioral learning theories, tended to exploit this feature through programs (tutorials, drill and practice) that *adapted* their behavior to different users' inputs by following different pre-programmed learning paths. Later, the development of constructionists' theories of learning (Papert & Harel, 1991) gave rise to the diffusion of learning environments of a *reactive* type, where the initiative is in the hands of the students who can build their own knowledge through an experiential approach. While the choice of adaptive software requires the teacher to take on board the teaching strategy implemented by the software author, using a learning environment with a constructivist approach is perhaps even more demanding: it entails the assumption that learning is essentially an active process of knowledge construction and, as a consequence, that the educator role is that of a coach who facilitates learning by providing suitable environments and stimuli. However, implementing constructivism is very rewarding in terms of the educational objectives that can be achieved: it allows deep understanding and competence development, as opposed to acquisition of information or application of procedural skills.

Another effective and perhaps more popular educational application of computers is when students are engaged in creative activities in which the computer plays the role of "cognitive amplifier," supporting several intellectual tasks such as data analysis, graph and diagram production, written composition, etc. In this case, the software tools employed are not specifically designed for educational purposes: word processors, spreadsheets, database management systems, Web-page editors, audio and video production tools. These are usually collaborative projects, inspired by social constructivist models of learning, where the teacher guides the students and keeps them on track, leaving them free to give shape to the products of their learning process. Whatever the end-product, learning takes place while designing and producing it and, as a consequence, it is the process and not the quality of the result that matters. Facilitating constructivist learning is a difficult and time-consuming task, so teachers who choose this approach should be fully aware of potential gains versus effort involved.

Computers, Contents, and Goals

Learning environments have been developed in several fields: physics, chemistry, and science simulation environments are very popular, as are micro-worlds for learning artificial languages and formalisms of various kinds (for example mathematical logic or programming languages). In the humanities, multimedia applications are available to learn foreign languages, word-processors and multimedia dictionaries help develop linguistic skills and there are programs for music production and editing, etc. All of these applications have proved useful both from the cognitive and affective viewpoints.

Computers, Target Population, and Learning Context

As to the classroom setting, computer use tends to induce a shift away from lecture-style layout to a more "workshop" style, to allow group work to alternate with individual study and teacher directed activities. Many schools have set up computer labs and regulate students' access to them. However, this layout has demonstrated limits, especially when regulations and time constraints constitute a barrier to use. Ideally, every student and teacher ought to have computer access whenever needed, free of any restrictions. Furthermore, when thinking along these lines, it becomes clear that the problem is not only the distribution of technology in schools but the whole logistical set up and organization of the education system, including the grouping of students into classes, timetabling, etc. Accordingly, many researchers claim that the introduction of technology triggers a revolution of the whole education system.

Computers and Production Context

Producing educational software at a professional level calls for a variety of skills and requires time and resources (Persico, 1997). It is perhaps for this reason that not many teachers take on this task and prefer to resort to existing resources, especially open source software, learning environments, and content-independent packages.

Computer Networks

Communication technology offers schools unprecedented opportunities for accessing information and communicating with the rest of the world, therefore enlarging their social network to other countries, settings and institutions that would otherwise be far beyond students' reach.

The Web as an Information Source

The Web is a huge, anarchically developed network hosting a wealth of multimedia resources. Using it in education may mean a number of different things and entail different strategies. One possible use sees the Web as a source of information, either for the teacher or for the students, and/or as a tool for publishing and spreading information. In this light, there are no limits, at least in principle, to the nature of content, educational aims and target population: suitable Web-based resources can be produced and selected for practically any subject. Of course, mature students will be able to develop more subtle navigation skills and therefore search or browse the Web very effectively on their own. Younger pupils, instead, will need more guidance, or at least some indication of interesting resources to start with. The use of the Web with young pupils, in particular, requires careful planning to avoid frustration and de-motivation, mainly because of the high risk of their getting stuck with unsuitable material. These problems should not prevent teachers from using the Web in the classroom: information hunting and retrieval are essential meta-cognitive skills for surviving in a knowledge society and the ability to identify reliable sources and trustworthy data is essential for personal development (Caviglia, 2002). To this regard, it is important that suitable strategies are adopted to avoid uncritical use of the information found. Examples of interesting ways to implement rich and productive Web-based learning activities that do not incur in this problem are the so called WebQuests (Dodge, 1995).

Considerations about the educational setting are similar to those reported for the use of computers: schools of the future should allow ubiquitous access to the Web. Production constraints are perhaps less strict: there is now a wealth of tools that allow development of simple Web sites or Weblogs without specialized competence.

To conclude, the decision to use the Web in education is mainly determined by the objectives and by the choice of a corresponding learning strategy. The added value provided by the network, though, should inform the decision: the need for up-to-date data, for authentic or multiple information sources are important factors in this decision.

Computer Networks and Interpersonal Communication

Educational use of tools that support interpersonal communication, including e-mail and computer-mediated communication (CMC) systems, has a great potential for implementing projects where classes collaborate at a distance, possibly involving external institutions or individuals that can contribute to the learning process. In applications of this type the nature of the interaction differs substantially from what we have examined so far: indeed, CMC is communication among individuals and not between an individual and a computer. The characteristics of this interaction vary according to learning requirements and the software used: communication can be synchronous or asynchronous, textual or multimedia. Synchronous communication lends itself better to quick interactions and decision making, while the features of asynchronous communication, in particular message persistence, make it more suited to in-depth discussions. The choice of textual or audio-video interaction should be informed by the previously described features of these communication channels, bearing in mind that video conferencing systems usually manage smaller numbers of interlocutors than text based ones. The choice to exploit the potential of the net for interpersonal communication goes hand in hand with teachers' beliefs about the nature of learning. The theoretical grounds for this kind of approach are provided by the already mentioned social-constructivist theories of learning. In this view the influence of cultural and social contexts in learning is emphasized, assuming "that we actively construct meanings socially through language" (Kanuka & Anderson, 1999, p. 9). These projects require an evaluation of the added value provided by the development of a learning community. Undeniably, some content areas are ideally suited to this kind of approach: language learning, for example, or any other subject where confrontation with others with different cultures and ideas may significantly foster learning. According to Trentin (2004), the learning strategies typical of this approach often guarantee a return on investment that justifies the heavy commitment required, by both students and teachers. In order to reduce the time and effort needed to set up and run interdisciplinary projects involving several institutions and therefore requiring considerable time and resources, teachers can resort to specialist Web sites that propose and run activities of this kind. Examples can be found in the Webscuola and the European Schoolnet portals (http://www.webscuola.it/ and http://www.eun.org/portal/index-en.cfm).

Conclusion

The variables influencing media selection include the educational purpose, the type of contents, the features of the target population, and the constraints imposed by the contexts of production and use. Face-to-face lessons can be greatly enhanced by the effective use of images, text and audio/video reproduction, especially if the adopted approach doesn't entail passive fruition by the students. The study of the educational potential of computers and communication technology falls outside the classic scheme of the three communication codes. These tools are best exploited to create learning environments where students learn through an experiential approach, by doing things and interacting with peers, teachers and experts, rather than passively absorbing information. The decision to use this kind of environment is therefore tied in with the adoption of constructivist learning strategies. As a consequence, integrating educational technology in education means exposing schools to the "destabilizing" effect of the new media and being prepared to rethink spaces, timing and ways of educating. From the point of view of the teacher, this may appear to be a rather time-consuming approach, both in the design phase, and in the implementation one. Nevertheless, the return on investment is guaranteed thanks to added value in terms of the "acquisition of skills, knowledge, methods and attitudes that go beyond the *mere* learning of contents" (Trentin, 2004, p.299).

Future Trends

This chapter starts from the assumption that there is no reason to favor one educational medium over another *on principle*: there is no *best* medium, rather each different situation calls for evaluation of the cost-benefit ratio related to the various choices available. Paradoxically, even the decision to eschew all educational mediating tools is now a methodological choice to be made in full awareness: technology can simplify or accelerate many teaching tasks, can reduce learning effort and enable the construction of learning environments that would otherwise not be possible. However, the competence needed to make decisions on media choice is quite complex and can only be built up through experience and a good amount of reflection on the advantages and disadvantages of the different tools available and the approaches to be implemented through them.

Research into the adoption of educational technology shows that in spite of the wide penetration of infrastructures and a reasonable average level of competence in its use, at least among young teachers, use of technology in schools still encounters several problems (MIUR, 2004; EURYDICE, 2004). The reasons for this may lie with both logistical and cultural factors. On both aspects much work can still be done. Logistical issues must be tackled by re-thinking aspects of school organization in such a way that resource based learning is more straightforward and is not hindered by the time and place constraints imposed by school regulations. Several countries are experimenting with new types of school organization that may favor experiential learning in general, not only easy access to technology when and where needed. Research in the field of ubiquitous computing should also inform these developments.

Cultural resistance is even harder to tackle. Teacher training is an effective way to make teachers more confident about the potential of educational technology. In addition, many efforts are devoted to make information easily available to teachers about educational audio-visual and software tools, as well as learning initiatives of interest for their students. However, documentation services such as those mentioned earlier in this chapter are only a starting point for the continuous professional development of teachers, which is a necessary condition for a wider uptake of educational technology in schools. Indeed, more should be done to combat resistance and lack of interest and increase trust towards technology enhanced learning. Theories about innovation spreading and uptake suggest that the key actors in dissemination of innovation in education are pioneer teachers (Midoro & Admiraal, 2003), whose action and success may encourage others to adopt educational technology. To foster the process of innovation, we need collaboration among teachers and sharing of good practice more than formal training. For this reason, the birth and the development of teachers' communities of practice is a very promising direction to go in, especially for the development of higher order abilities such as instructional design and media selection, where a collaborative and experiential approach appears to be the ideal way to deal with the complexity of the decision making criteria. Some of these virtual meeting places for teachers, such as Tapped in (Web site at http://tappedin.org/tappedin/) and Webheads (Almeida d'Eca, 2004) have already achieved worldwide impact.

References

Almeida d'Eca, T. (2004). Web-heads in Action (WiA): An online community for professional development—from past to present. *Humanizing Language Teaching, 6*(1). Retrieved April 15 2005, from http://www.hltmag.co.uk/jan04/sart10.htm

Bates, A. W. (1991). Interactivity as a criterion for media selection in distance education. *Never Too Far, 16*, 5-9.

Boud, D., & Prosser, M. (2002) Appraising new technologies for learning: A framework for development. *Educational Media International, 39*(3-4), 237-245.

Bloom, B. J. (1956). *Taxonomy of educational objectives, Handbook I: Cognitive domain*. New York: David McKay Company.

Caviglia, F. (2002). Lie detecting as a step towards critical literacy. *L1-Educational Studies in Language and Literature, 2*(3), 179-220.

Collins, A., Neville, P., & Bielaczyc, K. (2000). The role of different media in designing learning environments. *International Journal of Artificial Intelligence in Education, 11*, 144-162.

Dodge, B. (1995). *Some thoughts about WebQuests*. Retrieved April 15, 2005, from http://webquest.sdsu.edu/about_webquests.html

EURYDICE. (2004). *Key data on information and communication technology in schools in Europe—2004 edition*. Retrieved April 15, 2005, from http://www.eurydice.org/Doc_intermediaires/indicators/en/frameset_key_data.html

Kanuka, H., & Anderson, T. (1999). Using constructivism in technology-mediated learning: Constructing order out of the chaos in the literature. *Radical Pedagogy, 1*(2). Retrieved April 15, 2005, from http://radicalpedagogy.icaap.org/content/issue1_2/02kanuka1_2.html

Kirkwood, A. (1994). Selection and use of media for open and distance learning. In F. Lockwood (Ed.), *Materials production in open and distance learning*. London: Paul Chapman Publishing Ltd.

Laurillard, D. (1993). *Rethinking university teaching*. London: Routledge.

Maragliano, R. (1994). *Manuale di didattica multimediale*. Roma-Bari, Italy: Laterza.

Midoro, V., & Admiraal W. (2003). *Pioneer teachers: A key factor in European school innovation*. Ortona (Chieti), Italy: Menabò Edizioni.

MIUR. (2004). *Ministero Istruzione Università e Ricerca, Monitoraggio tecnologie didattiche: Sintesi 2004*. Retrieved April 15, 2005 from, http://www.istruzione.it/innovazione/tecnologie/monitoraggi.shtml

Papert, S., & Harel, I. (1991). *Constructionism*. Norwood, NJ: Ablex Publishing Corporation.

Persico, D. (1997). Methodological constants in courseware design. *British Journal of Educational Technology, 28*(2), 111-124.

Reiser, R. A., & Gagné, R. M. (1982). Characteristics of media selection models. *Review of Educational Research, 52*(4), 499-512.

Romiszowski, A. J. (1988). *The selection and use of instructional media*. London: Kogan Page.

Rowntree, D. (1994). *Preparing materials for open, distance, and flexible learning*. London: Kogan Page.

Schlager M. S., & Fusco J. (2003). Teacher professional development, technology, and communities of practice: Are we putting the cart before the horse? *The Information Society, 19*(3), 203-220.

Trentin, G. (2004). Networked collaborative learning in the study of modern history and literature. *Computers and the Humanities, 38*(2), 299-315.

Wenger, E., McDermott R., & Snyder W. (2002). *Cultivating communities of practice*. Cambridge, MA: Harvard Business School Press.

About the Authors

Antonio Cartelli is a researcher in didactics and special pedagogy at the Faculty of Humanities, University of Cassino, Italy. He graduated with a degree in mathematics at La Sapienza University in Rome (1976) and took the after degree special school diploma in physics at the same University (1983). He teaches educational and learning technologies and ICT literacy in the science education courses of his faculty. Cartelli also manages the Faculty Centre for ICT and online teaching and is a member of the scientific committees of several ICT publications. His most recent publications include collaborations to Idea Group Inc. (e.g., *Technology and Literacy Application in Learning* by D. Carbonara, 2005) and encyclopedias (*Distance Learning, Database Technologies and Applications*, and *Communities of Practice and Virtual Communities*). His main fields of interest are ICT in the teaching/learning processes, ICT in KM, Web technologies in education, and e-learning.

*   *   *

Rozz Albon is an associate professor and director of teaching and learning at Curtin University of Technology's Miri campus in Sarawak, Malaysia. Her PhD from Charles Sturt University, Australia was in the area of gifted education, but her research now focuses on e-learning and technology in higher education. Her 15 years of teaching has embraced research interests within the field of educational psychology, particularly social situational learning, constructivism, mediated learning, motivation, assessment, and self-regulated learning.

Paolo Ardizzone is a researcher in didactics at the Catholic University of Milan, Italy, since 1999. He has 20 years of teaching experience in the school, especially in media education and e-learning. He is the author of the following books: *Didattica e tecnologie dell'istruzione e dell'apprendimento* (Milano, 2002) and *Didattiche per l'e-learning* (co-authored with Pier Cesare Rivoltella, Roma 2003). His main fields of interest are media education and e-learning with special attention to university teaching and communities of learners.

John A. Clarke is currently a senior research assistant and formerly an associate professor in the School of Learning and Professional Studies, Queensland University of Technology, Australia. He has a history of working and research-ing in the fields of classroom learning, interaction, and learning environments, particularly at the tertiary level. He also has an interest in research methodology and has integrated this with learning environment research through the develop-ment and refinement of an instrument for gathering students' perceptions of what helps and hinders their learning. His current research interests include flexible, distance, and online learning environments.

Salvatore Colazzo is an associate professor at the University of Lecce (Italy), Faculty of Educational Sciences, where he teaches experimental pedagogy. He is the author of the book *Didattica Multimediale* (2001). For several years he has dealt with new technologies applied to education. He planned and carried out multimedia application for learning. Among other things, he designed and implemented a post-graduate course for "E-learning Mediators: Experts in Distance Education." He also teaches methods and techniques of distance learning in the special degree in pedagogical sciences at the University of Lecce.

Micheál Colhoun is a consultant on team work and management change and is affiliated with the University of Galway, Ireland. Originating from a back-ground in physics and astronomical instrumentation, he has spent more than 12 years in the applied physics and computer industry. He has been involved in many IT start-ups and research projects, including projects in retail and hospitality, tourism, financial services and human resources. He is chief architect and program manager of ViRTeCo, and has presented the concepts of virtual learning environments to academic institutes and the corporate world from Ireland to the UK to as far away as Korea.

Carmen de Pablos Heredero is a full-time professor in the area of manage-ment information systems at the Rey Juan Carlos University in Madrid, Spain. She carried out research on the impact of information and communication technologies over organizational performance and has long published in this issue. Amongst her publications are some co-authored books such as *Managing*

Information Systems in the Firm (2001, ESIC, Madrid) and *Computers for Business* (2000, ESIC, Madrid). More recent publications are "The Human Side of Information Systems: Managing the Systems," in the *Encyclopedia of Information Systems* (The Free Press, New York, 2002), "The Internet and Future Entrepreneurs: An Empirical Analysis," in *Entrepreneurship and Innovation Management* (Inderscience, 2004), "Does Technology Impact on Teaching Styles or Do Teaching Styles Impact on Technology in the Delivery of Higher Education?" in the *Journal of Informing Science and Information Technology* (2004) and *Some Spanish Cases of the Implementation of IT* (2004, ESIC, Madrid).

Jordi Hernandez received a BA in media and communications and an MSc in interactive media from the University of Limerick (2000 and 2001, respectively). He has previously worked in the e-learning industry and is currently a lecturer of user centered design and a PhD student at the National University of Ireland, Galway, Ireland. His research interests include collaborative virtual environments, 3D gaming, HCI, and auditory displays. He is currently investigating the classification of CVE related events into dynamic auditory hierarchies of significance in order to enhance user awareness.

Tony Jewels has been an IT industry professional for more than 30 years, much of that time operating his own IT consultancy business. Jewels now lectures undergraduate and postgraduate IT project management units at Queensland University of Technology, Australia. His PhD research concerns the management of knowledge in IT projects and his publications, which span the areas of project management and the science of teaching, include book chapters, journals and conference papers.

Zlatko J. Kovačić (PhD, The University of Belgrade) is a senior lecturer in the School of Information and Social Sciences at The Open Polytechnic of New Zealand, New Zealand. Dr. Kovačić has a varied academic background and research interests ranging from core interests relating to IT careers, learning and teaching, e-commerce, e-learning, time series analysis, and multivariate analysis. His current research is focused on cognitive processes in distance education using computers, information and communication technologies, and on social and cultural aspects of e-government.

Yair Levy is an assistant professor of MIS at the Graduate School of Computer and Information Sciences at Nova Southeastern University, USA. Prior to joining the school, Dr. Levy was instructor and director of online learning at

Florida International University. During the mid- to late-1990s, Dr. Levy assisted NASA in developing e-learning platforms as well as managing Internet and Web infrastructures. He earned his undergraduate degree in aerospace engineering from the Technion (Israel Institute of Technology). He received his MBA with MIS concentration and PhD in MIS from Florida International University. His research includes value of IS, e-learning systems, and system's effectiveness. He published several peer-reviewed papers in journals, conference proceedings, and book chapters. Dr. Levy has been serving as a referee reviewer for numerous scientific journals, conference proceedings, and books. He is also a frequent speaker at national and international meetings on MIS and e-learning topics.

Maria Apparecida Mamede-Neves was born in Rio de Janeiro, Brazil (1936). Her academic position is full professor at Catholic University of Rio de Janeiro (PUC-Rio), Brazil, where she is also pedagogical coordinator of Central Coordination for Distance Learning (CCEAD PUC-Rio). She has a PhD in psychology, an MA in psychology, an MA in education and also specialized in psychopedagogy. As a researcher of Brazilian National Research Council (CNPq), her main interest is distance learning and the relationship between youth and Web. She is the author of several books and international and national articles about these subjects.

Niall Naughton was conferred with a master's degree in applied computing and information technology in November 2004 from the National University of Ireland, Galway, Ireland. Having originally obtained his primary degree at the University in 1989, in applied physics, Niaughton worked for several years within the fields of quality assurance and product research and development. During this period, he developed a keen interest in the software development sector and returned to university to pursue his professional and academic interests. Having additional creative and artistic qualities, Naughton has a strong interest in the application of computer graphics and multimedia to enhance computer-based training and computer mediated communication.

Damien Noonan joined the ViRTeCo project after completing a bachelor's degree in information technology at the National University of Ireland, Galway, Ireland. ViRTeCo (Virtual Reality Teleworking Communities) was established after limitations associated with remote collaborative work were identified. These limitations are focused on in greater detail in Noonan's MSc thesis "The Importance of Awareness within a Shared Visual Space for Distributed Work."

Marco Pedroni graduated in agricultural sciences in 1982. In 1984, he started teaching computer science and organized courses for digital literacy. In 1992, he founded a software house and applied his competency and skills as a computer programmer in the production of Learning Objects and interactive environments for e-learning (mostly adopting Java language). He also teaches digital communication and databases, communication systems and technologies, information streams' management, and digital technologies for distance learning in the CARID, at the University of Ferrara, Italy. Among his research interests are knowledge management systems, concept map representation, and Web ontology construction.

Donatella Persico is a researcher at the Institute for Educational Technology of the Italian National Research Council, Italy. Since 1981, she has been active in the field of educational and training technology, its theory and its applications. Her major research interests include instructional design, online learning, and teacher training. She has developed educational material of various kinds (books, educational software, multimedia material) and is also the author of several research papers concerning aspects of educational technology. She is a member of the editorial board of international and national journals on educational technology and has been in charge of several national and international projects.

Hitendra Pillay is an associate professor in the School of Learning and Professional Studies, Queensland University of Technology, Australia. He has researched and consulted in the areas of information technology and learning. His ongoing research has highlighted the significance of cognitive interactions within ICT-rich learning environments by focusing on the understanding of cognitive maneuvers such as inferential reasoning and anticipation and has been aimed at developing a more holistic understanding of human learning. To this end, he is also researching and publishing on learners' conceptions, beliefs, and approaches to learning in traditional learning environments.

Angela Piu, a research graduate in training models, is currently a specialist teacher working in a lower secondary (junior high) school providing support for children with special needs. She is also a part-time university teacher of assessment in the degree course at the Faculty of Primary Education, University of Calabria, Italy. She carried out studies and research into planning and didactic assessment and, at the moment, she is involved in a research project on the use of simulation in training. She also contributed to the scientific debate through a number of publications, including a monograph *Processi Formativi e Simulazione. Fondamenti Teorici e Dimensioni Operative—Training and Simulation. Theoretical Bases and Practical Dimensions* (2002; Rome: Monolite).

Giorgio Poletti graduated in mathematics from the University of Ferrara. For the development of his thesis on "collision proton-antiproton in constant magnetic field" he worked as a computer scientist at the CERN (European Center for the Nuclear research) of Geneva. Since 1989, he has been a teacher in various school level courses. In 1999, he become a professor at the CARID (Academic Centre for Didactic Research and Innovation), University of Ferrara, Italy, where he manages the Multimedia Department. Disciplines he teaches are: elements of computer science, project and multimedia production, and laboratory: project of the communication with digital technologies. Among his interests are knowledge structuring, meta-languages, XML-based, and the project and production of Learning Objects.

Sam Redfern is a lecturer in the IT Department of the National University of Ireland, Galway, Ireland. His postgraduate and postdoctoral research career encompasses some 13 years of applied technical research in areas such as simulation, real-time graphics and multimedia, digital image processing, and pattern recognition. His current research interests include the nature and support of online community, and collaborative virtual environments as distributed platforms for computer supported cooperative work.

Giuseppe Refrigeri is a full-time professor in didactics and special pedagogy at the University of Cassino, Italy, study course of educational sciences. His scientific interests are mainly devoted to analysis of experimental pedagogical knowledge, both from quantitative and qualitative perspectives and teaching/learning communication processes with special attention to planning, programming, and evaluating of processes and educational systems. Among his publications are the following books: *Educazione civica e cultura costituzionale* (in cooperation with L. Corradini), Bologna: Il Mulino (2000); *Bruner nell'educazione post-industriale*, Napoli: Tecnodid (1998); *Come si fa un tema di pedagogia*, Firenze: Giunti-Lisciani (1995); *Scienza e pedagogia dell'educazione corporea*, Firenze: Giunti-Lisciani (1990).

Pier Cesare Rivoltella, Philosophy Doctor, is a professor of technology of education at Catholic University of Milan, Italy. He is scientific director of a master in education and communication media education. Rivoltella is a member of the Scientific Committee of CEPAD (Centre for Permanent and Distance Education) at Catholic University and of the Italian Society of e-Learning (SIe-l). His main interests of research are in the area of e-learning and media education. He wrote and edited 24 books and more than 80 articles, and is a member of the scientific committee of several education reviews.

Nicoletta Sala received her degree in physics and applied cybernetics at State University of Milan (Italy). She received her PhD in communication science at the University of Italian Switzerland of Lugano (Switzerland). Postgraduates (two years for each): "Didactics of the communication and multimedia technologies" and "Journalism and mass media." She is a professor in mathematics and teaches mathematics in arts and in architecture and computer graphics and new media at the Academy of Architecture of Mendrisio (University of Italian Switzerland). She studies the new media in education and in particular the use of virtual reality in architecture and design. She has written 16 mathematics and information technology textbooks and several scientific papers dedicated to new media in education.

Manfred Schertler studied business education and human resources at the University of Erlangen-Nuremberg, Germany. He graduated in 1998 and joined the research staff of the Department of Information Systems, where he obtained his PhD in 2004. His research activities focus on knowledge management, e-learning applications, and teacher support in distributed learning environments. Between 2000 and 2004 he was in charge of several e-learning projects together with the Virtual University of Bavaria, Germany. Since 2004 he has also worked at a management consultancy company where he oversees projects in the scope of e-learning and knowledge portals.

Peter G. Taylor is a professor and director of Bond University's Institute for Learning Communities and is currently affiliated with Queensland University of Technology, Australia. His interests and expertise are focused on the application of constructivist thinking about learning to a range of issues including the design of effective learning environments, and the promotion of learning within communities of practice. In the last five years this has involved projects on the design of learning spaces, organization level evaluation of innovations, and the use of information and communication technologies to support learning.

Index